Bhangra and
Asian Underground

FALU BAKRANIA

Bhangra and Asian Underground

South Asian Music and the Politics of Belonging in Britain

Duke University Press   Durham and London   2013

© 2013 Duke University Press. All rights reserved. Printed in the United States of America on acid-free paper ∞. Designed by Courtney Leigh Baker and typeset in Arno Pro by Keystone Typesetting, Inc.

Library of Congress Cataloging-in-Publication Data
Bakrania, Falu Pravin.
Bhangra and Asian Underground : South Asian music and
the politics of belonging in Britain / Falu Bakrania.
pages cm
Includes bibliographical references and index.
ISBN 978-0-8223-5301-0 (cloth : alk. paper)
ISBN 978-0-8223-5317-1 (pbk. : alk. paper)
1. South Asians—Great Britain—Ethnic identity.
2. South Asians—Music—Social aspects—Great Britain.
3. South Asians—Great Britain—Music.
4. Nightclubs—Great Britain.   I. Title.
DA125.S57B35 2013
305.8914′041—dc23
2013009710

For my family.

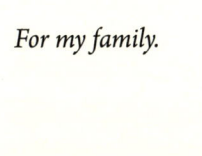

Contents

Preface ix
Acknowledgments xiii
Introduction 1

PART I. The Politics of Production

CHAPTER ONE. Mainstreaming Masculinity
Bhangra Boyz and Belonging in Britain 33

CHAPTER TWO. From the Margins to the Mainstream
Asian Underground Artists and the Politics of Not Being Political 70

PART II. The Club Cultures of Consumption

CHAPTER THREE. The Troubling Subject of Wayward Asian Girls
Working-Class Women and Bhangra Club Going 117

CHAPTER FOUR. Roomful of Asha
Middle-Class Women and Asian Underground Club Going 160

Conclusion
Bhangra and Asian Underground in the 2000s 187

Notes 203
Bibliography 227
Index 237

Preface

One afternoon in the summer of 1991 my cousins played a remix track for me; it was Bally Sagoo's "Star Megamix" from the album *Wham Bam: Bhangra Remixes*, released in 1990 in Birmingham, England. "Star Megamix" was unlike anything I had heard before. More than nine minutes long, the track layered and tacked back and forth between diverse musical forms such as classic bhangra, funk, and hip hop, and diverse vocal samples from American and British popular culture. I loved it; it was fun and funky. Indeed, the album that "Star Megamix" is featured on is billed as fun, party music (the liner notes claim it is "specially designed to fill any dance floor"). But more than this, the track brought together a range of South Asian sounds in a way I'd never heard growing up as a second-generation South Asian in the United States. My experiences contrasted with those of my cousins, who were always hip to the latest popular culture of South Asia and its diaspora: in their early teens they had moved from India to a heavily South Asian neighborhood in Los Angeles and were able to frequent the South Asian shops that lined their streets.

Particularly striking to me was how "Star Megamix" claimed a space for itself and subtly expressed a political consciousness, most notably through its use of black voices and music. For example, the track begins with a black British man stating, "Now we play bhangra *my* way," and then laughing menacingly. This is later followed by another black British man asking, "What do you think about r—*bhangra* music?" (The singer is about to say "rap," but Sagoo substitutes a sample from a South Asian man saying "bhangra.") Following this, in rhythmic succession, is the line "Now is the time!," sampled from a speech by Martin Luther King Jr. The track then builds on the theme of power by including the sampled lines "I've got the power!" (from "Power" by Snap), and "Shout, shout, let it all out!" (from "Shout" by Tears for Fears). One of the final lines, spoken in an official voice by a white, British male radio newscaster, expresses the conceit common to hip-hop songs that announce their own success: "This cut has been analytically designed to break on radio, and it will." After a pause, however, the newscaster adds the qualification, "sooner or later"—raising a question, and even a sense of struggle, about whether the track will break or not.

I later learned that the black and South Asian voices in "Star Megamix" reflect the racially diverse working-class population of Birmingham, England, where Sagoo grew up. In a move that was innovative both culturally and politically, he had remixed musical elements to create a new formation of sound that could not be easily characterized as British, South Asian, or black. Sagoo went on to become one of the pioneers of what has been termed British bhangra—a form that many claim expresses a uniquely British Asian identity because of the way it mixes British and Asian music.

As I listened to "Star Megamix," I brought my love of music and dancing and my experiences of race in the United States. Popular music, especially hip-hop, had played an important role in my struggles with identity; in high school I felt particularly alienated by the mostly white student body, among whom the use of racial epithets was common. I eventually met and became friends with the few South Asian Americans attending nearby high schools, and we began making every effort we could to meet others, which usually meant traveling for hours on weekends to attend small parties organized around music. Though this music was not South Asian–influenced, it still played a critical role: we were bonded by a shared relationship to American popular culture based on our collective experience of feeling different. These gatherings helped ease a sense of alienation for those of us who felt neither fully South Asian nor American. Years later Sagoo's track, which came from a diasporic community whose migration experiences were shaped by Britain's long history of colonial rule, sparked my interest in exploring the social formations shaping this music. Not only did the music "groove" me, but the political consciousness and racial affiliations suggested by Sagoo's remix captured my imagination.

Many years later, as a graduate student in cultural anthropology, I embarked on research on the British Asian music scene in London—a scene that included genres in addition to British bhangra. During this research I began noticing gender inequalities and class divides that had gone largely unremarked upon in much of the scholarship on this music. I also saw that, in going to clubs and making music, young people were actively constructing the identities that other scholars asserted this music was expressing. I started to focus on how young people crafted these identities and how conflicts among youth further shaped them. My interest was not in exposing the underside of youth communities; indeed, the politics of representing South Asians in the United Kingdom was already complicated since they had endured a long history of oppression. Rather, my interest was in calling attention to inequalities that were central to the struggles for justice that played an important role in these youth cultures. Ethnic or racial movements, and scholarship about those movements, have often sublimated questions of gender and class inequality, seeing them as detracting from the supposedly primary issues of race and ethnicity. Similarly, in racially politicized forms of cultural production it is tempting to read off racial politics from the productions themselves. But these approaches can elide contradictions, not only in the texts but also in the social formations that produce and consume those texts—that is, in their social life. In an effort to create a more nuanced view of British Asian youth identity, I analyzed the cultural politics of bhangra and Asian Underground, the two forms of British Asian music that came to dominate youth culture in the late 1990s. As I listened to producers and fans themselves, I heard vivid stories of conflict and community. This book represents my effort to do justice to their stories.

Acknowledgments

This book, which took many years to complete, owes so much to so many. My first and most heartfelt thanks goes to all of the music fans, artists, activists, and others who shared their perspectives and lives with me. This book would not have been possible without their incredible generosity. My deep gratitude goes to the friends, who as artists, shed light on the politics of producing "ethnic" art in Britain. I especially thank Parv Bancil, Ameet Chana, Polomi Desai, Ravinder Gill, Iqbal Hussein, Sonia Mehta, and Shazia Nizam for many enlightening conversations. During my fieldwork I was sustained by the humor and insight of Jatinder Barn, Hitesh Chauhan, Farzana and Rokhsana Fiaz, Rajinder Kumar, Sangeeta Matu, Kishori Panchali, Sophia Raja, and Sofia and Nadia Shah. Sophia has been there for me since we met on the dance floor through several follow-up trips to London; she has so greatly enriched my time in London. I am indebted to Hitesh, who helped me in innumerable ways: from technical help to insanely last-minute rides to the airport and much-needed downtime at the local pub. He and the staff at Tara Arts, headed by Jatinder Verma, also provided office support at several critical moments. My fieldwork was aided by the warmth and hospitality of Daud Ali, Zahed Amanullah, and Abida Riaz, Jyoti and Manoj Ambasna, Bhavna and Devesh Gundecha, and Carlo and Lella Ruzza, all of whom provided homes away from home. In London, my dear friend, Rashmi Sadana, not only helped me find my way, but also made some critical introductions.

The seeds of this project began when I was a graduate student at Harvard University. There, I was inspired by the work of Joan Fujimura and by my fellow students Nick Popovich and Joe Swingle; our conversations deepened my interest in feminist and ethnographic work. As I began developing this study as a graduate student at Stanford University, Paula Ebron, Joan Fujimura, Akhil Gupta, Purnima Mankekar, and Sylvia Yanagisako gave me critical intellectual guidance and support without which this project would not have been possible. Paulla Ebron and Joan Fujimura, supported me throughout the research and writing phases; for their unwavering faith in me, I cannot thank them enough.

I also learned a great deal from collaborations, workshops, and dialogues with fellow students; many of these relationships have lasted well beyond the days of graduate school. I am indebted to Lalaie Ameeriar, Robin Balliger, Kathleen Coll, Bakirathi Mani, Vivek Narayanan, Patricia Pender, Lok Siu, Miriam Ticktin, and Elizabeth Tunstall for their always keen insights. Lalaie, Robin, Kathleen, Baki, Trisha, and Miriam gave me trenchant feedback on several chapter drafts. As a graduate fellow at the Institute for Research on Women and Gender, I also received extremely helpful suggestions from the other members. I especially thank Trisha, who I first met through the Institute, for helping me transform my writing and for being such a great source of inspiration through her unflagging commitment to feminism.

A number of other brilliant colleagues and wonderful friends have given me their creative and thoughtful comments at various stages of this project, some of whom have reviewed several (if not all) of my chapters, and often more than once: Raphael Allen, Malathi de Alwis, Monisha Das Gupta, Lieba Faier, Paul Frymer, Kathleen Hall, Ronak Kapadia, Ritty Lukose, Naomi Murakawa, Anand Pandian, Nicholas Popovich, Amit Rai, Rashmi Sadana, Joe Swingle, Rajiv Vrudhula, and Eric Weisbard. Naomi, I have benefited so much from your incisiveness about matters in and beyond this book. Rashmi, our journeys together, in the United States, in India, and in Britain, have informed this work in deep ways.

I further developed my manuscript at SUNY-Binghamton, where my colleagues in the departments of Sociology, Asian American Studies, Anthropology, and History, provided a supportive and intellectually enriching environment. My deepest appreciation goes to Nancy Appelbaum, Deborah Elliston, Doug Glick, Michael Hames-Garcia, Ernesto Martinez, and Benita Roth who not only helped me advance my project, but whose friendships and humor sustained me.

At San Francisco State University (SFSU), where I completed the manuscript, I learned a tremendous amount from a remarkable community of scholars who generously discussed several of my chapters with me. These scholars include Joanne Barker, Clay Dumont, and Amy Suyeoshi in the College of Ethnic Studies and those I came to know through our work as part of the South Asians Studies Institute (SASI): Sanjoy Banerjee, Christopher Chekuri, Ashok Das, Santhi Kavuri-Bauer, Kasturi Ray, and Prithvi Datta Chandra Shobhi. I owe an immeasurable debt to Santhi and Kasturi—the writing group we formed helped me significantly revise and critically, complete the manuscript. I gained a great deal from their acute insights about the politics of art, gender, and South Asian identity. This project owes much to Kathy Chetkovich and Laura Helper-Ferris, who provided crucial developmental editing and taught me about storytelling. I thank Honely Hinnaniban and Elizabeth Keenan, who provided key bibliographic help, and to Owen Limbach, who helped with the final touches.

Many of the ideas in this book evolved in presentations at the University of Pennsylvania, Swarthmore College, and the University of San Diego at California, as well as at conferences, including those of South Asian Studies at the University of Hawaii at Manoa, the Asian American Studies Association, the American Anthropological Association, the Society for Cultural Anthropology, the National Association for Ethnic Studies, and South Asian Studies at the University of California at Berkeley and the University of Madison at Wisconsin. I thank the panelists and audiences for their critical engagement.

In learning about the world of music, I've profited from the insights of Anthony Filetto and Musahid Ahmed. My sister, Bella Bakrania, has taught me much about the gender politics of producing popular music. I give my love and thanks to my dear friends Priya Jagannathan, Nidhi Jain, Manisha Masher, Mona Shah, and Shipra Shukla. They have sustained me throughout the period of research and writing, providing unflagging love and support—they are like sisters to me. They have also been interlocutors, helping me develop my arguments.

I am grateful to the institutions whose financial support made this book possible. Funding for the early stages of this project was provided by the Center for European Studies at Stanford University and a Mellon Fellowship. I conducted the main fieldwork for this project with grants from the Woodrow Wilson Foundation, the Wenner-Gren Foundation for Anthropological Research, and the Joint Committee on Western Europe of the American Council of Learned Societies and the Social Science Research Council (with funds provided by the Ford and Mellon Foundations). The Institute for Research on Women and Gender at Stanford, the South Asia Initiative at Stanford's Asia/Pacific Research Center, and the Mellon Foundation provided funds for the initial write-up. Follow-up trips to London were enabled by a faculty research grant, an Individual Development award, and a Dean's Research Grant, all from SUNY-Binghamton, as well as a faculty research grant from SFSU. Two Affirmative Action awards from SFSU helped give me the time I needed to complete the manuscript.

I owe special thanks to Ken Wissoker for helping me understand what it means to write a book, introducing me to the Experience Music Project, and making a dream come true. I'd also like to thank the three anonymous reviewers during the review stage—their comments helped me strengthen my manuscript considerably.

My parents, Pravin and Veena Bakrania, have been extraordinarily supportive; they have been there for me through all of the difficulties and triumphs of completing this book and more. They are also simply extraordinary people without whose wisdom and love, this book (and much else) would not have been possible. Bella, my younger sister, has given me much inspiration through her own creativity and political engagements. Though I met Ronald Prasad when I was finishing the manuscript, his love, patience, and nurturing sustained me at those critical moments. As this book was nearing completion, he and I were blessed with the news that we were going to have a son. Sameen, you have brought us more joy than we could have imagined. This book is dedicated to all of my family, with my love.

A portion of chapter 4 was first published in my essay "Roomful of Asha: Gendered Productions of Ethnicity in Britain's Asian Underground," in *Transnational South Asians: The Making of a Neo-Diaspora*, edited by Susan Koshy and R. Radhakrishnan (Oxford University Press, 2008), 215–43. This essay has been reprinted in *Electronica, Dance and Club Music*, edited by Mark Butler (Farnham, Surrey: Ashgate, 2012), 357–85. A section of chapter 2 originally appeared in earlier versions in "Negotiating Art, Ethnicity, and Politics: Asian Underground Artists and the Commercial Public Sphere," *The Subcontinental: The Journal of South Asian American Public Affairs* 2, no. 2 (2004): 11–18 and in "'Asian Underground' Music and the Politics of Production," *sagar: A South Asia Research Journal* 6 (December 1997): 97–106.

Introduction

> For once Asians can conduct themselves with other Asians in a way they would never dream of doing in front of their parents. Coming to the Wag reassures me that I'm not the only one suffering from a cultural identity crisis.—**RAJAN MISTRY**, "Bombay Nights"

Getting into Bombay Jungle was no easy task. There were typically eight hundred people inside the club, and eight hundred more trying to get in, with lines that stretched well beyond the length of the building. One evening during a preliminary research trip I made to London in the summer of 1994 I eagerly waited with some friends in the long queue to enter. Once inside, we found the excitement in the club palpable, energized by thumping bass and rounds of beer. The deejays on the bottom floor played swing, soul, and hip-hop, while on the top floor they played remixes of bhangra. All of the deejays at Bombay Jungle were young men save for DJ Ritu, the only woman in the bhangra scene at the time. These deejays showed incredible technical skills, mixing in music that ranged widely in beats per minute and tempo. The crowd, comprised mostly of teens, danced along, mimicking the creativity and variety of the music in their steps. Club-goers moved fluidly between the dance floors as they changed their music preferences throughout the evening. But most of the women congregated on the hip-hop floor while the men exuberantly took center stage on the bhangra floor. Young people's clothing styles borrowed from those of commercial hip-hop, the men wearing baggy pants and flashy jewelry and even styling their hair with cornrows à la Snoop Dogg. While most women wore the requisite feminine, tight-fitting outfits, some also sported "hard" looks with baseball hats and puffed jackets. The class background of the crowd was not obvious, as their club gear was somewhat uniform. But I later learned that it was mostly working class, reflecting the demographic that was often drawn to bhangra. Though a generally friendly crowd, it was not without some attitude, the worst of which would lead to occasional fights erupting on the dance floor—mostly between men performing tough masculinities.

Bombay Jungle wasn't a club proper but a club night, a temporary arrangement that a venue would schedule to attract a specific audience. Three deejays, Mark, Mitts, and Dee, started the weekly event at the well-known London venue the Wag Club in the fall of 1993.[1] Known primarily as a bhangra night, it quickly became the hottest event on the British Asian music scene. Bhangra, originally a Punjabi folk music, had become increasingly popular with youth of South Asian descent who had, from the 1980s on, been creatively remixing it to create new music forms, often referred to as British bhangra (or just bhangra).[2] This new music combined the classic features of the genre of bhangra—such as the distinctive rhythms of the *dhol* (a wooden barrel drum) and Punjabi lyrics in couplet form (or *boliyan*)—with the instrumentation and sampled lyrics of popular music like R&B and hip-hop. Many of the young people involved in the scene as well as some scholars celebrated the music for expressing a uniquely British Asian identity.

By the mid-1990s, London had already seen many one-off bhangra club nights boasting audiences of up to five thousand. Young people would come not only from all over London, but also from all over England, arriving in buses. Bombay Jungle, however, was unique in several ways. It was the first regularly scheduled club night, and its success had led to the opening of several similar clubs. It was located in Leicester Square, the heart of London's bustling nightlife, where mainstream clubs had often denied young British Asians entry. As Dee said, "We were . . . breaking boundaries. . . . Being Asian, you used to just walk up to a [club] door, and they would be like, 'Naw, naw, you can't get in.' Whereas a couple of white people next to you would walk in." Journalists, who eagerly interviewed club-goers, interpreted the enthusiasm shown for Bombay Jungle differently: they saw mass rebellion by a group they assumed was trodden down by South Asian tradition. Although these media stories reinforced (post)-colonial stereotypes of South Asian culture, the popularity of Bombay Jungle heightened the visibility of British Asians. For many, its success represented a breakthrough.

When I went back to London in the fall of 1997 to commence a two-year period of research on the British Asian music scene, my return coincided with the arrival of what was to become the second major form of music to gain widespread attention, Asian Underground (AU).

As was the case at Bombay Jungle, the lines to get into Anokha, a club night featuring AU music, were long. And the media were again, eager to interview club-goers. But otherwise the experience of attending an AU club like Anokha bore little resemblance to attending a bhangra one. To get to Anokha I took the London tube to the East End, away from the commercial center of Leicester Square (other AU clubs that opened were likewise located outside of the city center). At the entrance, there were no extensive security checks like the ones that had started taking place at bhangra clubs, whose reputation for being violent had grown. The venue that hosted Anokha, the Blue Note, was small, representing the "boutique" feel of club nights striving to differentiate themselves from mass, commercial ones. On entering the club, I noticed that the audience was multiracial, including British Asians, blacks, and whites, and in their twenties and thirties, a slightly older demographic than that at bhangra clubs. I also later learned that it was generally middle class. At Anokha, fashion took an overtly fusion feel, most of the patrons mixing signifiers of East and West. For Asian women, this could mean wearing a *kurti* (top) with jeans, while for white women it could mean donning *mehndi* (henna tattoos), *bindis* (decorative dots on the forehead), and saris. Unlike the performances of masculinity at bhangra clubs, here in the arty, counterculture atmosphere, a few men experimented with gender bending through their club gear. Most, if not all, of the deejays, however, were men, with women appearing mostly as sampled vocalists on tracks. Groups of friends danced with one another, doing their own versions of fusion dance styles. But dancing by oneself was also a norm here, where appreciating the music, rather than meeting someone, appeared to be the primary focus.

Talvin Singh, a British Asian tabla player trained in classical Indian music, started Anokha, which means "unique" in Hindi, at the end of 1995. The club featured music that synthesized South Asian vocals and instrumentation (often classical forms) with Western breakbeats such as hip hop, jungle, and drum 'n' bass. In part to promote the club, Singh released a compilation album in June 1997 titled, *Anokha: Soundz of the Asian Underground*. As the popularity of the club and its music grew, British newspapers, music press, and style magazines seized on the label Asian Underground, using it to categorize and often promote the music. This label soon became the name of a new genre and was sometimes used by the British media, much to the chagrin of so-called AU artists, to subsume artists who ranged widely in their influences but who produced music not identifiable as bhangra. Thus, while bhangra had certain features that identified it as a genre (see chapter 1), AU music was much less easily definable and referred more to the kinds of music artists were remixing as opposed to a particular form they followed. For example, two releases that were considered club anthems of the AU scene—State of Bengal's "Flight IC 408" and Talvin Singh's "Jaan"—are more similar to each other than most AU tracks are. Yet they have little in common with regard to genre other than that they are forms of drum 'n' bass that use South Asian instrumentation (see chapter 4 for further discussion of both songs).

Within a short time AU music, like bhangra, garnered public attention. And the scene grew, with other clubs such as Swaraj joining Anokha, and AU record labels like Outcaste releasing compilation albums. But, unlike bhangra, AU became successful during the late 1990s as a mainstream form of music. In fact, its widespread recognition and mainstream acceptance as British Asian music were unprecedented. The press regularly featured it as a form that could be enjoyed by all, Asians and non-Asians alike, and many AU artists received some of the British music industry's top awards.[3] Indeed, the rising popularity of this music was evidenced in a phrase bandied about at the time: brown is the new black.[4] As was the case with bhangra, many youth and scholars claimed that *this* music expressed a uniquely British Asian identity.

THE EXPERIENCES OF youth of South Asian descent in Britain—a group I will refer to as postcolonial youth—shed light on the politics of belonging in a world shaped by empire and globalization. Youth has long been a socially and politically charged category; as a "metaphor for perceived social change and its projected consequences," it is often "an enduring locus for displaced social anxieties."[5] Thus I use *youth* to refer not only to an age cohort but also to an experiential category. Here, it refers to a sense of being in the second generation, that is, of having different sets of experiences from one's parents, who were settlers. As the largest ex-colonial, minority population of a two-centuries-long empire that was one of the biggest formal and far-reaching ones the world has seen, South Asians in Britain represent one of the most significant postcolonial communities today.[6] The experiences of the sizable and growing population of British Asians can help one understand how postcolonial youth face competing demands on them, such as those of a racist state and of ethnic communities invested in maintaining their cultures. Their predicament resonates with that of the vast numbers of other young people who hail from communities that their nations consider other.

The South Asian diaspora in Britain is a particularly rich site in which to explore how postcolonial youth negotiate identities through art and popular culture. Perhaps because of a confluence of factors—the high numbers and concentration of South Asian communities, their length of residence, and ongoing racial oppression—young people have been prolific, producing much film, comedy, literature, theater, dance, and music. And British Asians are forerunners: compared to other youth populations in the diaspora, they are often the first to work with specific forms, they commonly produce the most, and their work is frequently very influential. Perhaps owing to the relative accessibility of music technology and to music's mass appeal, music is an especially significant cultural product produced and consumed by British Asians. As Andrew Ross comments in an early anthology on "youth music," "The level of attention and meaning invested in music by youth is still unmatched by almost any other organized activity in society. . . . As a daily companion, social bible, commercial guide and spiritual source, youth music is still *the* place of faith, hope and refuge. In the forty-odd years since 'youth culture' was created as a consumer category, music remains the medium for the most creative and powerful stories about those things that often seem to count the most in our daily lives."[7] Ross's point applies to British Asians, who have produced many kinds of music in the past several decades. Of these forms, bhangra and AU are central. Not only do large numbers of young people create and enjoy these styles, but they have attracted attention in Britain's mainstream and have circulated transnationally, connecting diasporic communities in such locales as Britain, Canada, and the United States and even "returning" to South Asia.

In this book, an ethnographic examination of the practices of male music producers and female club-goers, I show that British Asian music is an intensely contested site through which competing notions of identity are played out. As such, this is a study of how postcolonial youth perform "hybrid" identities in diaspora. I place the word *hybrid* in quotation marks because, although I find it useful as a descriptor of cultural intermixture, scholars typically use it to refer to the mixing of two distinct cultural forms, in this case, British and Asian. My research questions the assumption that these two categories exist as separate cultures, that are singular and homogenous, and that all young people do is simply combine the two (albeit in some creative fashion). Music seems to be a literal example of this: bhangra and AU can be seen as a fusion of British and Asian music that produces a new hybrid form. I show instead that British and Asian are constructed categories and that young people interpret them through gendered and classed meanings of tradition and modernity, which in turn shapes how they craft hybrid identities through music. Cultural nationalism informs their use of these terms, such that they imagine tradition, or ethnic authenticity, to be the purview of women, and modernity to be the purview of men. Furthermore, given the predominantly working-class character of the South Asian diaspora in Britain, cultural nationalism is so deeply interwoven with class that ethnic authenticity is normatively associated with working-class status. Young people negotiate these norms in the bhangra and AU scenes, which are themselves differently inflected by gender and class: while British bhangra is associated with a working-class masculinity that trades in commercial hip-hop, AU, most of which is break-beat music, is ostensibly gender neutral and, because of its use of classical South Asian music, can be associated with the middle class.

By examining cultural nationalism as both an organizing idea and a principle in lived experience, one sees that it plays out differently for men, who are the main producers of this music, than for women, who, owing to their marginalization in music production, participate primarily as club-goers. Namely, they face distinct burdens of representation: male artists face the demand to be a certain kind of community representative, and female club-goers face the demand to maintain their ethnic authenticity. These groups deal with these expectations in ways that both challenge and reinscribe configurations of power. Their practices take shapes that, despite the politically celebratory rhetoric that marks much discussion of British Asian music, have exclusionary consequences for ethnic, racial, and national belonging. In the late 1990s the emergence of the AU scene, whose success augmented a crisis of slumping sales in the bhangra scene, revealed the increasing gendered and classed complexities of the British Asian community, unraveling unitary definitions of *British Asian* and celebratory discourses of resistance.

As this book explores South Asian belonging in Britain, it rereads a historical moment. In many ways the late 1990s represented what Arun Kundnani calls "the high point of progress against racism in Britain."[8] During that time Britain made dramatic and systemic policy changes as a result of the reopened investigation of the murder of Stephen Lawrence, a young black teenager who was stabbed to death by white youth in April 1993 while he was waiting for a bus. The original investigation by the Metropolitan police did not lead to any prosecutions. But the later, official inquiry into the case, headed by Sir William Macpherson, resulted in the publication in 1999 of the Macpherson Report, which declared that the police force was institutionally racist and demanded a number of policy changes. The report, the issuance of which has been described as one of the most important moments in the modern history of criminal justice in Britain, had an impact on policy areas beyond that of policing, as it called for reform in the British Civil Service, the National Health Service, education, and housing.

Changes were also occurring in the realm of public culture. In 1997 the Labour Party, which branded itself New Labour to distinguish itself as being modern, won the general election with a landslide majority, ending eighteen years of Conservative Party rule. In an article written in 1996, the journalist Stryker McGuire coined the term *Cool Britannia* to encapsulate the excitement in Britain, driven in part by the cultural diversity being expressed in London. Writing about that time in retrospect, he says, "Back then, the City [London] was the engine of our prosperity, British music, nightlife, art and fashion were the best in the world, and a young, dynamic Tony Blair was about to topple the Tories.... If loss of empire was once a drag on the spirit of the British people, the immigration that resulted in part from that loss had by the mid-1990s become a major driving force behind the richly multicultural London blossoming before our eyes."[9] In conjunction with increasing multiculturalism, British Asians were making major inroads in public culture: AU music was hitting the headlines, leading people to claim the arrival of a new "Asian Kool," and the British press "seized upon [AU] music as the sonic embodiment of Tony Blair's new, multi-ethnic Britain."[10] In television, the show *Goodness Gracious Me*, a sketch comedy by and about British Asians that parodied both South Asian and white culture became enormously popular among the public during its run on the BBC from 1998 to 2001. Kundnani says, "Comedy is a huge thing in Britain. So, being able to go into school and have other kids laugh at South Asian comedians who are on the BBC—that's a significant change that wouldn't have been imaginable when I was at school." He explains that such changes signaled "a sense that street culture could include South Asian communities in a way that worked." In tandem, "there seemed to be an opening of a space where there was a more interesting discussion about being British and about identity."[11]

After 2001 the landscape shifted. In the summer of 2001 race riots took place, predominantly between British Asian Muslim and white youth in cities such as Oldham, Bradford, and Leeds. After the riots came the events of 9/11 and 7/7, which refers to July 7, 2005, when four young men detonated bombs on London Underground trains, injuring and killing civilians. Three of the suspects were British Asian Muslims of Pakistani descent who came of age in Leeds. In response to these events, the cultural politics of British Asian identity changed, as Muslim identity became racialized, the state increasingly disciplined Muslims, and non-Muslim Asians responded by identifying less as Asian and more along the lines of religious affiliation. But these changes did not occur across Britain uniformly: a geographical aspect emerged, as the heightening of racialization along religious lines occurred more in the northern mill towns than in areas such as London, where the discourses of cultural diversity and multiculturalism continued to have a relatively more active life. And despite the changes that occurred in the bhangra and AU music scenes in the 2000s, British Asian music continues to be a site where the viability and crafting of the identity *British Asian* are ongoing (see the conclusion).

From the vantage point of today, the late 1990s seem to represent an idyllic time in which the state lauded cultural diversity and British Asians forged a unity. In other words, there appears to be a teleology in which the situation facing British Asians moved from good to bad. Yet, as this book shows, articulations of British Asian identity during the height of antiracism and state-sanctioned multiculturalism were incredibly power laden, shaped by both state racism and by internal lines of fissure. Thus, although the cultural politics of British Asian identity changed in the 2000s, the project of claiming such an identity has never been straightforward. By rereading the late 1990s, my book reinserts this period into the genealogy of the present. As Kundnani says, in light of the impact of 9/11 "there's a danger that you forget that [earlier] history. Nowadays, a lot of people think history started on 9/11; that's always the reference point."[12]

Apart from these historicized reasons for the import of this study, the discourse of fusion, which characterizes much discussion about British Asian music and its relationship to identity and which this book critiques, has far outlived the height of antiracism and multiculturalism in Britain. The term continues to be used in countless music promotions, media stories, academic studies, and fan blogs. I show how deeply problematic this term is, offering a set of analytical tools for understanding the ways in which British Asians and other minorities negotiate ethnic, racial, and national belonging through the hybrid popular culture they produce and consume.

Resistance

The bhangra and AU scenes differ in a number of ways, most obviously in their music, audience demographics, club dynamics, media coverage, and mainstream success. Yet many characterize the music and the clubs in which it is played as a utopia in which East meets West. Echoing the caught-between-two-cultures framework that some scholars have used to describe bicultural youth,[13] fans see this music's mix of Asian and Western elements as representing their own dual identities and thereby helping them resolve the identity crises they experience as being a part of two different worlds. As Rajan Mistry says in the epigraph to this introduction, attending Bombay Jungle assured him that he is "not the only one suffering from a cultural identity crisis." Several years later Krishnendu Majumdar, a young journalist and fan of AU music, described his experiences of attending Anokha in an elaborate essay posted on the Internet: "It was the first time I . . . felt truly proud of my heritage: it was incredible. The clash of cultures in me—born in Wales with a western education at school, entwined with a Bengali upbringing at home—was no longer a force pulling me apart. I was glowing and felt that this is where I belonged."[14] Notably, in both narratives club going is not only a site of healing injuries from culture clashes and identity crises but is a key site of actualizing ethnic and national belonging. Media produced by British Asians echo these narratives: the filmmaker Gurinder Chadha, who became well known in 2002 with *Bend It Like Beckham*, directed *I'm British But . . .* (1989) early in her career. One of the first films about British Asian music, it features the testimonies of young fans and artists throughout the United Kingdom on how this music expresses their bicultural heritage.

Studies have been sounding the theme of expression for at least ten years, part of a larger movement in which scholars have focused on youth agency to counter studies that have historically cast young people as deviant, pathological, or crisis ridden. They have held up young people's use of popular culture to celebrate youth creativity and contestation.[15] Accordingly, studies of British Asian music have overwhelmingly characterized it as a form of resistance to ethnic absolutism in Britain.[16] Scholars interpret lyrics and performance styles as calling into question culturally essentialist notions of Asian identity and racially essentialist notions of British identity. Using a framework adopted by many, for example, George Lipsitz writes, "The very existence of music demonstrating the interconnectedness between the culture of immigrants and the culture of their host country helps us understand how the actual lived experiences of immigrants are much more dynamic and complex than most existing models of immigration and assimilation admit."[17] Such scholarship is also fueled by a now long-standing emphasis in anthropology, cultural studies, and postcolonial studies on the ways in which hybridity enacts resistance.[18]

In contrast, my book demonstrates that multiple forms of "re-fusing" are at the heart of what is generally considered fusion. The "re" in *re-fusing* signals that people construct identity in an ongoing way; identity is never a finished or static product. Inherent in that process is not only a remaking but also a rejection (or refusal) of that which is not seen as part of the self. But while this rejection may resist power relations, it can also be complicit in them. On a broader level, then, *re-fusing* signals my own refusal of the fusion metaphor on the grounds that it collapses music and identity. This book refuses the direct mapping of one onto the other—a mapping that ignores the profound complexities and contingencies of making identity through popular culture.

Histories/Stakes

South Asian emigration to Britain, which has been performed mainly by Indians, Pakistanis, and Bangladeshis and which has been profoundly shaped by colonialism, illuminates the issues at stake in political assessments of British Asian music. While there is evidence that South Asians arrived in England as early as 1616, the major waves took place in the aftermath of the Second World War.[19] India gained independence from Britain in 1947, but the devastated economies of the newly created countries of India, Pakistan, and, after 1971, Bangladesh compelled South Asians to answer calls from Britain as it reached toward its former colonies for labor to rebuild its manufacturing base. These mostly rural immigrants arrived from the 1950s to the early 1960s from districts that had had an imperial relationship to Britain. And on arrival they confronted extensive race and class discrimination. As Avtar Brah states, "From the beginning ... the encounter between Asians and the white population was circumscribed by colonial precedents."[20] Further, immigrants took on what Shinder Thandi terms "3-d" jobs, jobs that were dangerous, dirty, and demanding and that white workers considered undesirable.[21] Because of the location of their jobs, their inability to afford expensive housing, and racist housing policies, South Asians settled in low-income areas. White Britons quickly associated problems in these areas with "the immigrants."[22]

These early groups were later augmented by family reunification and by another wave of South Asians—often referred to in scholarship as "twice migrants"[23]—who arrived in the late 1960s and early 1970s from the East African countries of Kenya, Tanzania, and Uganda. These populations left for countries like England because of the Africanization policies their home countries pursued upon gaining their independence from colonial rule. These groups too met with discrimination on their arrival: a mass racial hysteria erupted in the late 1960s in reaction to the supposed threat of Asians arriving from Kenya. Notably, these immigrants differed from the earlier ones: they came largely from urban areas and were middle class. This second wave of immigration thus marked the deepening of class stratification within the South Asian communities in Britain. Yet despite their class privilege, immigrants from East Africa, like their predecessors, became subject to discrimination and racial abuse. In fact, in the face of the growing numbers of Asians there was a corresponding increase in racialization. As a result, emigrants as well as scholars often refer to a singular Asian community, where *Asian* describes primarily South Asians, because of the plight that the diverse groups share.[24] With the addition of immigrants from East Africa, South Asians quickly became Britain's largest minority population. In the Census of 2001, the combined Indian, Pakistani, and Bangladeshi populations numbered more than 2 million (or 3.6 percent of the total population of the United Kingdom of some 58 million). Together, they made up nearly half of the total nonwhite population of 4.6 million.[25] (The 2011 census of England and Wales shows that Indians, Pakistanis, and Bangladeshis now make up close to 3 million or 5.3 percent of the total population in those countries.)[26]

Racism not only was a constitutive aspect of the daily lives of South Asians but also became institutionalized in national legislation aimed at curtailing the immigration and citizenship rights of nonwhites.[27] This legislation increasingly tied British identity to whiteness through such categories as ancestry, descent, and blood. For example, as a result of the anti-Kenyan hysteria, Parliament passed the Commonwealth Immigration Act of 1968 in a matter of days. Introducing ancestral notions of belonging into British immigration law, this act reinforced boundaries of race between Britain and its former colonies: it allowed entry into the United Kingdom only to those who held British passports and who could claim *ancestral connection* by proving that one parent or grandparent had been born or naturalized in the United Kingdom. As a result, white settlers from Kenya holding British passports were welcomed while South Asians were not only denied entry but also rendered stateless. The Immigration Act of 1971 further established the importance of white ancestry and introduced the notion of patrilineal descent by distinguishing "patrials" from "nonpatrials": only patrials, which meant British or Commonwealth citizens who were born in the United Kingdom or who had fathers or grandfathers born or naturalized there, were not subject to immigration control. The British Nationality Act of 1981 went even further: seeking to restrict the rights of British-born Asians, it declared that a person's citizenship was exclusively based on that of her or his parents, encoding citizenship no longer in the "law of the soil" (being born in Britain) but in the "law of the blood."

Another key characteristic of racism in Britain is its dependence on what scholars have termed cultural racism. While scientific or biological racism is based on an ideology of so-called genetic differences between racial groups, cultural racism argues that races are *culturally* different from each other, thereby attempting to make its claims with less obviously racist language.[28] Those who deploy cultural racism thus couch claims about the incommensurability of ethnic and racial groups by drawing attention to differences in social customs, religious practices, and language. In Britain, nativists have used these differences to argue that the culture of minorities threatens the majority's natural cohesiveness; their invention of a national tradition elides a history of diversity in Britain.[29] Former prime minister Margaret Thatcher's famous (or infamous) television statement in 1978 about the threat of Britain's being "swamped" by immigrants is a prime example of how state officials have deployed cultural racism to naturalize their goal of a white Britain: "People are really rather afraid that this country might be swamped by people of another culture. The British character has done so much for democracy, for law, and done so much throughout the world that if there is any fear that it might be swamped, then people are going to be rather hostile to those coming in. . . . We are a British nation with British characteristics. Every nation can take some minorities, and in many ways they add to the richness and variety of this country. But the moment a minority threatens to become a big one, people get frightened."[30]

As in the past, contemporary racism takes a variety of forms, including institutional, cultural, national, and violent.[31] As Kathleen Hall states, "In the post-colonial era, belief in the insurmountability of cultural differences has strengthened, while faith that cultural others will remain separate or assimilate has weakened, generating fears that nonwhite ex-colonial 'others' threaten the dominant (white) British way of life."[32] For example, in April 1990 the "Tebbit test" or "cricket test" became a way to police South Asians. In an interview with the *Los Angeles Times*, Norman Tebbit, a Conservative politician, suggested that immigrants who root for their native countries in cricket competitions rather than for England were not sufficiently loyal to their new country: "A large proportion of Britain's Asian population fail to pass the cricket test. Which side do they cheer for? It's an interesting test. Are you still harking back to where you came from or where you are?" Such racism often intersects with other categories of difference. For example, during the Rushdie affair in 1989—when Ayatollah Khomeini of Iran placed a fatwah on Salman Rushdie after he published his novel *The Satanic Verses* and many Muslims in Britain protested his work—nationally explosive debates about nonwhite others ignited and became an occasion for white Britons to condemn the fundamentalism of Muslim communities. Racism continues to show up in statistics about hate crimes. The Census of 2001 reports that South Asians, especially Pakistanis and Bangladeshis, who tend to be Muslim and of lower socioeconomic status than other groups, are disproportionately the victims of racially motivated violence.[33] These figures have since risen in light of increasing Islamophobia after 9/11 and 7/7.

But South Asian emigrants have resisted: intense struggle marks their history, as both women and men have waged battles across a number of fronts. These include the industrial disputes of the 1960s, in which women were in the front lines; the battles over religious rights, such as Sikhs fighting for the right to wear turbans at their workplaces; the antiracist protests that have taken place in majority South Asian areas such as Southall, in which protestors have endured police brutality[34]; the struggles of those like Satpal Ram and the Bradford 12 who have defended themselves against racist attacks; and the work of such organizations as the Newham Asian Women's Project, Women Against Fundamentalism, and the antidomestic violence organization Southall Black Sisters, all of which have aimed to redress gender inequalities.[35] A distinctive feature of the South Asian diaspora in Britain has been its collaboration with black Africans and black Caribbeans, the other major nonwhite groups that have endured histories of colonial and postcolonial oppression. Having been collectively and derogatorily labeled black by the white British, Asian and black groups have often joined forces, above all in the 1970s, appropriating the term *black* as a politicized category through which they have combated racism.[36]

As a new generation of British-born Asian youth started coming of age in the 1970s, they faced their own struggles. Though some of their experiences overlapped with those of their parents, they were in many ways distinct: on the one hand, young people encountered racism in schools and on the streets. On the other hand, not having experienced the homelands their parents remember, they could not look to these homes in the same ways their parents could. Many also faced their parents' desires for them to retain a South Asian identity, in many cases by marrying within the group.

Thus, young people found themselves struggling against both a racially intolerant nation-state and first-generation migrants who held onto rigid notions of Asianness. That British Asian music is seen as a panacea for these profound problems is a significant claim. At stake are crucial questions of *belonging in Britain*—a phrase that refers simultaneously to belonging to Britain, belonging to a South Asian community in the racially hostile context of Britain, and the fraught relationship between the two.

Refusing Resistance: An Ethnography of Intersections

Assertions that British Asian music is a site of resistance deserve close attention, not only because of the issues at stake but also because such statements resonate with celebrations of the hybrid cultural products of other minority groups. Using an ethnographic approach that attends to the social relations and local meanings that shape music production and consumption, I set out to explore the cultural politics of British Asian music. Central to my study is the use of methods like participant observation and intensive interviewing. But these are more than simply methods: they are a theoretical approach, as they help uncover the rich layers of on-the-ground realities that are not available from textual sources such as lyrics, recordings, and images. Ethnography took me quickly beyond these sources into the scenes themselves. Here, my work was in conversation with a number of ethnographies of popular music in which scholars have examined music as social practice and process.[37]

I went to England with several working understandings of identity and inequality. First, I saw British Asian music not as a straightforward expression of preconstituted identities that can be read off of such textual sources as lyrics but as an arena in which people dynamically construct identities.[38] This assumption was borne out in youth narratives: alongside their accounts of British Asian music representing their experience was evidence that the music played a kind of pedagogical role, helping them to learn who they "really" are. For example, the well-known bhangra deejay Ameet Chana interwove stories that naturalized bhangra ("it's in my blood") with accounts of bhangra's educational impact: "Bhangra's most important because it gives you something to hold on to, culturally. Because when bhangra started coming here, the younger generation started going 'All right.' 'Cause before bhangra, how many young kids used to listen to Indian music? . . . People went out, and they started listening to songs . . . and picking up words . . . they learned the language." As these statements show, young people have a mutually shaping relationship to British Asian music in which they shape it and it shapes them—not, as they more often claim, an unmediated or unidirectional one. The fact that young people see this music as an expression of their identity and that, in addition, it aids them in realizing that identity renders it especially powerful for them in the context of a racist Britain.

Second, when I started my research I looked for ways in which British Asian youth culture might be exclusionary, as claims to identity necessarily entail boundary making.[39] Third, I saw agency not as a matter of individuals exercising choice but as a matter of subjects negotiating social structures in ways that can both challenge and reproduce them; and here, resistance is often tethered to the conditions of constraint.[40] My understanding of identity and agency informed a fourth aspect of my approach: exploring both production and consumption practices. While studies of popular music typically see production as the site of hegemonic power and locate resistance in acts of consumption, I wanted to interrogate this binary by examining both sites.[41] I conducted a multisited ethnography by traveling across diverse domains and following the connections between different actors and discourses.

Fifth, I understood the ways in which people experience inequality and craft identity through the lens of intersectionality, which insists that categories such as race, class, gender, sexuality, and nation intersect in complex ways.[42] My use of ethnographic methods was critical here: they enabled me to explore the experiences of women, who, in male-dominated music industries, are often more present in spaces of consumption but who are still crucial to any assessment of the cultural politics of that music. Talking to both working- and middle-class men located in production and to working- and middle-class women located in consumption enabled me to analyze the imbrications of gender and class. In other words, instead of studying women or the working class, as gender and class, respectively, are sometimes understood, I examined the production of masculinity and femininity relationally and as they intersected with cross-class relations.

As I pursued ethnographic research by attending clubs, talking to clubgoers and artists, and listening to the music, I found the bhangra and AU scenes more intricate, much richer, and more contradictory than celebratory discourse suggests. Most immediately, it was clear that the two scenes attracted not only different groups of people but ones who claimed disparate kinds of identities. And the scenes were in conversation, even conflict: during the late 1990s the mainstream rise of the AU and simultaneous downturn in bhangra ignited a number of debates, debates that a focus on only one scene might erase. In fact, it was impossible to talk about one without the other. One way in which participants in one scene distinguished their sense of identity, for example, was to contrast features of their scene with those of the other.

Going forward, multiple layers of identity and inequality became apparent to me, signaling that the two scenes were shaped by disparity and power internally as well as in resistance to mainstream discrimination. I found unexpected alliances and unaccounted-for divisions: bhangra club-goers and artists deployed certain forms of black music and styles, while those in the AU did so less and almost never called attention to it; most of the artists from both scenes, certainly the popular ones, were men; there were strong class dissimilarities between the scenes; the experiences of women club-goers differed markedly from media images and public discourses about them, whether in the increasingly violent bhangra scene or the "chill" vibe of the AU. Indeed, the range of differences within and between each of the scenes raised fundamental questions: exactly how were British Asian audiences and artists using music to negotiate belonging in Britain? and what were the consequences of such uses?

The Hybridity of Postcolonial Youth Culture

In a generational, diasporic, and postcolonial problematic of belonging, many British Asians feel compelled to create or listen to music that fuses the two cultures of British and Asian, a process they normatively see as the fusing of modernity with tradition or authenticity. As they struggle to construct a hybrid identity in their production and consumption practices, gender and class in particular shape these struggles.[43]

Authenticity is often a central concern of communities living in conditions that they perceive as threatening to their cultural norms. In response, these communities can create essentialist notions of culture and demand that members remain culturally authentic. Maintaining authenticity here means not only saving a culture that its members fear is in danger of dying but also resisting oppressors. These demands take gendered forms in the South Asian diaspora.[44] Many communities task women with carrying on tradition, but the South Asian case has a specific history.[45] In the mid-nineteenth century, as Partha Chatterjee shows, Indian nationalists resolved the conflicting pulls of tradition and modernity by separating the domain of culture into two spheres: the material, associated with the Western world, and the spiritual, associated with the essence of Indian culture.[46] While they would need to learn Western forms of science, technology, economics, and statecraft in order to overcome colonization, they needed to preserve a self-identity, which they located in inner, spiritual life.[47] In practice, these realms became associated with gender roles: "Applying the inner/outer distinction to the matter of concrete day-to-day living separates the social space into *ghar* and *bahir*, the home and the world.... The world is a treacherous terrain of the pursuit of material interests, where practical considerations reign supreme. It is also typically the domain of the male. The home in its essence must remain un-affected by profane activities of the material world—and woman is its representation."[48]

Because, nationalists claimed, the West had "failed to colonize the inner, essential, identity of the East ... the crucial need was to protect, preserve and strengthen the inner core of the national culture.... In the world, imitation of and adaptation to Western norms was a necessity; at home, they were tantamount to annihilation of one's very identity."[49] Women therefore bore an immense ideological burden: their performance of femininity was equivalent to national survival. In their daily lives, women needed to embody gendered, upper-class notions of modesty: a woman could traverse such public spheres as education, employment, and travel as long as she displayed certain qualities, including refinement, chastity, self-sacrifice, submission, devotion, kindness, and patience.[50] She had to make these visible in her dress, eating habits, social demeanor, and religiosity. In these respects, she needed to distinguish herself from the westernized woman, seen as being brazen and lacking in feminine virtues; the lower-class woman, seen as being shameless but also coarse, vulgar, and loud; and the traditional woman, seen as being oppressed by a degenerate tradition.

South Asian diasporic communities continue to be impacted by an ideology that views women as bearers of tradition and sanctions only certain versions of femininity—an ideology that scholarship discusses as "cultural nationalism."[51] Heteronormativity shapes demands on women, as it did historically: they are charged with reproducing tradition by marrying and having families with the appropriate South Asian men.[52] Cultural nationalism surfaces in bhangra and AU youth cultures, which mobilize tradition and modernity in alignment with Chatterjee's theory, normatively associating tradition with *Asian* and the purview of women, and modernity with *British* and the purview of men.

But the two youth cultures force an entirely new consideration of cultural nationalism in diaspora, revising applications of Chatterjee's framework in serious ways. If young people are to be both British and Asian, how can women perform modernity without risking being seen as traitorous? And how can men perform authenticity without being emasculated? In other words, the struggles of British Asian youth force one to examine generation as a critical axis of how cultural nationalism works. They also necessitate a fuller examination of gender, not as a synonym for women but as a relational construct. Both axes are elided in current scholarship, which largely focuses on women, ignoring the generational differences among them, and eliding masculinity altogether. These studies mirror the lack of attention to masculinity in Chatterjee's work: because it assumes that men perform certain roles in the public sphere and are shorn of the responsibility to preserve culture, it says little about South Asian diasporic masculinity. Immediately, then, British Asian youth culture reveals that the overlapping dichotomies offered in Chatterjee's analysis—such as spiritual/material, inner/outer, home/world, female/male—cannot be seamlessly applied to contexts in which postcolonial youth struggle to perform hybrid identities on a national stage.

There's another level of complication: the history of South Asian emigration to England, which has been shaped by British colonialism, has been *primarily* working class. Tradition is thereby often associated with working-class status, and modernity with middle-class status. These constructs intersect with cultural nationalism to produce distinctive subject positions: working-class women, for example, might occupy a class status that is considered authentic, yet they are also inauthentic when they are subject to middle-class notions of respectability. Thus bhangra and AU youth cultures also ask one to examine the intricate intersections of cultural nationalism with gender and class.[53] Indeed, a class analysis was critical to Chatterjee's own work, another axis of difference that studies of cultural nationalism in the South Asian diaspora largely elide.[54]

In the British Asian music scene these intersections dovetailed with questions of authenticity that arise in the world of popular music, questions that have played a central role since the punk era of the late 1970s. Some struggles over authenticity and the related notion of selling out are debates about commercialization, that is, about whether an artist is being true to a music form or altering it in order to become more commercially successful. In other cases, a genre of music may be performed by a group not regarded as that music's authentic ethnic, racial, or national community. Examples of this include rock performed by African Americans and Tibetan refugees and jazz, hip-hop, and dancehall reggae performed by Japanese artists.[55]

The cases of bhangra and AU are slightly different: these two forms of music are performed by the group they ostensibly represent. But because of the fissures among British Asians and in the two scenes, both the questions of selling out and of being the appropriate group to produce the music emerge. For a while bhangra was *the* British Asian music; but while it purported to represent all, its demographic was mostly working class. It also represented a hard, roots masculinity, and as young people remixed it with commercial hip-hop it became laced with notions of black identity. But then along came AU music, which was imbued with an entirely variant set of meanings: because most artists remixed classical South Asian music with electronica, it acquired the meanings of those two forms. Many British Asians, for example, didn't see AU as roots music, let alone as working class. Because of the historical collaborations of white and South Asian artists working with similar forms, AU music was susceptible to being critiqued as well for being white. Furthermore, the AU scene appeared to be gender neutral: it did not witness the sexual harassment of women that plagued the bhangra scene, and it also appeared to be open to nonheteronormative identities. The success of the AU sparked divisions, each scene accusing the other of selling out by performing a music not authentic to the community. But while these conflicts appear to be solely ethnic or racial, I found that they were also gendered and classed. The debates between the scenes occurred most publicly and obviously between the male artists. But female club-goers also constructed themselves in ways that relied on class divisions.

A final set of complications is that tradition, modernity, and their associated terms have unstable, plural meanings that are in practice quite inflected, pliable, and contested. In its positive rendition, tradition can represent loyalty to one's culture, while in its negative rendition it is a sign of being backward or stuck, a construction reminiscent of colonial portrayals of the "natives." Modernity, on the other hand, can positively be a site of newness and negatively a sign of siding with whites and therefore being a traitor to community. In chart form, the categories look something like this:

	tradition	modernity
positive rendition	authentic; roots; loyalty	innovative; new; progressive
negative rendition	stuck; old; backward	white; traitor; betrayal

On the one hand, this is a structure that appears stable and that, for male producers and female club-goers of each scene, presents entirely different burdens of representation involved in becoming British Asian. But, on the other hand, this structure is unstable and therefore negotiable. As men and women work through the expectations they face, they sometimes contest the modalities of power they face and at other times reinscribe them. That is, as they re-fuse (or remake) British Asian identities, they refuse (or reject and accept) gender and class scripts that have uneven consequences in regard to ethnic, racial, and national belonging.

Recent ethnographies of popular music—for example, E. Taylor Atkins's *Blue Nippon* (2001), Ian Condry's *Hip-Hop Japan* (2006), Keila Diehl's *Echoes from Dharamsala* (2002), Maureen Mahon's *Right to Rock* (2004), and Marvin Sterling's *Babylon East* (2010)—have critically brought attention to how music is a site of struggle over such categories of identity as ethnicity, race, and nation; how these struggles can both reproduce and challenge dominant notions of identity; and how such practices counter romanticized readings of hybridity, of black cultural appropriation, and of resistance. My work is indebted to this scholarship and hopes to contribute to it in four ways. First, I show how categories such as ethnicity, race, and nation are mediated by class, gender, and sexuality. Instead of examining gender by focusing on the few and relatively unknown women artists in the bhangra and AU scenes, I explore how ideas about masculinity, femininity, and class infuse the very notions of ethnic authenticity with which male artists and female club-goers grapple and that they in turn craft.

Second, I extend the questions above to the issues with which postcolonial youth such as British Asians struggle. Studies like those of Atkins, Condry, and Sterling largely discuss musicians and fans who racially and nationally belong to the country in which they are based but who are drawn to music genres that are not considered authentic to that country. Mahon discusses a group considered racial others in a country from which they hail (blacks in the United States) who perform music (rock) considered inauthentic to them. Diehl explores a community (Tibetans in Dharamsala) that feels displaced from its homeland and desires to return to it. British Asians, however, are young people whose parents arrived in Britain as racialized immigrants and who feel caught between the two worlds of their ethnic communities and their home nations. As such, they produce and consume music that they feel reflects their bicultural identities. In analyzing these practices, this book extends the questions of authenticity above to a context in which questions of fusing tradition and modernity become salient, showing that these categories are associated with very specific notions of ethnicity, race, nation, class, gender, and sexuality.

Third, because of my interest in the intersections of gender with other categories of difference, I give equal attention to club-goers and to artists; with some exceptions, artists tend to be the focus of popular music scholarship. Fourth and finally, I extend discussions of the use of black cultural forms by examining a community that has had direct, sustained cultural and political relations with blacks.[56] In other words, British Asians have come of age in a context in which Asians have shared forms of race and class disenfranchisement with Afro-Caribbeans and in which there is a long history of black British politics. Yet, as I show, such relations do not guarantee resistant musical practices.

London's Geographies

The dynamism of British Asian identity played out on the unique terrain of London. I focused my research in London not only because 90 percent of the activities of Britain's music industry are located there, but also because it was a central area in which young people produced and consumed bhangra and AU music.[57] It had a history of hosting bhangra performances, with bands performing for audiences of up to five thousand in some of the largest venues, and the first regularly scheduled club night, Bombay Jungle, opened there and also occasioned the creation of others in the city. Moreover, the AU scene emerged in London, where all of the clubs and nearly all of the artists were based. In the context of the established popularity of bhangra and the rising popularity of AU music, London was a prime location in which to base this study. During my research in the late 1990s some bhangra clubs shut down, but the most popular ones remained open. And AU clubs, in the meantime, proliferated. In both cases, public consumption practices were salient and easy to observe.

London was also an ideal site because of the sheer numbers of South Asians who live there. It has the largest concentration of Asian people in Britain, a pattern that has not changed much since the 1970s.[58] This, combined with the growing birth rate, meant that in the late 1990s large numbers of British Asians were coming of age in London.[59]

In addition, London in the late 1990s, and the British Asians who resided there, held important positions in the country. A cosmopolitan city, it was a place where Prime Minister Tony Blair and the Labour government staged attempts at improving the United Kingdom's image globally, especially through a discourse of multiculturalism. From today's vantage point, after the race riots of 2001 and the events of 9/11 and 7/7, the turn of the millennium, as I discussed earlier, was indeed a poignant moment in Britain: coming after Thatcher yet before the full-fledged development of a security state, it was a moment in which the state lauded cultural diversity for its potential to enable the state's success. And London's Asian communities were central to this success. The mayor of London, Ken Livingstone, for example, linked London's growing "Asian creative industries" to the future success of London nationally and of England globally. After noting evidence that the creative sector was the strongest emerging force in the capital's economy, he said in the foreword of a report he commissioned, titled *Play It Right: Asian Creative Industries in London*, "Key to this success is London's cultural diversity. . . . The Asian presence within London's creative industries is a huge asset, with the potential to improve the competitiveness of the sector, and forge and sustain unique links between London and several of the world's fastest growing economies, including India and China. . . . This new generation of young London Asian entrepreneurs are [sic] also fusing cultures and styles in music and fashion that appeals [sic] to a wider mainstream market."[60] The report highlights "music and the performing arts" as one of the creative industries' critical sectors: "Asian music is currently fusing western styles [in a way] that is likely to widen its appeal to a larger market. In addition, the current explosion of Asian song samples within the hip-hop music genre has increased demand for Asian music in the UK."[61] In sum, London was an ideal site for this study because of its significance as a location for British Asian music practices.

But in the course of my research London's race and class geography also came to matter, revealing the critical role they played in the relationship between British Asian music and identity. Notwithstanding the state's use of a multicultural discourse, within London the politics of racial identity are spatialized, as Londoners across the board often map the city in terms of its black, Asian, and refugee populations; in the late 1990s the latest so-called problem populations included Somalis and Afghanis. Such racial segregation is a direct result of discriminatory housing acts introduced in the 1960s—the height of minority settlement in Britain—that channeled new settlers into concentrated places of manual or semiskilled work, including factories, mills, and airports. Specific areas of London, for example, Southall and Hounslow in the southwest, Wembley in the northwest, the East End, and parts of South London such as Croydon, are among the largest settlements of South Asians outside of South Asia and in the West.

Moreover, London's South Asian communities are stratified by class. The jostling between youth of diverse class backgrounds was real as well as imagined. For example, those who grew up in middle-class non-Asian areas often felt both guilt and nostalgia for not being Asian enough, and in traversing the city they would run into other Asians who they imagined were truly authentic. In contrast, those who grew up in working-class Asian areas often had a love–hate relationship with them: liking being with their own ethnic community but disliking the oppressive conditions they faced and the stigma they sometimes bore. Yet upward mobility seemed not only difficult but also undesirable, as it meant entering into alienating life worlds.

This race and class geography had a deep impact on how British Asian youth experienced the meanings of British and Asian and crafted British Asian identities. It produced subtle tensions among youth residing inside versus outside of majority Asian areas, tensions that youth expressed through conflicting notions of cultural identity, racial pride, tradition, and progress. These conflicts found their expression in contests around British Asian music, which often functioned as a flashpoint.

The geography of London and its impact on identity are more complicated than studies of race relations in Britain suggest. Certainly, the racial terror Asian and black youth experience in the streets of London finds its expressions in a literal mapping of space.[62] As Barnor Hesse suggests, racial segregation is one of many levels of racial harassment that secures the hegemony of whiteness as a form of governmentality.[63] But by focusing on race only in terms of racism, one learns less about the impact of these geographies on the production of identity.[64]

Methodology

I conducted ethnographic fieldwork in London during the summers of 1994 and 1996 and for a period of twenty months during 1997 and 1998, followed by brief follow-up trips in the summers of 2004 and 2006. I used participant observation not only as a theoretical tool of questioning, as noted earlier, but also as a methodology, as it is more usually understood. I also made extensive use of interviewing; this enabled me to explore the interpretive dimensions of how youth made and enjoyed music, which are critical to understanding the relationship between music and identity. Also, while participant observation made sense as an accompanying method for studying club dynamics, because I wasn't studying how artists made music, in my study of producers I relied more on interviews. In general, I was particularly interested in how young people understood and conveyed their identities in the ways they invoked such categories as British, Asian, modernity, and tradition. I approached these categories as both a concern of discourse and an attitude of self-consciousness. While I relied on people's discussions, I regarded them as mediated, not as transparent evidence of experience.[65] For example, when an AU artist told me "those bhangra guys are so backwards," I neither dismissed it as racism nor embraced it as an objective description. Rather, I explored it as a positioned critique that illuminated how social inequalities shaped negotiations of identity.

Because of my specific interest in this kind of production, I paid less attention to how people actually produce music. That is, instead of attending to the more technical aspects of how these music industries are structured and how artists make and record music, I focused on such areas as the key players and the general relationships of the bhangra and AU music business worlds to the mainstream. Likewise, because the music is indeed an important vehicle of identification and definition, I describe it throughout the book (although, again, it is easier to describe the elements of a bhangra track than those of an AU track as bhangra actually shares more generic elements). I have not, however, discussed this music in highly technical or ethnomusicological terms because my interests lay in theorizing young people's engagement with music. Moreover, a primary aspect and contribution of my work is examining the realms of both production and consumption; extending technical discussions of how artists produce music and the music risks exacerbating the bias of current ethnographies of popular music.

In order to explore the experiences of artists and industry folks, I interviewed pivotal individuals in the AU and bhangra music industries and club scenes. The interviews included eighteen artists, that is, musicians and deejays, and ten industry members, among them club staff, public relations and marketing specialists, record company staff, music shop owners, and music magazine editors. I also examined debates about bhangra and AU music in print media. In order to grasp how young people consumed music, I examined club going, a public form of consumption in which young people collectively staged British Asian identities. Along with observing club dynamics, I interviewed club promoters and staff and more than twenty regular women club-goers. I located avid club-goers by frequenting clubs, posting signs, and getting help from club staff; I was able to cultivate relationships with and formally interview a wide range of women in both bhangra and AU club settings.

Throughout my fieldwork I monitored mainstream and British Asian media for stories on youth. Mainstream media that I examined included television specials, documentary films, and print media, ranging from daily tabloids like the *Sun* and the *Mirror* to more conventional newspapers like the *Guardian* and the *Independent*. British Asian television I followed included shows such as *Café 21*, *Network East*, and the enormously popular weekly comedy *Goodness Gracious Me*. Together, these shows offered a sense of the various discourses that shape the identities of young people. British Asian print media, such as the glossies *Snoop* and *2nd Generation* as well as newspapers like *Eastern Eye* were a prime source of news regarding music events and covered ongoing debates about British Asian music. In order to understand more fully the struggles of South Asian communities in Britain, I regularly attended political demonstrations and conferences. I also interviewed, informally and formally, fifteen activists in race relations, women's, and youth organizations.

In the course of my research, I met, and in many cases made friends with, British Asian artists outside the music industry, including actors, dancers, and writers. They provided invaluable support as well as insight into the social inequalities British Asians face and the politics of producing so-called ethnic art. Because many of the artists deal with concerns similar to those of musicians, discussions with them afforded me a broader sense of the discourses that frame British Asian experiences and the issues that motivate artists' work. By knowing a wide range of cultural producers, I was also able to have ongoing conversations about the politics of British Asian music and other cultural production. These producers comprised an interpretive community that offered a diversity of opinions about contemporary events and contexts for debate. Finally, in that British Asian art constitutes a relatively small part of the arts industry in Britain, many producers know one another and often work together. Hence my relationships with diverse artists helped me obtain a sense of both the similarities in concerns and the different sensibilities that fracture groups.

Terminology

The South Asian diaspora to which I've referred here is a complex object of knowledge, as it encompasses an incredible diversity of movement and community formation. So complicated is this formation that the phrase *South Asian diaspora* has at times come under critique: many have shown that diasporic invocations of South Asia, though gesturing toward a pan–South Asian identity and politics, in reality represent the narrow interests of an Indian hegemony. The term has also come under criticism for referring to a singular diaspora, rather than to plural diasporas thereby running the risk of conflating incredibly diverse histories of migration and displacement on the basis of national origin. In addition, *diaspora* typically connotes an orientation toward and desire to return to a homeland, often at the expense of understanding the oftentimes equally important, transnational connections between diasporic communities.

Certainly, then, the South Asian diaspora in Britain is likewise complex. As I've discussed, it is composed of many communities—the main ones being the Indian, Pakistani, and Bangladeshi—who have arrived under a range of conditions and with varying socioeconomic capital. There are also diverse religious affiliations, so when people define themselves ethnically they sometimes use a combination of ethnicity or nationality with religion, for example, Punjabi Hindu, Punjabi Sikh, Pakistani Muslim, and so forth. In this book, I at times attend to these specificities within the category of British Asian, but one of my main findings is that these differences were not theoretically important to the ways in which men and women engaged with the bhangra and AU scenes—especially since most were crafting British Asian identities in ways that purposely erased diversity. In fact, a number of artists' biographies specify very little about their background, and in my interviews artists did likewise. Thus I refrain from naming the ethnic and religious background of each actor I mention, as that could mislead readers as to the significance of that information. Furthermore, much research on South Asians in Britain has tended to follow an ethnic community model, whereby certain communities, such as Gujaratis or Punjabis, are studied in isolation from others; this is a problematic model since these groups often interact with one another. A persistent focus on such categories of difference, especially in areas in which they do not matter, may reproduce the questionable logic of these studies.

In this book I mostly use the descriptor *British Asian* to refer specifically to youth of South Asian descent who have come of age in Britain. I use that locution descriptively where appropriate, that is, when it is used by people, including youth themselves, to characterize their identities and cultural productions. But because my goal is to show how youth construct this identity, I also use it as an aspirational and interpellative category. In Britain, *Asian* can be a shorthand term used to refer to South Asians of all generations. When necessary, I clarify its generational usage in the text.

Structure of the Book

The book is divided into two parts. Part 1, "The Politics of Production," explores the cultural politics of production among men in the music industry. Part 2, "The Club Cultures of Consumption," investigates the cultural politics of club going among women who go dancing. This breakdown is not meant to reify a dichotomy of male equals production and female equals consumption. There were in fact exceptions to this dichotomy, the main example of which is DJ Ritu, who played a strong role as both a businesswoman and an artist: she was a deejay at Bombay Jungle and a cofounder of the AU record label Outcaste.[66] But because she is only one example and her time in the bhangra and AU scenes that I chart here was brief, her experience does not allow for a sustained analysis of women's role in production. Furthermore, British Asian men were certainly consumers of both bhangra and AU music (in chapter 3, the examples of male violence in bhangra clubs make that clear). But my theoretical concerns (along with others, such as my safety in bhangra clubs) led to me to focus on female club-goers.

In chapters 1 and 2 I examine how the predominantly male artists and industry folks in the bhangra and AU scenes dealt with the British mainstream, a site that ambivalently symbolizes to them national belonging. As these men negotiated the burdens of representation that shaped their respective scenes, they reworked such categories as tradition, modernity, culture, and politics, constructing masculinities that can resist racism but that also write others, including women, queers, blacks, and working-class people, out of the script of national belonging.

Chapter 1 focuses on a time of crisis in the bhangra industry, when the rise of the AU only deepened men's frustrations about bhangra's ongoing lack of mainstream success, at times causing them to repudiate the mainstream altogether. Drawing on industry interviews and news media, I examine how men understood this lack and crafted ways to cross over. Because bhangra is seen as roots music, the dream of it crossing over has strong appeal. Yet, because authenticity is seen as the purview of women and bhangra is a historically masculine music, its male producers face the challenge of performing their British Asian identities—or both ethnic authenticity and modernity—in ways that are not emasculating. As they refashion tradition into a property of men they resist class oppression but reproduce other social inequalities.[67]

While bhangra artists didn't achieve crossover success (and in 2013, still

Introduction **27**

hasn't), AU did. In that process, they faced the demand that they engage in protest politics, that is, that they express desires for racial equality in lyrics, interviews, and performances. But many of them disavowed an interest in politics, even as they cared about empowerment. How, then, did AU artistis negotiate the expectations they faced and with what consequences? Chapter 2 shows how the insistent requests made of artists as well as artists' responses contest commonsense understandings of what is and is not political. The trope of the angry Asian encapsulated the burdens placed upon them by the press, scholars, and activists; while it appears to be racial, it in fact reproduces patriarchal norms of national belonging. Three well-known AU artists—Nitin Sawhney, Badmarsh, and Joi—dealt with the demands placed on them by engaging in a creative dance with community empowerment and liberal humanism, a dance that simultaneously rejected the angry Asian trope and resisted racist nationalism. Yet they replaced this trope with others that recentered men as agents and subjects of the nation.

In chapters 3 and 4, as I move from men in the industry to women clubgoers, my goal is not simply to write women back into the story of British Asian battles for belonging. Rather, it is to show how class shapes women's struggles with the cultural nationalist demand to be good Asian girls. British Asian women are asked to reproduce tradition, but class complicates this expectation. South Asians in Britain often see being ethnically authentic as being working class. Yet women are expected to reproduce this authenticity by being respectable (virtuous), which is considered a property of the middle and upper classes. Working-class and middle-class women therefore face disparate conundrums, which I show they negotiate with uneven consequences. Their club-going practices not only illuminate the complexity of women's agency but also challenge utopian narratives that cast British Asian clubs as "diasporic public spheres" that represent racial liberation.[68]

Chapter 3 explores the club-going practices of the predominantly working-class women who frequent bhangra clubs. It focuses on a club night called Masala that was held in central London.[69] In the late 1990s Masala was one of the few club nights still in operation, as others had closed down because of ongoing violence. Women's club going reveals a multi-layered story about women's agency and shows that bhangra clubs are shaped by racialized heteronormativity and gendered violence, some forms of which authorities sanction. Women attend clubs in part to find men to marry on their own, that is, to exercise agency in the demand to be a good girl. (Indeed, Mistry, in the epigraph to this introduction, alludes to performances of sexuality—necessarily imbued with power—that studies of British Asian music have largely elided.) But this strategy was inherently contradictory, as it subjected them to the stigma of being a bad girl. Women dealt with this contradiction in ways that simultaneously resisted racism and cultural nationalism but that also reinscribed gendered power relations.

In chapter 4 I turn to the club-going practices of the predominantly middle-class women who frequent AU clubs. It focuses on clubs like Anokha, Club Outcaste, and Swaraj, which received the most attention from clubgoers and mainstream media. Having grown up within the middle class or experienced upward class mobility, many of these women dealt with accusations that they are not ethnically authentic, an accusation that is doubly difficult given that women are directed to carry on tradition. Women participated in AU clubs in ways that enabled them to critique essentialist and gendered notions of Asian identity and also to produce themselves as legitimate Asians to Asians and non-Asians alike. In the process, they contested cultural nationalism. Yet women's strategies risked naturalizing class privilege and showed little evidence of black British politics. Further, the AU club scene's commercialism threatened to reproduce (post)colonial race and gender hierarchies.

In the concluding chapter I examine some of the shifts in the cultural politics of British Asian identity that took place in the 2000s, in the aftermath of the "race riots" of 2001, and the events of 9/11 and 7/7. I juxtapose these shifts with the major changes that took place in the bhangra and AU scenes.

These chapters show that as British Asian youth craft identities through music, they engage in complex kinds of re-fusing that have profoundly uneven consequences for belonging in Britain.

PART I. **The Politics of Production**

Chapter One

Mainstreaming Masculinity
Bhangra Boyz and Belonging in Britain

In 1998 I met with Sunny Suri, the son of the owner of Metro Music, a well-known South Asian music shop in Southall, London. I wanted to discuss the state of the bhangra industry with him. As we sat down, he said, "I don't know how many people must have told you the bhangra industry is going down, or has gone down, and it's suddenly picking up, or is going to pick up.... Everyone's trying to be a pundit and forecast what bhangra is going to be like."

Fast forward to more than a decade later. In 2009 Bobby Friction, the host of a weekly radio show on the BBC Asian Network, moderated a one-hour debate with four bhangra producers. Friction opened with the central question, "Where is bhangra in 2009? Is it healthy?" The panelists quickly focused on how the industry had "gone down" and whose fault it was, sustaining that theme for most of the hour. Midway through, Gurshuran Chana, a former journalist and deejay, voiced a small protest. "Bhangra music... will never die," he said. "It will always be there. We've had this debate many times. Like when I was a journalist twenty years ago when Pardesi released their 'Pump Up the Bhangra,' people said, 'Oh, this is terrible!... It's going to kill bhangra music!' But it didn't. It revitalized it."

INDUSTRY FOLKS HAVE long discussed the state of bhangra, usually quite anxiously. Music journalists, promoters, artists, record label heads, and music shop staff regularly express frustration, describing bhangra almost as a patient in failing health. Accordingly, they diagnose its problems by identifying its symptoms, who or what is to blame, and possible treatments. A central problem for them is bhangra's lack of sustained crossover, or mainstream, success—a long-standing goal that signifies to them national recognition and, in turn, belonging in Britain. Such goals necessarily raise questions of race, nation, and, I argue, gender.

As with the hybrid productions of other "bicultural" youth, popular and scholarly discourse often sees bhangra as a straightforward expression of young people's hybrid identities, in this case, as British and Asian. But as bhangra artists perform British Asian identities they have to follow implicit rules. As I discuss in the introduction, young people often associate the categories of Asian and British with tradition and modernity, respectively, each of which has a double valence and is therefore an unstable signifier. In its positive rendition, tradition is seen as ethnic authenticity, while negatively it is understood as being backward or stuck in a premodern moment, a familiar trope of colonial discourse. In contrast, modernity, in its positive rendition, is seen as newness or innovation, but in the context of British racism it can be negatively associated with whiteness. The challenge for artists aiming at the national stage, therefore, is to perform a British Asian identity that is authentic and new, not backward or white.

Performing bhangra in the public sphere of the British mainstream, moreover, involves further challenges. Having been historically performed by men in the agricultural regions of Punjab—a heavily masculinized space in contemporary Indian imagination—bhangra is often seen as roots (or traditional) music and is associated with a tough male identity. This history is reflected in the British bhangra industry, in which men, including both the older pioneers and a new generation of young artists, dominate music production. Yet the idea that they can seamlessly perform ethnic authenticity in the public sphere is complicated, as South Asian communities in Britain normatively task women with reproducing Asian tradition, locating that activity in the private sphere of the home.[1] The injunction for artists, then, is to perform their Asian identities in the public sphere in ways that do not emasculate them. Inherent in artists' struggles therefore is a particular crisis of masculinity.

During my fieldwork in the late 1990s disappointment within the bhangra industry heightened: not only had bhangra sales plummeted, but, by contrast, Asian Underground (AU) music, a genre that bhangra fans often saw as catering to whites, was enjoying increasing mainstream popularity. This dissatisfaction energized young men's negotiation of the aforementioned identity categories, and in addition people in the bhangra industry developed a somewhat unstable relationship to the mainstream: they mostly continued to view it as a desired site of modernity, but in light of AU music's success, they at times cast it as white and therefore as a site only so-called ethnic traitors occupied. The mainstream itself thereby became doubly valenced: at once a sign of national acceptance of racial difference and a space of whiteness that can eclipse that difference.

In such a tenuous time, how did young industry men negotiate their desires for bhangra to enter the mainstream and with what consequences to the community and the nation? As I traced the discussions of music journalists, promoters, artists, record label heads, and music shop staff through my interviews and through stories in the popular British Asian weekly *Eastern Eye*, it became clear to me that postcolonial anxieties about Asian masculinity shaped their desires for bhangra's national success.[2] They blamed bhangra's lack of success on such figures as the businessmen and the old-timer artists, who, they felt, failed because they left tradition mired in femininity. In tension with these critiques, however, were the ways in which they disparaged figures of success like the AU artist, represented by Nitin Sawhney, and the bhangra artist Apache Indian. In these cases they used gendered notions of racial mimicry to accuse them of not being Asian enough. Since discourses of impossibility and hope often need each other (perhaps especially so in a frustrated music industry), bhangra folks also celebrated two kinds of artists—I call them the cultured hard boy and the lad-like boy band—who they hoped could lead bhangra into the future. Here, too, gender norms were central. In both their disappointments and hopes young men in the bhangra industry drew on masculinity to negotiate the overlapping dichotomies that shaped their reach for the mainstream—dichotomies like tradition and modernity, Asian and British, private and public—in ways that construct the feminine and queer as other.

Before I turn to industry folks' criticisms and hopes, I want to provide a brief history of bhangra to explain why many youth consider bhangra to be synonymous with British Asian identity and why they want it to become mainstream. While there were moments in which bhangra seemed it might attain mainstream success, it didn't, and the rise of the AU only deepened anxieties within the bhangra industry. I explore how industry people understood bhangra's downfall and placed hope in its future, showing how notions of race, class, gender, and sexuality played a central role in these discussions. The multiple ways in which workers in the bhangra industry negotiated their desires illuminate how British Asian battles with ethnic and national belonging are complex. British Asian music is not a static form in which the preconstituted identities of British Asian youth are simply expressed through hybrid lyrics and performance styles. Rather, it is a dynamic site of social practice in which one finds differently positioned actors who face their particular struggles in ways that both resist and reproduce social inequalities.

British Bhangra, Identity, and the Mainstream
HISTORIES

Young fans of bhangra persistently and intensely engage in discussions about this music because they hear it as synonymous with British Asian identity. Bhangra originated as a folk song and dance genre from rural Punjab associated with *Vaisakhi*, a celebration of the harvest and the New Year. Typically performed by men, it is the counterpart to women's traditional song and dance form, *giddha*.[3] Sabita Banerji and Gerd Baumann, two music scholars who have written extensively about the early history of bhangra in Britain, describe its traditional form: "Bhangra is characterized by the distinctive rhythm of the *dholak*, a wooden barrel drum beaten with sticks, and the smaller *dholki* beaten by hand. The *dholak* drummer, with his instrument slung around his shoulders and therefore able to move around, is considered the 'leader' of the dance, with the principal singer as 'deputy leader.' The often humorous or romantic lyrics in couplet form may be improvised and end in a burst of the drums, to which dancers perform a vigorous, acrobatic display of their agility and strength."[4] Discussing bhangra's carnivalesque power, Banerji explains that it is "vibrant, rhythmic and joyfully hedonistic and the language in which it is sung has been described as 'the cockney of India.'"[5]

Bhangra was popular among the large numbers of Punjabi migrants to Britain, who, as they reinvented tradition in their new homes, began transforming it into a musically unique form. Early bhangra bands consisted of about ten to fifteen Punjabi men who were amateur musicians and commonly held full-time jobs. In the mid-1960s these bands performed traditional songs at weddings and cultural celebrations but also began using pop and disco instrumentation to remix bhangra. Labeling the newly emerging form British bhangra, most historical accounts locate its birth with Alaap's successful release of the album *Teri Chunni de Sitare* in 1984. For the next several years British bhangra developed in tandem with the changing technology of disco music, with artists making creative use of high-tech synthesizers.[6]

Although some of this new music narrated the hardships that migrants experienced in Britain, most of it remained jubilant in nature and narrated life experiences from the point of view of a male protagonist, similar to the bhangra popular in rural Punjab.[7] Baumann notes, "The texts of virtually all of these songs are celebratory in tone, and can focus on the beauties of the harvest season, on natural and human beauty, and on a range of, usually male, sentiments about attraction, companionship, friendship and love. A great many of the bhangra songs most popular in England celebrate experiences of infatuation and romantic love. They do so in a robust and worldly way which contrasts with the romanticism associated with the songs of Hindustani films."[8] Describing the "certain niche in Asian taste" that bhangra occupies in England, Suri said that it is seen as a dance genre because of its fast beat: "Bhangra is something that works well at parties. It's a more happy type of music, not something to be depressed to."

In the mid-1980s bhangra gained popularity among a cross-section of British Asian youth, many of whom, in turn, saw it not as a specifically Punjabi form but as a British Asian one. Banerji attributes part of this success to South Asians' widespread familiarity with the rhythm of the dholak: the dholak, "much more than the sitar, represents Indian music over a wide area of the subcontinent and at every level of musical activity, folk, classical and film music."[9] DJ Ritu credits bhangra's success to its "strong dance sensibility," which, she says, "lent itself to crossing over into a 'street style' pop music."[10] The increased interest among young British Asian deejays gave "wider exposure to the music, creating new audiences, new bands, and widespread interest."[11] New kinds of bhangra emerged as deejays remixed traditional elements with music as diverse as reggae, dancehall, soul, and hip-hop. Describing the growing excitement about bhangra and how young deejays and bands began to diversify musically, Suri said, "This was... when a new era in deejaying came in.... So you had this whole change in music. You had newer bands coming in, people like Pardesi and more sort of alternative bands like DCS as well... the market was generating phenomenal business; it was becoming a very major interest with a lot of companies."[12]

As musical styles were proliferating, however, the themes of bhangra lyrics, including the centrality of a male protagonist, remained the same. Comparing the older band Apna Sangeet with the younger DCS, DJ Ritu explains, "Whereas Apna Sangeet chose a very traditional bhangra style with their *dhol* player given pride of place centrestage, groups like DCS didn't feature a *dhol* player at all and concentrated instead on Westernising their sound as much as possible using keyboards, electric guitar, and conventional drum kit..... What they all had in common were Punjabi lyrics, largely centred on themes of drinking, dancing, chasing girls, or nationalistic pride, driven by pulsating, heavy rhythm percussion."[13] This consistency in themes has in part to do with the fact that bhangra, as men originally performed it, is a historically masculine music. In its reinvention in Britain this pattern has continued: there are a few well-known women artists, but the great majority are men. Virinder Kalra notes, "Certainly the male-dominated character of the Bhangra record industry, from musicians to studio owners and lyricists and producers has played a part in keeping the production of the music solely male."[14] The roles given to the few women singers are "mediated through what is expected or anticipated by male producers and consumers."[15] In other cases, women vocalists are not given due credit. DJ Ritu writes of the artist Bally Sagoo's compilation track with a woman vocalist, Satwinder Bitti, "No we don't know who she is, but Bally Sagoo still [*sic*] going strong with his brilliant compositions/remixes, momentous basslines and knack for finding great unknown vocalists, who remain unknown even after he's finished recording them."[16]

Furthermore, the lyrics are often sexist, patriarchal, and heteronormative. As Raminder Kaur and Virinder Kalra explain, "In conventional Bhangra texts, women tend to appear as fit and fashionable temptresses to be watched, teased, commented upon and owned; e.g. *goriye* (fair one), *soniye* (pretty one), *ni zara nach kuriye* (do a little dance, girlie), *shakeenan* (fashionable woman), *disco wichaari, fashion di maari* (fashion-obsessed disco queen)."[17] Moreover, songs that narrate the social conditions of migration, such as "the fact of dispersal, a sense of loss, [and] a yearning for home," are "crudely sexist in their content"[18]: the protagonist of these songs is usually a young South Asian man who journeys to the West to indulge in its pleasures, represented in part by the supposed free love on offer by its white women.[19] His family calls for "the young man to take his family (read kinship) responsibilities seriously and stop acting frivolously"—in other words, stop running around with inappropriate women.[20] These tales receive further scrutiny from Gayatri Gopinath, who shows that early bhangra music focuses on conflicts between fathers and sons, reproducing a model of diasporic identity based on "heteronormative paradigms of biological inheritance, oedipality, and blood-based affiliation."[21] This music forecloses female agency: diasporic identity is constituted through a longing for the homeland, but the subject of this identity is male, while its object of desire (homeland/tradition) is represented by female figures imagined as static and as sexually and morally pure.[22] Here I expand analyses of gender and diaspora by showing how gender shapes the production of bhangra music.[23]

IDENTITIES

As I discuss in the introduction, young fans of bhangra and AU music see their respective music forms as expressing their bicultural or hybrid identities. But for several reasons fans of bhangra make their claims particularly strongly. As the music marketer and publicist Rashmi Mahajan explained to me, bhangra was the *first* South Asian music that young people widely remixed, creating a form they saw as their own: "The reason why bhangra started in this country . . . is because a lot of young kids felt a sense of identity with this music . . . culturally they were living in the midst of two different cultures . . . and through this music, which was a complete fusion of their own, they created their own identity. . . . It was the first thing—the only thing—that was their own, and that's why people flocked to it. . . . For the first time they could be proud of who they were."[24] Because bhangra is a genre that originated in South Asia, specifically in its agricultural regions, and can therefore be traced to the homeland, many youth readily identify it as roots or traditional music, whereas they do not do so in the case of AU. As the deejay Ameet Chana said, "It's music that's been taken from a country where our people come from."

Due to bhangra's origins, fans see British bhangra as a source of comfort and belonging in the face of long-standing racism. I found it striking, for example, that the music promoter Vinay, who intensely disliked bhangra, said to me that no matter what, there will always be a need for this music because young British Asians will always feel the difference of being nonwhite: "You're always going to be brown, and you'll never get away from it."[25] The fact that bhangra hails from South Asia makes it an especially powerful resource in helping young people negotiate the feeling of being ethnically inauthentic. Comparing bhangra in South Asia with the music emerging in Britain, for example, Chana proudly proclaimed, "[Bhangra's] been brought into another country, and it's been made a huge success. . . . [T]he bhangra that they've got over there is nothing like the bhangra that we've got here. . . . This is British Bhangra!"

THE MAINSTREAM

During the mid- to late 1980s, the years in which bhangra emerged, there were tensions among the older artists: some wanted to professionalize the industry with the aim of entering the mainstream, but others wanted to retain the cultural roots and ethos of the music by keeping it within the community, that is, within private affairs such as community functions and weddings.[26] As young people became more involved in subsequent years, however, they fueled the movement for mainstream success. One of the strongest desires of young artists is that their music become mainstream. As Rishi Rich, a pop musician who is one of the few British Asians to have had a single in the British Top 40 chart and to perform on *Top of the Pops*, explained to me, "[Artists] want their record to chart . . . in the UK singles chart . . . that is every person who's in the Asian music industry's dream."[27]

Although Rich equates the mainstream with the singles chart, definitions of the mainstream can vary. As Suri said, "To some people, mainstream means getting into the Top 10, Top 40 . . . to others it may mean that you're being played on mainstream radio, like Capitol or Kiss 100. . . . [S]ome people have even said you're truly mainstream if you're on *Top of the Pops*." Notwithstanding these varying definitions, the underlying meaning of mainstream is national recognition of bhangra music.[28] As Suri explains, it is about "generally being recognized in the English [market]." The meaning of mainstream success has remained fairly consistent over the years. In 2006, for example, a radio program called *The Mainstream Dream* that aired on the BBC Asian Network and focused on "desi beats" (or South Asian-inspired beats) defined mainstream as "popular recognition across the British public" and being part of the "national media conversation."[29]

The wish for national recognition is not simply about having greater fame and wealth. Insofar as the mainstream is seen as representative of the British nation, this wish is also about a desire for being accepted in Britain, in short, a desire to belong. The *Oxford English Dictionary*'s definitions of *recognition* are useful here: to "show official appreciation of; reward formally" and to "acknowledge the existence, validity, or legality of." Drawing on these meanings, the "official appreciation" that is symbolized by inclusion in the mainstream charts in turn symbolizes an acknowledgment of existence and validity as part of the nation. As early as 1990 Banerji and Baumann stated, "Cross-over holds out the promise of recognition of Bhangra as part of British youth culture."[30] And mainstream acceptance of the music as British means acceptance of youth of South Asian descent as British as well.

Because of how bhangra has resonated in many South Asian communities in Britain, when artists succeed, both the artists and the communities see that success as reflecting on themselves. A good example is the case of Rich, a musician who creates pop music but who grew up in communities in which bhangra is popular and who often includes Punjabi lyrics in his music. He said that having a song on the singles chart certainly helped him gain credence in the British music world: "It makes it easier when you're going to radio stations. . . . They take you a bit seriously." But what these accomplishments meant to his family and community was of paramount importance to him. Discussing his performance on *Top of the Pops*, he said, "Growing up . . . I've always said, 'Mum, one day I'm going to be on *Top of the Pops*.' . . . [T]he first time we were on . . . it was like a dream come true. I took my mum there and said, 'Look!' . . . It's a big kind of achievement . . . because they're not letting [just] anyone on. The fact that you've charted, that means that your music has crossed over, in a sense. . . . The fact that you've got a track on *Top of the Pops*, which is . . . in Punjabi . . . that's a big thing for the community. . . . I know that people in Southall are watching this, and that Asian households are going, 'That's an Indian guy on *Top of the Pops*' . . . that's the reason why, for me, it makes it special." Performing on *Top of the Pops* not only earned Rich respect from his family but also became a mirror of success for Asian communities at large.

From the emergence of British bhangra in the mid-1980s to the late 1990s there were several moments when it seemed bhangra might cross over. When the music first emerged, for example, the British media covered the "new bhangra craze."[31] Although much of this reportage reinforced postcolonial stereotypes of British Asian youth as rebelling against oppressive, backward traditions, bhangra's appearance on a national stage nonetheless offered enthusiasts some hope. Then, in the early 1990s, the mainstream charts saw the arrival of Britain's "first Asian pop star," Apache Indian: he was the first bhangra artist to be signed by a major record label, Island Records, and his song "Boom-Shak-a-lak" reached an unprecedented No. 5 in the singles charts. Mainstream hopes were spurred even more in the late 1990s by the fact that British bhangra was becoming popular not only in Britain but also in the South Asian diaspora at large. As DJ Ritu writes in 2000 in the liner notes of the album *Rough Guide to Bhangra*, "Bhangra music is now Britain's major Asian export, accounting for huge sales across the world notably in other parts of the scattered Asian diaspora. A large industry supports this music with some thirty or so record labels, PR companies, radio programmes, magazines, and so on, not to mention an abundance of weekly gigs in all the UK's major cities. Album sales by top bhangra artists usually sell in excess of 100,000 units in the UK and beyond."[32] Despite these signs of increased popularity, however, bhangra did not cross over. As DJ Ritu laments in her notes, "[Bhangra] is still an industry and genre shunned by the mainstream media."

While its failure to cross over is a recurring complaint in the-state-of-bhangra discourse, the late 1990s were an especially bad time for bhangra music: although music production was high, sales were at an all-time low. As Suri explained to me, in the early 1990s a bad album would sell ten to fifteen thousand units (a unit being a CD or cassette), an average album around twenty thousand, and top titles anywhere from sixty to one hundred thousand. In the late 1990s, however, a bad title would sell only two to five thousand units, an average one fifteen thousand, and a good title thirty to forty thousand, representing a drop of anywhere from 50 to 80 percent in sales. The mainstream success of AU music only increased the bhangra industry's annoyance. Artists in the AU were everywhere: featuring in British style magazines, receiving some of the British music industry's top awards, and signing album deals with major record labels. As the well-known producer Sukhshinder Shinda said, "[Bhangra] did die down with the introduction of new British Asian Underground music. Bhangra had been at the forefront of British Asian music for ages and that pushed us back a bit."[33] Asian Underground had captured the mainstream. How did bhangra industry folks diagnose their "downfall"?

Unscrupulous Asians and the Pursuit of Profit

It seems that the past two years has been the cause of a downfall in the quarters of bhangra.... The bulk of the new bhangra releases over the past few months have had about as much appeal as a long, thin line of oil dripping down an oil-can.
—SHABBS, *Eastern Eye*

"The bhangra industry is stuck in a rut and the industry is not as big as it should be." That is all I hear these days.... We have been listening to bhangra music on a serious clubbing scale for over ten years now and it is still very small in comparison to mainstream artists. The question is why?—RAJ GHAI, *Eastern Eye*

One of the main criticisms of bhangra artists was that record companies and promoters were driven by pursuing profits, and they did so in unethical ways, at the expense of following professional standards and, most important, of developing bhangra music. A member of the long-standing band the Sahotas said, "Record companies aren't interested in music, they're businessmen. They just want you to churn out stuff, regardless of quality or consideration to fans, with the only aim to make a quick buck."[34] Younger artists, such as Panjabi MC, confirmed that view: "The biggest complaint bhangra artists have is that the record companies all-too-often play keymaster to their fortunes and deny the musicians the artistic license they crave."[35] Music writers agreed with these censures: a full-page story in *Eastern Eye* on how to succeed as a bhangra artist characterizes the industry as a "dicy [sic] old game," visually presenting it as a board game with squares one has to successively move through to succeed.[36] The squares are labeled with statements indicating excessive profiteering in the industry, such as, "A label is interested in you. You sign without thinking. Sure, they'll release your record—but any opportunity to bleed you dry, they will."[37] Artists also denounced the promoters. The well-known bhangra artist Balwinder Safri said, "I blame the promoters. There are one or two that are ruining the music for all of us and are running away with the money—they're fooling the public. . . . putting peoples names on flyers without any confirmations and not having the [proper] sound system. . . . all those so-called professional promoters out there—sort it out!"[38] Summing up artists' complaints, the famous singer Malkit Singh said, "All business affairs should be treated as a business not as an underground deal."[39]

Artists themselves were not safe from attack. Indicting artists for profit mongering, an anonymous shopkeeper said that one of the factors contributing to the fall was that "artists started moving around, going to different labels, doing a song here and there. They actually milked their own name and credibility as an artist." But artists returned the accusation: the Sahotas said they were reluctant to commit to one record company because companies in general showed a "lack of professionalism."[40] In light of the innumerable insults that industry insiders were hurling at one another, many felt that the bhangra industry had witnessed a shift from passion to profit. As Suri said, producing music had become "more of a business" and was no longer motivated by a "love for bhangra."

While one can conceive of similar charges being made about any music business, in my interviews industry folks laced their comments with cultural content. That is, even as they acknowledged that the mainstream industry is corrupt—as one interviewee said, "The problem with mainstream practices is that they're well hidden"—they saw the pursuit of profit in the bhangra business as reflecting a "typical Asian mentality" characterized as avaricious, unscrupulous, backwater, impassionate, derivative, and miserly. According to them, this mentality found its worst expression in parasitical behavior: as Mits Singh, a well-known promoter, said, "The typical Asian mentality for . . . the generation above us . . . is they come into the scene, they make a quick buck, but they don't want to stay there and invest in that scene . . . and it doesn't work like that. If you really want to push the scene up, take it to another level, you have to go in there; it's like a long-term investment."

The stories that industry people told about shopkeepers show how they recast what might be considered normal capitalist behavior as corruptly Asian. A persistent problem in the industry is that shopkeepers, who usually live on the edge of the economy and try to keep their costs down, do not carry bar code readers, and often bhangra albums don't have bar codes. As a result, they cannot track music sales, and, in turn, popular bhangra tracks cannot be registered in the mainstream charts.[41] Discussing this issue with me, Dev, who has long been involved in the industry, explained that shopkeepers had recently adopted new marketing strategies that negated the possibility of bhangra ever properly charting.[42] He said that shopkeepers had begun "jumping on the [bhangra] bandwagon" by forming their own record labels, and "since they released their own stuff, they'd only promote their own stuff." This was a shift from what he considered normal music industry practice: "In the past, you had . . . independent record labels releasing artists' work, selling it to shopkeepers . . . as a normal market, as in the mainstream market." According to Dev, shopkeepers' "abnormal" practices not only had led to the flooding of bad bhangra music into the market but also had exacerbated the problem of not charting. Blaming the "mentality" of Asians, Dev said, "If every main outlet [had bar code readers], you'll get at least a reasonable idea of what's selling. The mentality of Asians unfortunately is . . . ," at which point Dev used his hands to motion that they can barcode an item repeatedly. He continued, "If every music shop [recorded sales properly], it would benefit the whole industry. . . . But it also won't work. If most of these shopkeepers are their own labels, then each is going to want to till in their own titles." While one could view shopkeepers as following a normal capitalist strategy, Dev suggests that shopkeepers are acting in particularly corrupt ways attributable to their Asianness.[43]

In the context of Britain's South Asian communities, the qualifier "typical" generally signifies stereotypically ethnic and backward, or nonmodern, behavior, a fact underscored when the young use it as a generational critique of the old. Though young people in general may attribute a number of qualities to the state of being typical (see chapter 4), the young men in the bhangra industry use it to refer to greed and lack of ethics. Though not apparent, gender is central to these rebukes: their subtext is that the typical Asians responsible for bhangra's downfall fail in part because they do not perform a modern Asian masculinity. Although unspecified by fault finders, save for their occasional reference to businessmen, the actors they refer to are men. The picture they paint of these men resonates with the figure of the wily Oriental, which has a long life in Oriental discourse.[44] Colonists used this figure to refer to South Asian men as being deceitful, corrupt, and shrewd, deploying effeminacy as a way to condemn the natives for not being proper capitalists. Although the types of businessmen that industry folks refer to, including record company staff, promoters, and shopkeepers, differ in their class status, they are all seen as being wily.

Insofar as critics cast the typical Asian as parasitical, one can also productively read this figure through the metaphor of the Shylock. A product of European anti-Semitic discourse, the Shylock figure represents the parasitic Jew, the "idle and dependent other" or "middleman" who lives off the physical labor of working-class bodies.[45] In its propensity for economic opportunism and lack of social morality, the Shylock also represents an absence of allegiance to a fatherland.[46] Because normative capitalist masculinity reproduces patriarchal inheritance not by being avaricious but by circulating capital,[47] the Shylock figure is alternately impotent and effeminate ("dependent") but most of all, queer, that is, sucking on the blood of young men. Judith Halberstam underscores this point in her analysis of the resemblances between the Jew and the figure of the vampire: "The Jew, like the vampire—is not only parasitical upon the community's health and wealth, he is sick, nervous, a representation of the way that an unbalanced mind was supposed to produce behavior *at cross-purposes with nation, home, and healthful reproduction*" (emphasis added).[48] Showing how such parasitical behavior is linked to national treason, she continues, "The Jew and the vampire . . . both unite blood and gold in what is feared to be a conspiracy against nationhood."[49] Insofar as the typical Asian businessmen in the bhangra industry are seen as preying on male artists ("bleeding them dry"), one can likewise see how they might be read as not only parasitical but queer: that is, by preying on the blood of young men, businessmen are seen as exhibiting a nonnormative male identity. In parallel with the figures of the Jew and the vampire, critics see such parasitical, nonnormative behavior as a kind of disloyalty to nation: it prevents the bhangra industry from advancing into the mainstream, a project they align with actualizing national belonging.

The Old-Timers: Respect and the (Effeminate) Father

All you old-timers like Alaap, Sahotas, and Safri boys, go back to the 80s where you belong. A new generation needs new blood to survive.—RUBAYAT, *Eastern Eye*

For young men in the bhangra industry, a second site of failure was the old-timers, that is, the first generation of artists whom they considered to be musical pioneers and yet too "un-hip" to carry bhangra through to the mainstream. They poke fun, for example, at the stylistic choices of these bands, focusing on their clothing (white trousers and sequined shirts), hairstyles (perms), and general appearance (lack of youthfulness) (figs. 1.1, 1.2). (Though the images are from early albums, the stylistic choices of these artists have not changed much over the years.) For example, the music editor of *Eastern Eye*, Thufayel Ahmed, advises older artists to "take a serious look at their image": "white trousers will be out. Sequined shirts will be burned. White fake crocodile–skin shoes will be replaced by Adidas trainers and the 'hoi, hoi' chant will be silenced. . . . [I]f we want to go mainstream, we have to go with the flow."[50]

While Ahmed is aggressive in his rebuke ("Sequined shirts will be burned"), young men more commonly lodged criticisms against old-timers through a qualified kind of respect: they expressed shame and embarrassment about their style while also claiming to honor their virtuosity. Chana, for example, said that he and his friends respect the older generation of singers, not only because they are the "originators" but also because "they're still wicked to watch on stage . . . and are still amazingly good." But he said there is still a need for "Asian idols" because no young people want to *be* like them: "We used to go to bhangra gigs, have a really good time, and then say, 'Apna Sangeet are wicked, but they're all real kind of *pindus* . . .' nobody ever wanted to be like a *sardar*[51] from Apna Sangeet and have long, permed hair. . . . I'm not saying that should go, but that's the traditional side." Here, Chana is using *pindu*, which pejoratively connotes "from the village," to characterize the band as backward as opposed to modern.

Gender is central to this qualified respect: Chana valorizes his elders, respecting them as "father figures" of the scene, but at the same time rejects them for not providing an adequate male image. Indeed, the specific problem with the pindu and the perm is that they are decidedly unmodern, noncompetitive, and feminine. And by donning feminine style the elders risk becoming queer. Thus, young men in the bhangra industry interpret the old-timers' lack of "hipness" via gendered, heteronormative notions of tra-

FIGURES 1.1 and 1.2 *Apna Sangeet; Greatest Hits* (1988); *Diamonds from Heera* (1992)

dition and modernity that render elders "effeminate fathers" and therefore as partially failed figures of masculinity. Indeed, the qualified respect young men show to elders enables them to perform a patriarchal ethnic authenticity, that is, to have respect for the father yet also produce themselves as modern against the effeminate elder of whom they are also ashamed.

Whereas the wily Oriental/Shylock has no redeeming qualities, the old-timers are liminal figures occupying the line between being ethnically authentic, a good thing, and being backward, a bad thing. Aggressive attacks such as Rubayat's, for example, are met with consternation: the music editor Wicked Miah, responding to Rubayat, lauds experience as vital and argues that, in contrast to some older bands, many younger ones have stagnated.[52] His response hints that outright censure of old-timers sits uncomfortably with young men's ongoing desire to retain tradition, a desire that features prominently in their criticisms of certain success stories.

Barbarians and Babus: The Battle for Real Asianness

[In 1996] everyone was moaning that bhangra, nay Asian music as we knew it, was well and truly on the way out. The sales were downcast . . . the public interest [was] waning. . . . The whole surge of interest in Asian music was not just rekindled, but blazed into the fore, by one Talvin Singh—riding on the fiery back of the chariot called Anokha.
—WICKED MIAH, *Eastern Eye*

Next to the figures of failure (the shopkeepers, the old-timers) stand two examples of success: the AU artist and the bhangra artist Apache Indian. Paradoxically, the bhangra industry folks also find them to be figures of failed Asian masculinity, this time because they problematically occupy modernity. If members of the industry blamed typical Asians for causing the downfall of bhangra, thereby implying that Asian culture itself was the problem, they responded very differently to the mainstream success of AU music. A few noted this success with pride and found it an occasion to repeat their disappointments about the bhangra industry for being unprofessional,[53] but the more prominent response was to condemn AU enthusiasts for being sellouts or traitors and to defend bhangra as ethnically authentic. As debates ensued between both sides, they typically traded in the same terms: tradition and modernity. Recalling the multiple connotations of these terms I charted earlier, each side tried to construct the other negatively as backward and white, at the same time constructing itself positively as authentically Asian and innovative. Again, gender was central to the arguments that each made.

While the stances of each side are well illustrated in a host of letters sent by readers to *Eastern Eye*, they found greater elaboration in a published debate between the successful AU artist Sawhney and the bhangra artist DJ Sheikh in October 1997. (Though Sawhney dislikes the term *Asian Underground*, he was nevertheless positioned as an AU artist by the media.) Sawhney inaugurated the debate with an op-ed piece titled "It's Time to Move On."[54] He begins by suggesting that, contrary to popular opinion, bhangra is in fact a white music. Stating outright that it is a "coconut" form of music, that is, brown on the outside and white on the inside, he charges that bhangra has been "diluted beyond recognition for the pallets [sic] of the unmusical Westerners and hopelessly adopted by British Asians as all that is good and pure in the world." Using the traitor argument, he goes on to say that bhangra enthusiasts, by presenting bhangra as the only form of Asian culture rather than embracing the "diversity and richness of our cultural heritage," are perpetuating stereotypes: "The sort of thing that is used by racists to bully innocent children." Constructing bhangra fans as being stuck and ignorant, he addresses them directly: "Tablas were not invented to create boringly simplistic bhangra rhythms, believe it or not! Study and learn what you're talking about and stop embarrassing yourselves." Referring to these fans, he challenges, "How many of them would know about the complex and beautiful *taal* system?" Here and in his earlier charges that bhangra is coconut music, Sawhney is referring to the fact that bhangra has a 4/4 beat structure, lending itself to being remixed with much Western popular music. Taal, on the other hand, is a rhythm system whose structure can vary tremendously.

Sawhney contrasts bhangra, outmoded and unsophisticated, to the "new musical forms" which are part of a "genuine renaissance" through which "British Asians are making a real difference in every sphere of British life." One way they make a difference, he contends, is that they are actually able to inspire young British Asians to challenge racism: "For years we've been portrayed as victims—what is happening now is empowering our people—kids who get bullied at school don't have to take as much stick." This new music is so powerful, he argues, because it draws on real knowledge of Asian culture.

Sawhney dwells on bhangra being white (the bad rendition of modernity), since this is the main accusation that bhangra's staunch fans make of AU. He equates bhangra fans with "Westerners" and the AU with racial saviors by using "bully[ing]," an experience that stands for the history of young Asians being victimized by whites. Although bullying is theoretically gender neutral, I propose that Sawhney's use has male connotations, referring to a long history of young white men violently attacking young Asian men in schools. First, this is a form of violence to which Sawhney himself was subject and that he often discusses in interviews about his motivations in creating music (see chapter 2). Second, bullying gains purchase in a debate with bhangra fans because the contest between bhangra and the AU is in part a masculine one, bhangra typically positioning itself as the real site of virility. Reversing this notion, Sawhney suggests that bhangra actually enables bullying by perpetuating the stereotypes that motivate it. He thereby casts bhangra as empowering a white masculinity that threatens to annihilate Asian men. By contrast, he positions the AU as a form of empowerment that can counter bullying and, by implication, rescue the male Asian subject.[55] In doing so, he endows the AU with functional manliness: unlike the Shylock, for example, the AU artist is engaged in a system of paternal inheritance, passing on a model that other young men can use.

Sawhney's characterizations of bhangra fans as backward are only implicitly gendered. Those of other letter writers, however, are explicit. As one reader writes, "Most people seem to hold on to the bhangra scene because they think it means holding on to their culture. Rubbish, you grow up and move on. Otherwise everyone would still live in caves and carry spears . . . there's an alternative out there. Acts like Joi, Nitin Sawhney, Amar are holding on to their roots, but taking it into the space-age. If you don't join the future you'll be left behind with only a broken *dhol* to cry into."[56] Here, "caves" and "spears" signify a gendered trope of barbarianism that constructs bhangra fans as primitives and savages that need to be superseded. Crying also represents effeminacy: the injunction to bhangra fans is that if they don't modernize they will become even more resolutely effeminate.

DJ Sheikh's response to Sawhney, "Why Bhangra's Here to Stay," attempts to reverse all of Sawhney's charges.[57] Sheikh begins by constructing Sawhney, and by extension the AU scene, as elitist by conjuring an "average Asian kid" with whom, he hints, Sawhney is completely out of touch. Hinting at class divisions between the scenes, he calls Sawhney "pompous" and "holier-than-thou," saying that Asian kids just want "good music" and "don't really care about how music is made." He then uses the authenticity argument to laud bhangra, drawing on the old claim that bhangra is roots music: "Bhangra . . . is about giving young Asians who have grown up in Britain a chance to hold on to their roots." Because he cannot leave bhangra "mired" in tradition, however, he argues that bhangra strikes the right balance between East and West, that is, it is able both to hold on to culture and to be hip: "Bhangra fans are Asians who are proud to be Asian and want to have a good time to music that is not so Westernised it betrays identity and not so Easternised that it's *abbaji*'s [auntie's] cup of tea."

Notably, DJ Sheikh doesn't directly respond to Sawhney's charge that bhangra has less complex rhythms than taal. In fact, bhangra deejays enjoy this music precisely because they can easily remix it; they see bhangra as a site of opportunity, not of simplicity. They also contend that because bhangra club-goers want to hear a wide range of music, they need to have extensive skills to perform successfully. DJ Ritu explained that deejaying at a club that features only house music, for example, involves playing with one tempo and perhaps making slight pitch changes. But at bhangra clubs, deejays remix bhangra, Hindi film music, ragga, swing, jungle, soul, and hip-hop. Mixing jungle music, most of which is at 160 beats per minute (BPM), with a bhangra track, most of which is at 100 BPM, involves knowing not only how to play with pitch controls, but also how to deal with the complication that bhangra music often changes tempo *within* a track. DJ Ritu said, "It's not like house [music] where you've got like 'doint, doint, doint' . . . that's very clearly the kick drum, the snare. With bhangra, it's totally different, and so for your ears to pick out what beat you're going to synchronize with, it's a different kettle of fish all together."

Sheikh goes on to counter Sawhney's coconut charge by proposing that it is AU artists who make music for whites since they seem to require approval from whites to feel validated: "[Sawhney's] music is not talking to us, it is talking to the White youth who . . . see Asians as the new fad. 'Brown is the new black,' proudly pronounces the frighteningly funky rag *2nd Generation* . . . but who is that statement directed to? And what is it saying? 'Hey, White people see Black people as cool. Now we can be just as cool as them—thank you sahib, shall I kiss your feet?' "[58] He extends this portrayal of AU artists as pandering to a white British audience by juxtaposing them to the "average Asian kid" who could not be bothered by such concerns (or perhaps be in a position to even expect them): "All these AU artists are yearning for acceptance from Great Britain, and the music they are making will be praised by pseudo-cool club critics like the *Evening Standard*'s Tim Marsh, but your average Raj, Taz, and Hari will simply say, 'huh?' "

What emerges from Sheikh's response is an association of bhangra with an average kid who is male ("Raj, Taz, and Hari") and working class (not "pompous") and retains a sense of his roots. This average kid is a kind of lad, or young man who shares the interests of other young, working-class men.[59] By contrast, the AU scene is associated with upper-class men who pander to British men ("thank you sahib, shall I kiss your feet?") and who are therefore also effete, traitorous, and potentially queer. Since effeteness here inheres in purportedly effeminate qualities such as deference, gender and sexuality are instrumental to both Sawhney's and Sheikh's efforts to cast the other as white: while Sawhney uses bullying to cast bhangra as coconut music, Sheikh uses effeteness to do the same with the AU. Conspicuously, neither spends too much time on the question of who is more ethnically authentic. Rather, it seems easier to struggle over who is the traitor. In the one instance when Sheikh does discuss bhangra's retaining of Eastern qualities, however, he has to distance it from "abbaji's cup of tea," a feminine trope of tradition.

There is much history here. Sheik's construction of the AU as effete resonates with British colonists' ideologies of masculinity. Writing about their shape, Revathi Krishnaswamy observes that in response to anticolonial resistance in Bengal in the late nineteenth century, colonists constructed "Western-educated Indians, a large majority of whom were Bengali Hindus" as effeminate, referring to them as *babus*.[60] The stereotypical babu was an "urban, English-educated, alienated 'intellectual.' English education, it was widely believed, compounded the Bengali's inherent cowardliness to produce personal malice and political sedition."[61] Since the babu's mimicry of the British elite threatened their rule, the British, to counter the threat, cast that mimicry as a sign of weakness.[62] Sheikh in effect draws on the trope of the babu but does so in the service of a postcolonial and class analysis, using it to bring attention to how the AU's mainstream success might reinforce and in fact not threaten white, upper-class structures of power. But while this strategy aims to resist race and class power, by valorizing the average kid it replaces the effete Bengali babu with the virile Punjabi, reinforcing norms of masculinity and heterosexuality.

Sheikh concludes in a way that exposes a fundamental ambivalence at the heart of the project of becoming mainstream. In what becomes a mounting reprehension of white consumer capitalism, Sheikh refutes Sawhney's "AU-is-new" claim by arguing that English bands have been producing similar music for years—"English bands such as Loop Guru, Eat Static, and Transglobal Underground were mixing ethno-rhythms to Western beats yonks ago"—and that AU artists are getting attention simply because they satisfy whites' desires to consume ethnic difference. This line of argument, perhaps inevitably, leads him to paint mainstream success itself as white, even as crossing over has been a persistent goal of bhangra enthusiasts. He states that he is proud that Western radio stations haven't played bhangra music and that, unlike the AU, bhangra "is not weighted down by this cloak of cool, this aura of self-importance—its image is glitzy, fun, tongue-in-cheek." Far from being "stuck in a rut, refusing to move on," he claims, "we have found our pace and place in bhangra, we don't feel the need to tailor it for the White mainstream mentality."

Sheikh's near ceding of the mainstream in light of AU's mainstream success calls the unitary category of British Asian into question. What initially appears to be an issue of race and nation, that is, Asians trying to make it in a predominantly white market, now also appears as one of class and gender. In other words, the average or working-class Asian lads feel the need to produce themselves as ethnically authentic, fending off the accusations of not being modern enough that they themselves hurl at the old-timers. Such class splintering, however, gets prosecuted and defended on gendered grounds.

Notwithstanding the condemnation of white consumer capitalism implicit in Sheikh's response, as ongoing conversations in British Asian newspapers and radio shows reveal, the mainstream dream remains. In 2006, for example, a radio documentary, *The Mainstream Dream*, which, as noted, aired on the BBC's Asian Network, focused on why desi beats had not crossed over to the mainstream.[63] The question that arises from the bhangra industry's anxieties about performing tradition and modernity is, who is the right lad to champion bhangra?

Apache Indian: The Threat of Blackness

Controversy is Apache Indian's biggest groupie, following the *raggaman* wherever he goes.
—AUTHOR UNKNOWN, *Eastern Eye*

That lad could have been Apache Indian. Apache is one of the most significant second-generation bhangra artists, if not one of the most well-known British Asian artists altogether. As I noted earlier, Apache was among the first artists to appear on the mainstream charts and to be signed by a major record label. He is distinctive for creating unique remixes of bhangra: commonly described as bhangramuffin, his songs fuse reggae and bhangra, lyrically switching between Punjabi and patois and layering dhol beats with reggae rhythms. The cover of his debut album, *No Reservations* (1992) shows the influence of reggae on his performance style in its use of such signifiers as the backdrop of a Jamaican flag (fig. 1.3).

FIGURE 1.3 Apache Indian's album *No Reservations*

Beyond his popularity among youth, Apache has become something of an icon among scholars. Featured in more than a decade of work on British Asian music, Apache Indian has been used by scholars to theorize the hybrid identities of British Asian youth and the way this hybridity challenges British nationalism.[64] George Lipsitz argues, for example, that Apache calls attention not only to the shared victimization and politicization of Asians and Afro-Caribbeans as black, but also to their cultural connections: "Standing at the crossroads of Punjabi and Jamaican cultures, Apache Indian shows that Afro-Asian and Afro-Caribbean Britons share more than a common designation as Black people.... The music made by Apache Indian uses performance to call into being a community composed of Punjabis and Jamaicans, South Asians and West Indians, reggae fans and bhangra enthusiasts."[65] Lipsitz further contends that Apache Indian challenges the racially homogeneous norms of nation-states: "Apache Indian reads 'British' culture selectively ... proudly displaying the diverse identities that he has learned in its schools and streets. He creates problems for nation states with their narratives of discrete, homogeneous, and autonomous culture, but he solves problems for people who want cultural expressions as complex as the lives they live every day."[66]

Such scholarship sheds light on cultural intermixture in Britain and its political ramifications, but it also ignores the controversies about Apache's racial identity that have surrounded him throughout his career. To be sure, scholars' celebratory tone is echoed among industry folks, who praise him for becoming a mainstream success and for being even a kind of messiah. Shabbs, the *Eastern Eye* music editor, writes, "He hit the scene almost a decade ago and single-handedly showed the mainstream that Asians aren't just about waiting and serving—that they can boom-shakalak as well, if not better, than the rest."[67] On occasion they extend this praise by locating Apache in a black British political frame: an *Eastern Eye* reader writes, "This ragamuffin has sent out a message to all Whites telling them the way it is. His message . . . has blown all racial stereotypes and has laid the foundation for a better future. Thank you Apache for telling the whole world that we are Black!"[68]

However, some in the industry denigrate him because of his use of Afro-Caribbean cultural forms. Ethnic absolutism shapes many of these attacks, which cast Apache as adopting the wrong racial identity. Critics sometimes characterize Apache's "misguidance" as a product of his own confusion: "Apache is confused about his racial identity. . . . He sings reggae like a Black man. Apache Indian wants to be Black. He reckons his real name is Stephen. Apache Indian wants to be White."[69] But most often they see him as adopting black identity to the detriment of the Asian community and thereby undercutting the significance of his mainstream success. Reviewing the inroads British Asian artists have made into the mainstream, for example, one writer portrays Apache as a traitor: "We also had . . . Apache Indian. . . . But whose culture does he belong to—Black or Asian?"[70] In some instances he is seen as deliberately trading in his Asianness for blackness in order to become mainstream. As an anonymous music shop owner said, "He sold out, so they say. . . . Maybe because they felt he was doing tracks like *Arranged Marriage* and *Choke There* then suddenly does *Boom-shak-alak*, which is absolutely mainstream—technically, no Asian element in it, just an Asian guy singing it."

Perhaps the worst indictment of Apache is that his success not only meant little to other Asian artists and did not help them succeed, but also caused racial confusion among them. As Ahmed writes,

> For years and years people in the Asian music industry have been waiting for a messiah, someone to lead them out of the ghetto and into mainstream heaven. When Apache Indian burst onto the scene a few years ago many thought he was The Chosen One . . . but the problem is that he was never really seen as Asian . . . his ragga style dominated his identity. This meant that while he did well as an indi-

vidual, other Asians in the field couldn't benefit. In fact, just the opposite happened as confused bhangra stars tried to reach No. 1 by adding a few reggae beats to their traditional Punjabi tracks![71]

Although these charges pivot around the notion that Apache is "trying to be black," industry folks also expressed anxiety about his supposedly failed use of black music. Vinay and Rashmi, for example, were horribly embarrassed by what they characterized as Apache's lack of progression, by which they meant his inability to advance in his use of black music: "He had [heavy] black influence . . . and that's not a bad thing, but at the end of the day, he never progressed as well as the black people did. They progressed in a certain genre, in a certain style; he stayed there. He's laughable at this moment. His last album is just a joke." To summarize the different criticisms of Apache, they see him as failing because of his mimicry of blackness, whether this failure is about his own sense of identity, his use of blackness to enter the mainstream and thereby not helping others, or how he remixes black music itself.

While there are no overt references to masculinity in these indictments of Apache, one can productively read the accusations of his being "too black" through the prism of gender. Many young artists have remixed bhangra with dancehall, reggae, hip-hop, and jungle. Thus, bhangra's mainstream competition, in one sense, is commercial black music. Some of these forms, such as hip-hop, currently entail extreme performances of heteronormative male identity, with black men exhibiting prowess through physical violence, conspicuous consumption, and misogyny. Commercial videos, for example, often feature men toting guns, driving expensive cars, and being surrounded by skimpily clad and sexually available women.[72] A challenge for bhangra artists is to perform an Asian masculinity that can compete with these forms. This challenge is difficult because in Britain dominant notions of Asian and black men construct them relationally, wherein the Asian is seen as being effeminate and the black as hypermasculine.[73] Although South Asian men have not been constructed unilaterally and transhistorically as effeminate, in urban youth culture in Britain black masculinity remains a prominent signifier of hipness.[74]

One could imagine, then, that young people would roundly celebrate Apache as an artist who has successfully remixed South Asian and black music in ways that enable the performance of British Asianness on a mainstream stage. And yet indictments of him persist. I argue that masculinity is central to the reasons some youth find fault with him: they attack him not simply because they see him as performing the wrong racial identity but also because they see him as performing a black masculinity that threatens to eclipse an Asian one. As Shabbs intimates, young male artists see his success as lying in his ability to "conquer" the mainstream and therefore as part of a male contest: "He's managed to acquire their holy grail a long time ago—to conquer the mainstream. Name another Asian artist who has appeared on Top 40 more than twice? Case rested."[75] But they also see Apache's phallic power of conquering as redoubled because of his black-inflected style. As Apache said, "Man, I had to put up with that for years. Apache's riding on a novelty factor, he ain't pure, he's a wannabe, he's too big for his boots. I don't get it. Why are they so bothered? I don't even know these guys."[76]

Detractors' discussions of Apache further imply that they fear black masculinity, framing it not in terms of empowerment or a political identity of black British but in hegemonic terms as competitive and contaminating. Whereas a host of artists remix bhangra with black music, Apache is seen as trafficking in blackness in ways that are coeval to his Asian identity, as opposed to subjugating his black identity.[77] He is superseding the effeminate Asian man by becoming, at best, a dreaded sign of hybridity and, at worst, a hypermanly black man.

That critics adopted a hegemonic racial framework to condemn Apache is also evidenced by their complete lack of discussion of his use of Native American signifiers. While Apache claims he chose his stage name to honor the reggae superstar Wild Apache, his name clearly points to a Native American identity. Such trafficking is even more pronounced in the title of his album *No Reservations*, which can refer simultaneously to his having no reservations in expressing himself and also to his claiming that Native Americans should not be marginalized on reservations. One could argue that industry folks don't call attention to such usages because they read Apache through the antiethnic absolutist framework that Lipsitz and other scholars celebrate. However, the industry's lack of discussion, negative or otherwise, indicates that they read Native American (male) identity through a dominant framework as vanquished and therefore as able to be dismissed altogether.

Promising Lads

Considering the simultaneous presence of the varying critiques that bhangra industry folks make, a kind of Goldilocks problem emerges: while they disparage Asian culture in their discussions of businessmen and old-timers, who are too Asian, they laud it in discussions of the successful AU and bhangra artist, who are not Asian enough. And while they accuse successful AU artists for being too white, they cast the successful bhangra artist Apache Indian as being too black. Finally, although they desire mainstream success, in discussions of the AU they can equate it with whiteness and repudiate it altogether. Taken together, their stances expose the ambivalence at the heart of the project of becoming mainstream and the centrality of gender and sexuality to that ambivalence. They see figures of failure, for example, as exhibiting feminized and nearly queer backwardness: wily Orientals, parasitical Shylocks, and pindus with perms. In turn, they see figures of success as being racial traitors in ways that are gendered and sexualized: Sawhney is the effete, nearly queer babu who kisses the sahib's feet, whereas Apache is the hypermasculine wannabe black who threatens to eclipse Asian male identity altogether.

These censures show that young men's desire to enter the mainstream are fraught with impossibility. But men's frustrations are in a dialectic with hope. During the late 1990s they celebrated several artists for promising to lift bhangra out of its fallen state. One can glean from the aforementioned complaints that the successful artist has to perform both roots and modernity in a heteronormative, virile manner, and their modernity must be neither white nor black, although being able to compete with black music and masculinity is still important. He also needs to be of star quality in order to cross over while still being the regular lad, a notion that connotes working-class status. Two kinds of artists, whom I call the cultured hard boy and the lad-like boy band, offered a type of solution.

CULTURED HARD BOYS: PANJABI MC

The rapper, producer, and composer Panjabi MC (PMC) is the quintessential example of the cultured hard boy. Panjabi MC is well known for "Mundian To Bach Ke," a Punjabi rap song that became a hit among mainstream audiences in both the United States and Europe. Although he originally released this song on his album *Legalised* (1998), it became enormously successful after the rapper Jay-Z remixed it in 2003, debuting high on the music charts in the United Kingdom, the United States, and several European countries.[78] This success brought a new wave of hope that bhangra would become mainstream. The period I examine is late 1998, when PMC first began to be recognized outside of the Asian community.[79] At this point he dealt with the injunction to be traditional and modern in two ways: by repeatedly stating his pride in bhangra, his culture, and his roots, each of which functions as a metonym for the other, and by performing a masculinity that he claims is "black on the inside" (figs. 1.4–1.7).

As an example of the first strategy, a profile of him in *Eastern Eye* says, "Whilst many stars are screaming 'mainstream' to get away from the commercially unviable tag of bhangra, PMC is proud to be rooted in the scene that shot him to stardom."[80] This story sees PMC's real Asianness as being central to his relationship to black music, that is, it saves PMC from becoming lost in hard boy culture. For example, it lauds PMC for not slipping into "hard-man-of-bhangra" mode during a photo shoot and then quotes him as being truly "down" with his culture: "I'm never going to pretend I'm not down with [my culture]. I'm an Asian man, living in an Asian community. I can't go round shooting my mouth off to who I want. We've got elders in our community and we've got to give them respect. Our culture is so strong because we do respect each other."[81]

PMC does construct himself as having a male prowess, however, by condemning artists who mimic black rappers in their image and by claiming that he himself is somewhat black on the inside. Implicitly referring to the images of gun-toting black men featured on rap albums, he claims he does not need to appear to be a tough guy through imagery: "I don't need to have my picture taken with a legion of tough guys carrying guns. . . . [S]ure, I'm going to rap about how cool, tough and fly I am, but that's the nature of the music. Anyone can have a tough-looking picture taken."[82] But while PMC disregards fake forms of prowess, having prowess still remains of great import; he continues, "I'm down with who I am. No one in my hometown is gonna mess with me, my car or my crew."[83] He deflects the potential accusation that his identity is a form of black mimicry by linking the "average bhangra kid" to black music. Discussing his music, he said, "Of course I'm going to put in modern touches—but I don't see that as dilution—the average bhangra kid loves a bit of house, soul, swing, jungle."[84] Instead of taking refuge in a pure Asian form of music he is celebrating bhangra as an already mixed form, and, implicitly, himself as an artist who remixes it properly, presumably unlike artists like Apache, who are too black.

PMC performs male prowess as well by fashioning himself as being rooted in bhangra yet having a true knowledge of black music forms that enables him to outperform both black and white artists: "I'm down with the bhangra, but I'm into the cross-over. By that I don't mean sticking in samples for the sake of it. . . . [I]f you're gonna make it work you've got to understand the music you're slipping in. . . . Being the best in bhangra shouldn't be the only aim. My major aim is to blow away a White or Black

FIGURES 1.4 and 1.5 PMC's albums: *100% Proof* (1995), *Grass Roots* (1996),

FIGURES 1.6 and 1.7 *Legalised* (1998), and *Dhol Jageero Da* (2001)

artist off the stage."[85] The cultured hard boy is a practitioner of tradition because it is inside of him. Yet he is also modern because he is hard, a performance that entails claiming expertise of black music forms, the enjoyment of which he links to the "average young Asian guy." PMC thus constructs an identity that brings together the figures of the babu, or the educated side, and of the Punjabi, or the martial, hard side and does so in ways that are beyond black performers, not in alliance with them.

Other popular artists, such as the singer and producer Bindha Jatt, crafted their identities and were seen by music writers in similar ways. Though Jatt is from Canada, his music was popular in Britain. As Shabbs says of Jatt, reinforcing the disparagement of old-timers, "The aging bhangra music industry needs guys like him otherwise we will forever have to contend with white scarfs and grandpa beards."[86] Mirroring PMC's censure of the hard outer image some artists perform, Jatt said, "Underneath this guise, we're as desi and traditional as any one else, if not more, culture is something you hold on in the inside and that's what I want to try and put across to the fans."[87] Shabbs lauds Jatt, as he does PMC, for being the average Asian guy whose averageness inheres in his love of both bhangra and rap: "Bhinda is your average young Asian guy. He loves his pure desi bhangra, he loves his gangsta rap."[88] He, like PMC, is the cultured hard boy: being traditional inside, shunning outward guises of hard or black identity, yet retaining a love of gangsta rap, a choice that purportedly represents the average young Asian man. And yet it is precisely his expertise in gangsta rap that makes him not just average but a star.

The cultured hard boy's ethnic authenticity thus inheres in his love of bhangra. He's neither "abbaji's cup of tea," that is, in the effeminate tradition, nor Apache Indian, a wannabe black, because he finds fault with gun-toting black masculinity as farcical. However, he loves black music, an identity he fuses with his average Asianness. Even better, he knows black music in such a way that he can lead the industry into the mainstream, actualizing national belonging for British Asians. The cultured hard boy uses blackness to perform hipness so that bhangra isn't left mired in tradition. He naturalizes blackness as interior, conjoining it with an also interior Asianness, a move that works since, as the case of Apache reminds us, blackness can't appear as an uncontrolled outward expression. Moreover, blackness can be internal only if it resides together with Asianness. When figures in the industry imagine the mainstream as white, as DJ Sheikh does, they can denigrate it as a site that only ethnic traitors occupy. Yet when they imagine it as black, as PMC does, it represents a kind of arrival. But here the question becomes how to perform mastery of black music in ways that are not derivative, a word industry insiders often used in conversations, or a form of black mimicry, as the discourse about Apache Indian shows.

LAD-LIKE BOY BANDS: B21

So far it's been a B21 year... and at the moment everything those guys touch turns to Gold—as everyone saw at the Asian pop Awards.—**ANONYMOUS AUTHOR**, *Eastern Eye*

The second kind of artist that industry members celebrated during this time was the lad-like boy band, the quintessential example of which was the band B21 (figs. 1.8–1.11). In the late 1990s it was composed of three young men, the brothers Bally and Bhota Jagpal and Jassi Sidhu. They take their name from the postcode for Handsworth, the racially diverse, working-class city in Birmingham from which Apache Indian hails. The name B21 thus functions as a patriotic evocation of locality, especially given that many refer to the Midlands as the heartland of bhangra. The numerous awards B21 has received, including several for best newcomer and best album, reflected the fact that they held great promise.[89] How did B21 negotiate modernity and tradition through claims of race, class, and gender?

The industry lauds B21 for three reasons: its appearance, comportment, and use of Punjabi lyrics. Unlike the cultured hard boy, B21 models itself more on a traditional bhangra band than on the solo rapper. But as I've noted, one of the main indictments the bhangra industry made of the old-timers was that they failed because of the effeminate image they conveyed by their clothing and hairstyles. That young, aspiring bands were consumed with the question of image is revealed by their arguments for why *they* are the solution to the industry's problems. The band DIP said, for example, "With a typical band you're just listening to the music and that's it. With us it's a lot more, we've got an image and style to portray." Shabbs, in a profile of the band Intermix, said, "Intermix's added effort may just be what the choking bhangra scene needs to rev itself back into gear. Armed with a new image, and sexy as ever, Intermix are, as their mainstream counterparts *Take That!* once said, back for good."[90] Thus, a main challenge for a band like B21 is to perform a modern image.

To meet this challenge B21 projected an image that young fans saw as attractive and fashionable in a mainstream manner. For example, at a show featuring many young artists, B21 abandoned the Asian garb worn by others and appeared in long, sleek black suits and white shirts with oversized collars. According to Chana, such style choices encourage young audi-

FIGURES 1.8–1.11 B21's albums: *The Sound of B21* (1996), *Long Overdue* (2002),

and *Made in England* (2000; cover and inside image)

ences to identify in an aspiring way with this band more than they did with earlier ones: "People like B21 are quite important . . . initially, it was like . . . Apna Sangeet coming on with their *lunghis* and his long, curly, permed hair and stars all over their costumes. . . . But now, we've got people like B21, three young guys looking really clean-cut, fresh, looking quite sort of mainstream."

While Chana's narration seemed gender neutral, his discussion of another event indicates the centrality of gender to B21's appeal. He explained that the crowd at that event, including both women and men, rushed the stage "because you've got three guys, who can sing and produce and look good as well." When I questioned Chana, trying to understand the gendered basis of audience attraction to B21, he explained that the group functions in different, yet equally appealing, ways for young men and women: "The guys are responding to them because of their dress and their music and that, and the girls obviously like their music, and they think that the three of them are *all right* [attractive] as well." Bands like B21 therefore solved the problem of modernity by performing an Asian masculinity that young men felt they could aspire to and that purportedly fulfilled heterosexual codes of appeal for young, straight women.[91]

But there's more to this story. Central to B21's solution to the masculinity problem is their comportment as a particular kind of lad. The colloquial use of *lad* in Britain refers to "a young man characterized by his enjoyment of social drinking, sport, and other activities considered to be male-oriented, his engagement in casual sexual relationships, and often by attitudes or behaviour regarded as irresponsible, sexist, or boorish; (usually) one belonging to a close-knit social group."[92] Confirming this definition, an interviewee said that a standard definition of a lad is a young man who is brash and arrogant, who hangs around pubs, and who likes to "go out with the boys." Yet B21 positions itself and is positioned by others as a group of bad boys who are nevertheless respectable. For example, in a media profile titled, "21st Centyury [sic] Boys," the band members, trying to distinguish themselves from the emasculating label of boy band, said, "Boy bands are packaged with the right moves and the right image and go as quickly as they come. We are definitely a lads band on a student level. If you had to call us anything, it'd be a men behaving bad band!"[93] Wicked Miah, who wrote the profile, adds, "Hanging out with the B21 is like hanging out with your mates in a pub," and he goes on to hint that they are not rough working-class lads but down-to-earth guys who are "happy-go-lucky" and have a "simple, unpretentious philosophy."[94] The band appears to be composed of lads insofar as they are bad: that is, they drink with the boys and potentially play with the girls, but they display a noncompetitive masculinity. As in the case of PMC, the industry sees them not as the farcical hard boys but as the easy-going lads who nonetheless garner respect precisely because of their lack of pretension. A linked marker of their manliness is what the industry views as their genuine approach to music: in contrast to the wily Oriental and Shylock, B21, in Wicked Miah's view, produces music out of passion: "They're not in it purely for the money."[95]

Another ingredient of B21's success is its performance of tradition through their lyrical choices. According to Chana, bands like B21 and DCS became popular because they use simple Punjabi lyrics. Discussing DCS at length, Chana claims the band released "one of the best albums for years," *Punjabi Dance Nation*, not only because of its "really young, really fresh" images but also its lyrics: "The lyrics [have] been made simpler for the people that listen to it, which is cool, because it's still poetic, but . . . understandable to everyone." Chana contrasted these "simpler" lyrics to the "real sort of Punjabi folk singers who sing in quite strong Punjabi" and in dialects that are more traditional. B21 and DCS thereby seem to retain Punjabi, considered authentic to bhangra, but by simplifying lyrics allow for bhangra to be accessible to a larger audience and therefore to be more modern. Punjabi youth understand these lyrics, but so do other British Asian youth, as they often acquire a basic understanding of Punjabi through interethnic and interracial friendships. The added benefit is that this strategy follows market logic. In sum, the image, comportment, and lyrics of B21 contribute to its cross-generational appeal and, in turn, to its successful negotiation of the divides of tradition and modernity. As Chana explains, "They got the right mix . . . cause they're attracting *all* the crowds. Even the older lot like B21 . . . like I play it at home, and my mom likes their stuff." Given the importance of respect to successful Asian manliness, the band's broad appeal is key to its general success.

Conclusion

Promising artists fulfilled the implicit race, gender, and class rules of properly performing tradition and modernity. The cultured hard boys and lad-like boy bands, represented, respectively, by PMC and B21, did so by constructing their interiority as Asian, yet not effeminate; thus they could also be modern. PMC uses his love and knowledge of bhangra and black music, balanced in a controlled way, to deem himself to be an average Asian guy and as hip or modern. But his expertise in both music forms gives him crossover potential. He deflects the potential accusations of mimicking black men that are made of Apache by rejecting toughness as a guise that he, as someone who is truly "down" with his culture, doesn't need to perform. Alternatively, B21's use of simple Punjabi lyrics reflects the band members' interiority as traditional yet modern Asians. Their performance of lad identity also brings them back from the brink of femininity, that is, they are bad but not thugs because they are like mates. Their modernity inheres as well in their fashionable image. Here, their lad-like qualities nullify the threat of effeminacy that arises from being a fashionable boy band.

Despite the enormous success of PMC's "Mundian To Bach Ke" in 2003, bhangra has not crossed over into the mainstream. Yet the mainstream dream remains. As the radio show described at the beginning of this chapter indicates, debates within the scene continue. Significantly, however, discussions in the late 1990s, a moment of crisis in the industry, not only recentered masculinity as key to the performance of bhangra, but in fact rewrote it. In both their disappointments and their hopes, young men in the industry drew on gender norms to negotiate the overlapping dichotomies—tradition/modernity, Asian/British, private/public—that shaped their reach for the mainstream in ways that constructed femininity and queerness as other. In doing so, they worked toward reconfiguring the gendered relationship between diaspora and nation: rather than locating women in the traditional private sphere in the service of a postcolonial, diasporic struggle of national belonging, their actions risked situating women outside of this project altogether. However, they left the sexualized relationship between diaspora and nation intact, as queers have always been and are here kept outside the boundaries of national belonging.

BHANGRA INDUSTRY FOLKS had to contend with a particular crisis in masculinity: because their communities often associate traditional bhangra with roots and a robust male identity and yet, in Britain, saw tradition as the purview of women, young artists struggled with the question of how to perform British Asian identities in the public sphere of the mainstream in a manly way. As the next chapter shows, however, artists in the AU faced different burdens of representation. They were remixing classical music, which many South Asian communities saw as neither working class nor representative of their roots. Furthermore, because of such historically popular collaborations as that of Ravi Shankar and the Beatles, white Brits more readily recognized classical "fusion," and therefore AU music was more susceptible to being disparaged by South Asians for being white. Having made it into the mainstream but not performing community in any obvious way, AU artists had to deal with the accusation that they were not adequately representing their communities. Their entrance onto the mainstream stage also meant facing a number of other burdens of representation levied by various constituents, including record labels, activists, and the media. As in the bhangra industry, so in the AU music world masculinity played a key role, shaping both the expectations the artists faced and how they negotiated them. Here, middle-class notions of artistry also played a central role in their responses, leading to altogether different consequences for the project of belonging in Britain.

Chapter Two

From the Margins to the Mainstream
Asian Underground Artists and the Politics of Not Being Political

In late 1998 a large, racially diverse audience had gathered at Shepherds Bush Empire, a famed club in London with a capacity of two thousand, to watch Asian Dub Foundation (ADF) take center stage. Composed at the time of five young British Asian men—the bassist player Aniruddha Das, the deejay John Pandit, the rapper Deedar Zaman, the midi programmer Sanjay Gulabhai Tailor, and the guitarist Steve Chandra Savale—ADF was, said the media, one of the most important bands of the Asian Underground (AU). When ADF arrived on stage, they began singing songs, a mixture of dub, rapcore, dancehall, and rock, in a militant manner, calling attention to race and class oppression in Britain. Videos highlighting the struggles they sang about appeared behind them. Along the sides of the concert hall, activists had set up stalls to disseminate information about recent campaigns. One leaflet described a movement to release Satpal Ram, a South Asian man who was imprisoned for defending himself against a violent racist attack. In collaboration with the campaign, ADF crafted a song titled "Free Satpal Ram" that they sang with their characteristic energy and intensity. As at most of ADF's performances, the crowd was exuberant, jumping up and down to the music while collectively protesting social inequalities in Britain.

Across London, in the East End, another British Asian band whom the media also saw as part of the AU scene, took center stage. But this band, Joi, had a decidedly different aesthetic from that of ADF. Performing at a much smaller venue, the brothers Farouk and Haroun Shamser, the highly skilled artists who formed Joi, spun their mixes of South Asian instrumentation with drum and bass and techno. Playing music from their album *One and One Is One*, Joi's vibe that night was about bliss, love, and joy. True to their style of playing with signifiers of Asianness, their stage show included white women wearing the clothing of classical Indian dancers and performing classical dance steps to the music. The venue itself was decorated with spiritual art to match the aesthetic of the event. The audience, racially diverse like the one at the ADF concert, expressed their enjoyment by getting lost and content in their own world of dance. Here, there were no pronouncements about racism, no militancy.

Despite the popularity of both ADF and Joi, many who cared about racial justice made finer distinctions between them politically. As they saw it, ADF was challenging the long history of racism in Britain, but Joi was not.

THE LATE 1990S WITNESSED a sea change in the British Asian music scene. While bhangra artists continued to struggle to enter the mainstream, AU artists made major inroads. As I mentioned in the introduction, Talvin Singh's club night, Anokha, and his release of an accompanying compilation album, *Anokha: Soundz of the Asian Underground*, in 1997 launched AU music. Over the next several years AU music became so popular that the British media, including radio programs, music magazines, major papers, and television shows, featured it. By 1999 club nights similar to Anokha were scheduled for every night of the week, and the British music industry had given a number of AU artists some of its top awards. Furthermore, the hip and trendy images of British Asians that were circulating in promotions of AU music helped generate positive attention toward these youth in the public sphere, leading many to claim, "brown is the new black" (here, *black* referred to black popular culture as being hip).

While many British Asians were euphoric about the arrival of AU music, its mainstream success sparked fierce debates about its impact on racial inequality in Britain. Enthusiasts felt its popularity represented a long-awaited acceptance of Asians by Britain's white majority. Critics, however, argued that whites' attention to AU music was a symptom of the commodification of ethnicity (as the "flavor of the year").[1] John Pandit, an ADF band member, said, "The music industry is so important for British capitalism that they need to compartmentalize everything. They have their own markets like the gay market, the pink pound. Now there's the rupee pound, and Asian audience. It's the history of Western imperialism: let's talk about exotic Asians."[2] Critics argued that despite the AU's success, racial inequality, as evidenced in the high rates of violence against Asians, continued apace.

A related, yet different set of discussions centered not on the question of white acceptance but on the responsibilities of AU artists. These conversations often turned on the question of representation, that is, on whether AU artists were adequately acting on behalf of their communities culturally and politically. I found that many journalists, scholars, and activists celebrated only the artists they felt were political. On the one hand, their definition of political meant engaging with struggles around social justice, a definition I share. On the other hand, they held very specific ideas about what that engagement looks like: they lauded only those artists who involved themselves in what I call protest politics, that is, those who addressed social inequalities in their interviews, in the lyrical content of their songs, and in their stage performances.[3] Protest politics were thus a burden of representation with which AU artists had to grapple. By this yardstick a band like ADF is resolutely political and worthy of celebration, while artists such as Joi are neither.

The stances of AU artists themselves, however, complicated these normative evaluations of who is and isn't truly political. In my discussions with fifteen artists (a large percentage of the scene at the time), nearly all expressed disdain for the label political as a descriptor of their artistry. Themselves using a protest politics lens to interpret the term, they roundly voiced their disinterest in politics, countered demands that they should be political, and downplayed the importance of their ethnicity: they were first and foremost artists, not politicians and not Asian artists. Strikingly, however, they made these claims at the same time that they expressed a deep desire to empower Asians, a desire born of their concerns about racial injustice.

How, then, did AU artists negotiate the burdens of representation they faced as they entered the mainstream? And what consequences did their practices have with regard to racial equality and British Asian battles for belonging? As in the case of the young men in the bhangra industry (see chapter 1), the categories of race and nation are central to this negotiation, but so, I argue, are gender and class. Because AU artists made it into the mainstream, particular presses, activists, and scholars asked them to be spokespersons who engage in protest politics on behalf of their ethnic communities. Though other constituencies, like bhangra fans and AU record labels, were not interested in such politics, they still wanted AU artists to act as cultural representatives. While these requests may seem like straightforwardly ethnic and racial ones, they are in fact gendered, as all groups used a model of spokesperson or representative that relies on the patriarchal norms of liberalism and anticolonialism. Together, these norms situate politics in the public sphere, see men as the agents of politics, and cast militancy as properly political behavior. Well-known AU artists such as Nitin Sawhney, Badmarsh, and Joi struggled with these expectations, recognizing that taking on the roles of spokesperson or representative both enabled and threatened their success. They responded by reconciling their own desires to be understood as unique artists, not politicians who are part of a movement, with the demands of constituencies in ways that creatively enacted antiracism. In this way they expanded conventional notions of what constitutes artistic engagement with social inequality and therefore of politics. Yet their responses reproduced gender as well as class norms. The contradictions that emerge in the decisions and experiences of AU artists illuminate not only the multiple avenues through which British Asian youth grapple with ethnic, racial, and national belonging, but their uneven consequences for their battles to belong in Britain.

Burdens of Representation

Successful AU artists face a burden of representation whereby they are expected to symbolize the South Asian community in their work—a demand that problematically assumes this community is homogeneous, that it can be represented in a transparent manner, and that the role of the artist is to do just that.[4] These artists find themselves negotiating an "incitement to discourse"[5] through which others incessantly ask them not only to sing about and perform but also to discuss in interviews what it means to be a young Asian in Britain, often at the expense of their music.[6] As Rupa Huq explains, "All those involved are immediately seen as spokespersons for the 'community' and 'their generation.'"[7] In a postcolonial Britain deeply shaped by racial inequalities the call is to act as a particular kind of representative, that is, to engage in protest politics in interviews, music, and performances, as ADF does and Joi does not.

To be sure, the groups making requests of AU artists, and the underlying motives of these groups, vary. Groups with a strong presence include the mainstream British press, scholars of British Asian music, British Asian activists, fans of bhangra music, and British Asian record labels. Despite their differences, however, the patriarchal norms of liberalism shape their demands. Liberal philosophy is based on an opposition between the private and public spheres: while it imagines the private sphere as the space of domesticity and the family, it sees the public sphere as the space in which individuals, conceptualized as free and equal beings, engage in political and economic activities to protect their private interests and increase their property.[8] But it sees this individual as male, casting men as having the rationality requisite to be individuals in the first place. In contrast, it sees women's ability to bear children as positioning them closer to nature and as inhabiting the private or apolitical sphere.[9] These liberal assumptions, which locate politics in the public sphere and see men as its executors, structure the insistent requests made of AU artists.

But a second set of patriarchal norms is also at play. Those adhering to a protest politics model imagine men as the normative subjects but, in addition, see militancy as the normative behavior. These norms enact a Fanonesque script that centers men as the agents of anticolonial nationalism. As Qadri Ismail writes, for Frantz Fanon, anticolonial nationalism "is primarily about the native's imperative to assert a national identity when faced with the epistemic violence wreaked by colonialism which ... denies the colonized such an identity."[10] But, "the native here is male, and the native with agency is violent."[11] Fanon writes, "At the level of individuals, violence is a cleansing force. It frees the native from his inferiority complex and from his despair and inaction; it makes him fearless and restores his self-respect."[12] Here, the subject is male, and the recommended action is violence. The patriarchal ideals of both liberalism and anticolonialism shape, in different ways, the expectations AU artists faced.

THE MAINSTREAM BRITISH PRESS

The mainstream British press frequently characterizes popular British Asian bands that produce "post-bhangra" music as expressing their Asianness in music, in turn reifying their ethnicity and, by extension, their music as, in the words of Rehan Hyder, "an authentic marker of progressive political resistance."[13] Hyder calls this process "exotic politics," one in which "the cultural expressions of non-white minority groups are romanticized, stereotyped and interpreted as authentic articulations of a radical political vanguard."[14] The media viewed the four bands Hyder studied through the lens of "exotic politics," regardless of the bands' racial composition and at the expense of their music style. For example, the press called Cornershop "the voice of disaffected Asian youth," despite the fact that three of the band members are white.[15] In 1995 Fun'Da'Mental, a band whose lyrics are typically militant, released a purely instrumental album, *With Intent to Pervert the Cause of Justice*, a reinterpretation of their debut LP *Seize the Time* (1994), most of whose tracks lyrically comment on inequality. Although the political content of their music remained important to them, and instrumental music can be considered political—for example, avant-garde jazz challenged European conceptions of music—as Hyder explains, "One of the main purposes of releasing a lyric-less record was to focus primarily on the group's *music*."[16] The press, however, "ignored the album's musical content in favour of perpetuating the somewhat one-dimensional stereotype of Fun'Da'Mental simply as a forum for a radical political agenda."[17] The British media, Hyder argues, commodifies "exotic politics" as a form of difference that helps them market these bands. This marketing proliferates stereotypes, in particular the "angry Asian" and the "mystical Indian."[18] Cornershop, for example, changed its musical style over time, using less explicitly political lyrics than in its earlier days. But, as the band member Ben Ayres explains, the media, much to the band's annoyance, still called them "Angry Asian polemicists."[19]

Implicit in Hyder's analysis, though not spelled out, is that the political protest model that found its apotheosis in the angry Asian is highly gendered in that the media imagine this figure to be a man. Moreover, the angry Asian conjoins the norms of liberalism and anticolonialism: it is a masculine figure engaging in protest politics in the public sphere and doing so in a militant, or angry, way. One can test whether these angry Asians are necessarily men by asking if women artists faced this same burden of representation. There were no prominent women artists in the AU scene, but two well-known bands in the indie scene included British Asian women: the Voodoo Queens and Echobelly. These bands provide arguably stronger test cases given that one can easily read their music as a kind of protest politics in that it can be militant and the lyrics often directly contest sexism.

The all-female band Voodoo Queens is an illustrative example given how outspoken the lead singer, Anjali Bhatia, has been about the expectations she has faced.[20] Bhatia formed the band in 1992; it included her sister Rajni Bhatia, her cousin Anjula Bhaskar, and two non-Asians, Ella Guru and Stefania Lucchesini. As Hyder writes, the band played in a "guitar-based style in garage/punk tradition," their live performances were characterized by "high-energy performance and aggression," and their music often critiqued sexism. For example, their most popular release, "Supermodel, superficial" (1993) was "highly critical of the media and the fashion industry's perpetuation of thinness as the prerequisite of female beauty."[21] On the basis of their style, the media often associated them with the Riot Grrl scene.[22]

In light of the music and performances of the Voodoo Queens, the media could have characterized them as angry Asians. Instead, they were fascinated by the fact that the band was composed of outspoken Asian women. As Bhatia says, "[The press] took up on the fact that 'hey, they're Asians, women as well, what a brilliant press angle' so they just hyped us up to that, one as being Asians and one as being riot grrls.... I think the press is very racist and sexist as well."[23] These press reactions are not that surprising given the entrenchment of a colonial rescue discourse in Britain that sees Asian women as passive victims of an excessively sexist culture from which they need to be rescued by white men.[24] This discourse also shapes media reactions to Echobelly's lead singer, Sonya Aurora-Madan, who said, "Everyone expects me to be this Asian-female-escaped-from-an-arranged-marriage freak."[25] In the few instances in which the media did characterize the Voodoo Queens as political, they labeled them "the female Corner-shop," further testimony that the media normatively see the angry Asian as male.[26]

The liberal media often extolled the angry Asian man, but, true to the nature of stereotypes as ambivalent symbols of desire and disgust, they at times denounced this figure, interpreting the politics inherent in its anger as a sign of its lack of artistry.[27] A review of ADF's album *Rafi's Revenge* (1998) posted on the website of the prominent British magazine *National Music Express* is illustrative. While explicitly gendered terms don't appear in the review, the fact that the angry Asian to whom it is referring is male invites a reading of its denunciations as gendered.[28] The review tellingly opens with the statement that "no one would be interested in an Asian dub group preaching political change," signaling not only that the angry Asian man is a public trope, but also proclaiming the public's exhaustion with such a figure, a move that thereby emasculates it. The review then assures readers that ADF's politics are acceptable because they are not the politics that one typically expects from Asians, that is, Asian men; rather, they are the more interesting kind associated with white and black artists. By momentarily legitimizing ADF in this way, the review risks reinforcing stereotypes of Asian men as being effeminate. In another emasculating move, the review then dismisses the band's politics altogether by claiming that the political content of ADF's music is "not the first thing that hits you about this album. Nor is it the most interesting." The review then changes tone again by concluding that the album is "exactly the sort of confrontational and defiantly experimental music we've been missing" and seems to congratulate the British music industry for being enlightened multiculturalists by finally recognizing ADF. In concluding, however, it warns audiences to listen to the album in stages since the "harsh, hammering rhythms and percussion" and the accompanying "strength of [ADF's] convictions" might be too "overwhelming," as if ADF has an unschooled masculine prowess that might offend one's sensibilities. The manic dance this review performs around the political content of ADF's music—dismissing it, then rescuing it, then making it subservient—reveals not only that the media associate post-bhangra British Asian male artists with protest politics but also that they can simultaneously question whether the angry Asian man is a true artist.

Pandit sheds light on the other ramifications of the media's calling ADF political: "It's just like we get ... called 'political' as a tag. What the hell does it mean? ... They don't want to define what *they're* saying that defines *you* as political.... And why is it that ADF is 'political' when that song, 'Smack My Bitch Up' isn't?" He suggests that the label political at once narrows the meaning of the band's music and elides the ways in which, for example, sexist music, which the media do not label political, nevertheless has consequences vis-à-vis social inequality.

SCHOLARS

Scholars writing about post-bhangra music share the press's focus on protest politics bands, even as their focus stems from concerns about racial inequality.[29] Scholars devote a great deal of attention to bands like Fun'Da'Mental, Hustler's HC, Kaliphz, Black Star Liner, Cornershop, and ADF—some of which use militant-sounding music and all of which use lyrics that explicitly call attention to social inequality—lauding them for being truly political.[30] Like press coverage, scholarly attention is highly gendered. As Gayatri Gopinath argues, it "replicates a notion of diaspora that depends on dominant gender and sexual ideologies, in that it tracks forms of 'radical' cultural politics only insofar as they circulate between men and pass literally and metaphorically from fathers to sons."[31] She describes the ways in which scholars valorize the issues bands sing about, but overlook the ways in which those issues are gendered. Ashley Dawson, for example, celebrates ADF for its "resistance to the inequalities often generated by the globalization of the economy" but ignores how globalization generates inequalities along gendered lines.[32] Thus "men are once again the tacit subjects and objects of analysis."[33]

Moreover, scholarship disregards the involvement of several bands in a black nationalist politics that "may valorize a militant, tough Asian masculinity at the expense of female agency."[34] John Hutnyk, for example, argues, "The Kaliphz often seem caught up in a version of macho Gangsta rapping that is testosterone-fuelled and boyz-in-the-hood aggressive, yet their record in opposition of British fascist groups is considerable."[35] As Gopinath contends, for Hutnyk the music of Kaliphz "is radical *despite* the sometimes unfortunate conservatism of its gender and sexual ideologies. By simultaneously acknowledging and disavowing the limits of masculinist militancy, Hutnyk in effect subordinates gender as a terrain of struggle to the seemingly more urgent political project of antiracist organizing."[36] While Gopinath focuses on how such scholarship reinforces the heteronormative norms of diaspora theory, it also reproduces the patriarchal norms of liberal and anticolonial models of politics. That is, politics remain the purview of men who sing about social issues in the public sphere in a masculinist and militant manner and in ways that pertain only to them.

ACTIVISTS

By focusing repeatedly on particular bands for being "truly political," scholarship suggests that other bands are not engaged with social change. British Asian activists, however, make these distinctions explicitly. A range of political and cultural activists with whom I spoke felt strongly that AU artists have a responsibility to speak out about the racism that plagues South Asian communities in Britain.[37] They claimed that while the commercial music industry may have the power to neutralize artists' radical agendas, artists still have agency and should inhabit the mainstream in self-consciously political ways. For many of them, the majority of AU artists failed to exercise this agency well, instead using ethnicity opportunistically to sell their music. For example, Sofia, a prominent race-relations worker, distinguished between cultural Asian artists and political ones: "I don't even pretend to think they are political. Most of them are interested in being cultural Asians: they'll talk about identity to the mass media, but they are not committed to the project of eradicating racial discrimination." For her and other activists, only artists like ADF are political. In Sofia's words, "They *do* something." Sangeeta, an actor and photographer who works with disenfranchised youth, complained that, unlike ADF, most artists evaded the duties that come with claiming a British Asian identity: "*If these groups are going to use the fact that they are British Asians to sell their music, then they have a responsibility to articulate the political and historical contexts of Asians in this country.*" Voices such as these index a wider dismay among activists about how newly successful AU artists were inhabiting the mainstream; they felt that most had compromised any substantive political project.

These criticisms found their way into the public domain. In mid-1998 Watermans, a venue in West London that is historically important for hosting British Asian theater, comedy, music, and dance performances, featured a play titled *Made in England* by Parv Bancil. Because an interest in social critique shapes Bancil's long involvement with the theater as both an actor and writer, he can be situated as a cultural activist. The storyline, meant to be both humorous and hard-hitting, centers on a fictional British Asian musician, Bally Dingra, and narrates the changes he undergoes as his new record company transforms him into the star Billy India. While Bally used to play punk music with his British Asian friend Kes to express politicized concerns, he gradually begins creating South Asian remix music to attain commercial success.

Through the figure of Bally Dingra and his friendship with Kes, who remains true to his identity, *Made in England* dramatizes condemnations of AU artists who have found fame in the British mainstream. One of the messages of the play is that artists should refrain from remixing South Asian music simply because doing so is in at the moment, especially when other musical influences might have actually been more formative for them. As *Made in England* unfolds, it issues a twin rebuke: it denounces the music industry, encouraging all to be mindful of the potentially exploitative nature of its recent focus on British Asians. But it also takes artists to task, indicting those who believe their success has to do with their talent or who, even worse, opportunistically sell their ethnicity. The play applies these censures by contrasting Bally with Kes, who remains committed to his interest in music and social change even though he does not attain commercial success.

Key points in the play show that Bally used to care about the racial abuse Asians face, so much so that this concern informed all of his music. But as he changes to join the new fads, he loses all ethnic, artistic, and political integrity: he performs his Asianness in a nonpolitical way, adopting music styles that have become fashionable and that are in fact new to his repertoire. But, perhaps worse, he dismisses the impact of ethnicity on his success, claiming his fame is owing to his talent. Restaged at the Birmingham Rep in March 2004, *Made in England* makes statements that many found relevant several years after the heyday of the AU scene.

Activists may differ from scholars in their emphasis, yet both resort to gauging the degree of protest politics to distinguish between truly political bands and apolitical ones, relying on the patriarchal aspects of liberalism and anticolonial nationalism to do so: they locate politics in the public sphere, ascribe men the requisite agency to exercise these politics, and generally see politics as inhering in militant protest. That these assumptions are so widely shared underscores the ubiquity of the masculinist interpretation of politics used to judge AU artists and, in scholarship, to theorize diaspora altogether.

BHANGRA FANS

As evidenced in chapter 1, many bhangra fans too find fault with AU artists, seeing them as traitors who pander to the white mainstream. To them, only bhangra truly represents British Asian music and identity, the symbol of which, as noted, is the lad, or young, working-class man who retains a sense of his roots. Though the lad is not an explicit protest politics figure, he is a kind of political representative of antiracism insofar as bhangra fans contrast him with the AU artist, whom they see as selling out to whites. Consequently, their valorization of the lad relies on a male-centered liberal approach to politics, as their representative is a young man who can cross over to the public sphere of the mainstream (a crossing they don't see, in the case of the bhangra artist, as being compromised). While they don't require the lad to be the anticolonial hero embodied in the angry Asian, he still needs to portray a kind of masculine prowess. For example, they use gender and sexuality to contrast the AU artist with the bhangra lad: whereas the AU artist is upper class, effete, and queer, the bhangra lad is working class, manly, and heterosexual. In the lad's specific renditions as the cultured hard boy (Panjabi MC) and the lad-like boy band (B21), he performs prowess, in the former case by being hard, that is, tough and arguably militant, and in the latter by being bad, that is, having sexual power with women.

BRITISH ASIAN RECORD LABELS

The angry Asian man and the bhangra lad were not the only subject positions interpellating AU artists. The British Asian label Outcaste Records, the main label producing AU music in the late 1990s, only hired artists who refrained from engaging in protest politics. The label was created in the mid-1990s, and over the next several years signed a number of musicians, including Sawhney, Badmarsh, and Shri, who came to form the core of the AU scene. DJ Ritu, who helped create the label, told me she and the label's main founder, Shabs Jobanputra, wanted to promote British Asian artists to counter the "racism in the music industry and the fact that there are very few opportunities for Asian artists."[38] She said they were interested only in artists whose music was a "blend of East and West" but was not "overtly political," by which she was referring to the political protest model. Here, she juxtaposed Outcaste to Nation Records, a company created by Aki Nawaz in 1991 that was known for signing artists like Fun'Da'Mental who speak out about social inequality: "We set up Outcaste Records with the intention of working solely with South Asian artists who wanted to produce music that was very clearly about their Asianness and their Westernness—that very clear blend. . . . [W]e weren't going to be a bhangra label, and we weren't going to be Nation Records . . . [which] had a very overt political kind of message in its music and in its artists. . . . [Our emphasis was] purely on the music . . . as opposed to 'Are they saying the right thing in the lyrics?'"

If the founders of Outcaste saw themselves as creating new avenues for British Asian artists and challenging industry racism, their desire to sign those who were "blending Asianness and Westernness" yet were not political was also aimed at mainstreaming and profit making. Early in our discussion, for example, Ritu was critical of the mainstream media's coverage of AU music, saying that white journalists were writing about it because it was more accessible to them than other British Asian music, such as bhangra. Later, however, Ritu suggested that Outcaste was trying to achieve that same kind of accessibility: "Part of our agenda . . . was [to work] with music that we felt had more access points for non-Asians, because to us it was about spreading Asian music further but in a more accessible way."

Though Outcaste rejects the trope of the angry Asian, it arguably adheres to a liberal model more strongly than the other groups described above do. Given the public's association of post-bhangra male artists with protest politics, Outcaste's desire to sign those who did not have an "overt political . . . message" represents an attempt to deracialize them (or reracialize them as white, as it were) in order to gain greater accessibility to the mainstream. Because protest politics is associated with a militant masculinity, this strategy can also be seen as neutering artists, using gender to help reracialize them as white. One is still left with men—Outcaste did not sign any women—who are to take the lead in representing British Asians in the public sphere. Yet, by the same token, because their artists don't engage in protest politics they are less racialized as Asian. This strategy is squarely liberal because the normative subject of liberalism is not only male but also white.[39] In sum, while the agendas of various groups differ, the patriarchal aspects of liberalism and anticolonialism shape their notions of representation. And, as the examples of the bhangra fans and Outcaste Records show, these aspects shape even those agendas that appear to counter the framework of protest politics.

The Struggles of AU Artists

How did AU artists negotiate the various burdens of representation they faced as they stepped onto the mainstream stage? Sawhney, Badmarsh, and Joi, three very different but well-known artists, cared about empowering South Asian communities through their music, even as they disavowed politics. I analyze here the origin stories they told about their motivations as well as other stories about their work. They dealt with external pressures through these stories, which circulated among audiences alongside their music. As such, these stories represented ways in which artists performed identity and produced themselves for the public.

NITIN SAWHNEY: BEING BEYOND SKIN

Nitin Sawhney's career has taken him in a variety of directions, and he has been enormously successful. In the late 1990s Sawhney emerged as one of the most important artists in the media-labeled Asian Underground. Of Punjabi Indian background, Sawhney grew up north of London in Rochester. As a youth he studied piano and guitar, focusing on such music forms as classical, jazz, and flamenco. But he also pursued his interests in South Asian instruments like sitar and tabla. When he left his A-levels (standardized tests used to qualify entrance into a university), he started studying law but dropped out to tour with a jazz band, later forming his own band, the Jazztones. He sustained his interest in South Asian music and, with Talvin Singh, formed the band Tihai Trio, which featured indojazz fusion. Sawhney then trained to become a chartered accountant but left that career path to pursue music full time.

When I initially met Sawhney in 1994, he had released his first album, *Spirit Dance* (1993) on his own label. Outcaste subsequently signed him as its first artist, and he released three albums in the next several years: *Migration* (1995), *Displacing the Priest* (1996), and *Beyond Skin* (1999). Each album was more successful than the preceding one, *Beyond Skin* getting short-listed in 2000 for Britain's coveted Mercury Prize for best album of the year. Sawhney's music had launched him into the limelight of the British mainstream and Asian entertainment press, which began regularly promoting him as one of the most important British Asian artists that Britain had seen. Media coverage called attention to the way he mixes Eastern and Western musical elements and addresses societal issues. Sawhney is a uniquely outspoken artist who regularly discusses questions of racial inequality in interviews and newspaper editorials. How did he respond to the requests of communities, including British Asian bhangra fans and activists, corporations like the British Asian and mainstream music industries, and the press? Sawhney has deployed three different discourses—antiracist, essentialist, and liberal humanist—depending in part on his audience. These discourses both resist and reinscribe dominant ideas of British Asian identity.

Antiracism. In his interviews Sawhney often emphasizes the role personal experiences of racism play in shaping his artistry. His discussions reveal that he felt silenced during his childhood because he was regularly and violently attacked as a "Paki." These experiences motivate him to include Asian elements in all of his music in order to resignify Asianness as empowering and strong rather than as "a sign of weakness":

> I grew up in an all-white neighborhood, and I went to an all-white school where showing your Asian identity was seen as a sign of weakness and [made] you a potential victim or a target for attack or racial abuse.... I was regularly attacked on a daily basis, for two years, by the same group of people—physically assaulted, tied up, from the age of eleven to thirteen. I would walk into my class, before registration, eight people would actually grab me. They would wait for me to come in, and they would see it as a fun thing.... "Here comes the Paki, okay, let's get him." They'd jump on me, kick me on the ground, punch me in the face; they tied me up to a desk once and assaulted me while I was tied up.

> If people judge you on race, I do get really, really angry. I can't help it. It's a natural thing, because of that time.... I had to keep my mouth shut because I couldn't do anything. I couldn't fight back.... I think even now, I'm driven by a slight paranoia.... Definitely, because at that age, it really does affect you.... [The music I make] is kind of like showing what it *does* really mean to be Asian and how empowering that can be. It's about saying how strong that makes you. But at the time, I was being forced into a position of thinking of it as a sign of weakness.... [T]here are lots of different musical

forms that I play . . . [b]ut the one thing that I always try and do now in every single thing I do, I try and incorporate an Asian angle in, and that is just for that reason.

Sawhney's descriptions are poignant, reflecting not only the unabashed ways in which whites have terrorized Asians in school but also the real trauma it causes. Sawhney does not want to live an adult version of what he experienced in childhood; he doesn't want to disappear or be punished for his difference. Rather, he wants to draw attention to that ethnic experience which was previously silenced.

The way Sawhney includes an "Asian angle in his music can be seen on each track on his first Outcaste album, *Migration*. The album, whose name connotes the journey of South Asians to Britain or elsewhere, fuses such genres as jazz and instruments like the guitar and piano with classical South Asian instrumentation and vocals. The songs use tabla and *dholak* along with samples of the flute, *bin*,[40] and sounds of the marketplace that Sawhney collected in India. The vocals on the tracks, several of which are sung by the Indian classical vocalist Jayanta Bose, are in South Asian languages, the one exception being the track "Hope," which the artist Natacha Atlas sings in Arabic. In the liner notes, the jazz writer Linton Chiswick describes the weaving of classical South Asian music with other genres in the album's first track, "Migration": "Starting firmly in the East, with Aref Dervesh's propulsive tablas and some intricate, snake charming bin (played by a street musician from Chandigarh, whom Nitin recorded on a visit), the percussion stacks up gradually, locking the music into a nice bustling groove. Jayanta Boses's superb vocals lead the way through a journey to the West as, ever so gradually, the scenery changes, and tabla, dholak and vocals are transformed into funky drums, bass and Fender Rhodes. When the vocals and eastern instruments surface again later, the music seems to glance backward with a nebulous hazy awareness of its own history."

When I asked Sawhney why he worked with particular styles such as classical music and not with others such as bhangra, he said he wanted to challenge stereotypes of British Asian identity. He emphasized that British Asians are not interested solely in bhangra and expressed his frustration that many Asian music companies had signed only bhangra artists, while British companies tended not to sign British Asian artists at all, in the belief that all they produce is bhangra. Indicting the British industry for being racist, Sawhney said, "[They are] happy keeping all Asian music out by saying 'we're not interested in bhangra.'" In contrast, he felt that the creation of Outcaste Records was important since one of its goals was to counter the stereotypes to which other companies conformed. In fact, he and a number of British Asian artists who signed with Outcaste shared these goals: "That's why I made the music that I did, [to subvert stereotypes]; why I was so keen to put in . . . Indian classical sounds . . . and bring them to a wider platform, but also to have a real statement of identity, and I believed that Outcaste was completely in line with that, and so did everyone else. Shri was into that idea, Badmarsh was into that idea, Ges-E was into that idea, Niraj Chag was into that idea, Mo Magic was into that idea. All of us were with Outcaste."

Sawhney's eagerness to subvert stereotypes shapes his criticisms of the art-funding industry in Britain. In order to produce his first album, his only hope was to find grant money. During that time aspiring artists and independent arts organizations depended on subsidies from local and national funding bodies such as the London Arts Board, the Arts Council of England, and the National Lottery. These bodies earmarked some of their funding for cultural minorities and administered it by fulfilling quotas for Asians and other minority groups. But they often gave substantial amounts to a few well-known organizations, excluding smaller, less established ones. In turn, the Asian organizations that received funding tended to sponsor classical forms of South Asian art, featuring artists from South Asia as opposed to local talent.

In this funding environment Sawhney initially found it nearly impossible to acquire grant money. Indicting institutional arrangements for ultimately serving the elite in Britain, he said, "[Asian music organizations in England] would just put on elitist concerts for doctors and so on . . . and they would get a quarter of a million pounds a year to do that." With the recent media attention AU artists have enjoyed, Sawhney claimed that new opportunities were opening up: "I think there is a *genuine* renaissance going on. There is an awakening, a change that is happening that is based on substance, on the fact that I think we have an opportunity to learn the true depth of our culture without having to be kind of too tokenistic about it, which I think we have been forced into a position of being." These shifts allowed Sawhney to state that the arts-funding establishment and the organizations it funded were reproducing "tokenistic" notions of Asian culture represented by classical forms rather than fully exploring its "true depth." By implication, his music offers that depth.

Sawhney contests racial inequality on multiple levels: his origin stories raise awareness of racial violence, and he uses an Asian angle in his music to empower youth. He speaks out against essentialist notions of South Asian culture promulgated by bhangra labels, classical South Asian arts organizations, and the British arts-funding enterprise, itself fueled by state-sponsored multiculturalism. His contestations arguably extend beyond the stories he tells, as his music, which draws on South Asian classical music in innovative ways, was (and continues to be) highly regarded, potentially empowering British Asian youth. Moreover, the strategies he has used to navigate the music and art industries, for example, producing his first album and signing with Outcaste, resist their racialized economies.

Essentialism. As a forerunner in the AU scene, Sawhney bore the brunt of accusations by bhangra fans that AU music is culturally inauthentic and therefore musically illegitimate. Fans made these accusations in the Asian press, such as in letters to the *Eastern Eye* and at *melas*, or cultural festivals. Sawhney, for example, described a mela at which the emcee was riling up the audience, urging fans to shout, "We want bhangra!" before Sawhney was to appear onstage (a hostile response that I, too, witnessed at several AU performances). Given Britain's history of racism, accusations of ethnic inauthenticity are extremely powerful: they carry the force of betrayal of the community.

Sawhney countered bhangra fans by arguing that artists need to incorporate South Asian music in their songs with integrity, by which he means with a true understanding of South Asian culture. He positioned artists who are classically trained (such as himself) as having this knowledge:

> In the letters pages of *Eastern Eye*, there are people writing . . . "What is Talvin Singh? What is Nitin Sawhney about? We want to hear about *our* culture. We want to hear about bhangra." And I'm sitting there thinking that's so funny, because what Talvin knows about tabla playing, bhangra people couldn't learn in a million years, it's so enormously complex!

> I've studied a breadth of different types of forms from India and worked with those extensively and try and incorporate them in what I do. And that's *true*, that's not *diluting* them, that's *understanding* them, spending time even learning to speak the patterns, learning to count the rhythms. But bhangra . . . is so simple, it's unreal. Bhangra is four-four music, it's perfect for Western ears, and that's why it's received such interest is because it is, in *fact*, without people realizing it, it's probably about the most Westernized kind of music.

> I get [upset by] the fact that . . . there is within our own Asian community this whole thing of thinking that bhangra is the only thing . . . and that if you don't use that, you're not being true to your culture. . . . They don't know what we do. . . . This is actually something that *is* from a *genuine* angle, and it has *integrity* and it's not just about trying to be tokenistic or whatever.

Culture is fluid and power-laden. Yet rather than questioning the narrow notion of cultural authenticity that some bhangra fans espouse, Sawhney's counterargument retains the terms of the debate—that is, that there *can* be an authentic expression of culture—engaging in its own competitive invention of tradition.[41] In doing so, it risks reproducing class and race norms: in arguing that it is classically trained artists who pay proper respect to South Asian cultural forms, Sawhney's responses show that the incitement to authenticity is a matter of aesthetic mastery, that is, having sufficient training to understand tradition. This requirement privileges the classical musician over the deejay whose sampling is seen as not being true to the genealogy of the sampled elements. It also privileges the classical musician over the bhangra fan who is seen as not being sufficiently educated. Becoming classically trained is expensive: it requires extensive lessons and, often, costly equipment. Though one could argue that bhangra uses less complex time signatures than classical Indian forms, Sawhney's narrative transposes this difference onto "bhangra people," whom it likewise sees as simplistic. In doing so, it also treads dangerously close to colonialist uses of barbarianism. Casting bhangra as westernized draws on the anticolonial strategy of positioning the West as corrupt and the East as pure, a formulation that problematically essentializes both. While AU artists such as Sawhney aimed to empower British Asians, then, they sometimes adopted strategies that worked against that goal. Sawhney, for example, countered the demands of bhangra fans in ways that arguably narrowed rather than expanded notions of British Asian identity. These strategies reinforce essentialist ideologies of culture that he and other AU artists have tried to contest.

Liberal Humanism. Sawhney's portrayals of his artistry to the British mainstream perhaps necessarily differed greatly from the ones he used with bhangra fans. Instead of emphasizing that he has true access to South Asian culture, he drew on liberal humanist notions of identity to stress his individuality and to position himself outside of community. Though renditions of liberal humanism vary historically, it "proposes that the subject is the free, unconstrained author of meaning and action, the origin of history."[42] Sawhney's liberal humanist stance is recognizable in his liner notes for *Beyond Skin*:

> I am Indian. To be more accurate, I was raised in England, but my parents came from India . . . "Indian"—what does that mean? At this time, the government of India is testing nuclear weapons—Am I less Indian if I don't defend their actions? . . . Less Indian for being born and raised in Britain?—For not speaking Hindi? Am I not English because of my cultural heritage? Or the colour of my skin? Who decides?
>
> The BJP in India.[43] The BNP in England.[44] The first would define me by my religious heritage, the latter by the colour of my skin.
>
> I believe in Hindu philosophy. I am not religious. I am a pacifist. I am a British Asian.
>
> My identity and my history are defined only by myself—beyond politics, beyond nationality, beyond religion, and Beyond Skin.

Here, Sawhney first mobilizes the category of British Asian to unsettle the essentialist ideas of identity that both Hindu nationalists in India, represented by the Bharatiya Janata Party, and right-wing xenophobic political parties in Britain, represented by the British National Party, espouse. Yet his claim to be a British Asian is an individualistic one: after questioning who defines identity, he adopts a liberal humanist position, claiming that only he defines himself and that he is therefore beyond politics, nationality, religion, and skin.

Sawhney's strategy sat uneasily with the heads of Outcaste Records: even though they wanted to contest stereotypes of British Asians, as a label "British Asian" offered them a tool to market their artists to both Asian and non-Asian audiences. One can see this tension in Jobanputra's follow-up to Sawhney's notes: "This LP is Outcaste Records' finest musical achievement to date. Our search to find a new sound which emanates from British Asian culture looks achievable upon listening to this. A seamless, emotional and beautiful testament to our lives as British Asian people." Whereas Sawhney sees himself as an individual, Jobanputra positions him as an informant of British Asian culture.

Liberal humanism was in fact foundational to Sawhney's work in the late 1990s and early 2000s. As his albums transitioned from *Migration* to

Human, which he produced in 2003, after leaving Outcaste, liberal humanist discourse increasingly frames them (figs. 2.1–2.4).

The title *Migration* refers to immigrants' experiences, as does the album cover, which shows a bisected footprint, suggesting travel across two spaces. *Displacing the Priest* begins to adopt liberal humanism as it confronts groupthink by implying the need to displace the heads of organized religion. His later albums more explicitly use liberal humanist language and images to promote the idea that society should be colorblind. For example, the title and cover of *Beyond Skin* connote a man who is trapped by his skin and who wants to be seen for his uniqueness, outside of socially constructed categories. *Human* represents an even stronger use of liberal humanism in its title and especially its cover, in which the figure is even less decipherable (though it is still legible as a man's). Emphasizing the similarities that all people share on the basis of their biology, *Human* moves away from the language of race altogether ("I am a human, not an 'Asian'"; "we are all, in fact, human").[45] A story produced by National Public Radio in January 2010, over a decade after the heyday of the AU, shows how the albums he produced in the 2000s continue to bolster color-blind discourse: "What he's trying to say is that we should be colorblind in terms of our sort of cultural understanding of Britain and London," says Laura Barnett, an arts editor who profiled Sawhney for the British newspaper the *Guardian*. "We're all Londoners. We're all British. We're not British-Asians, we're not white, we're not black; we're just people."[46]

Sawhney speaks from a liberal humanist stance in interviews as well. For example, he often expresses disdain about the media's situating him as part of a larger British Asian "movement," instead using the rhetoric of individualism: "I have a huge problem with people who make assumptions about me and that are interested in talking to me only as part of a movement and not as an individual." In a more elaborate statement, he maintains, "I'm trying to express my own identity, which is I'm a British Asian. I happen to be one, but my own identity is what I'm coming from. People can choose to relate to it or not relate to it. I'm not trying to say this is what British Asians are, I'm trying to say this is what I am."

One can link Sawhney's use of such language to his disdain for politics. As Huq reports, "Sawhney has rejected any such resistive responsibility in his work declaring: 'I hate everything about politics. To me politics was [*sic*] about white, middle-aged men. I don't wanna preach to people. I don't think I've got the right to preach anymore than anyone else.'"[47] Sawhney's rejection of politics is twofold: he denounces the formal arena of

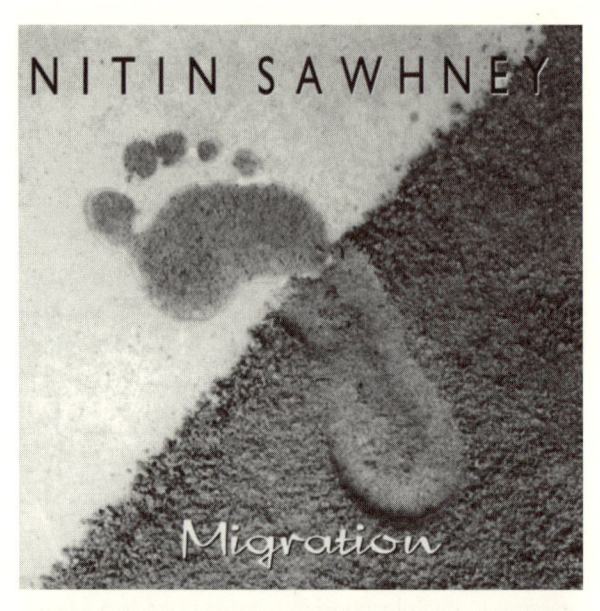

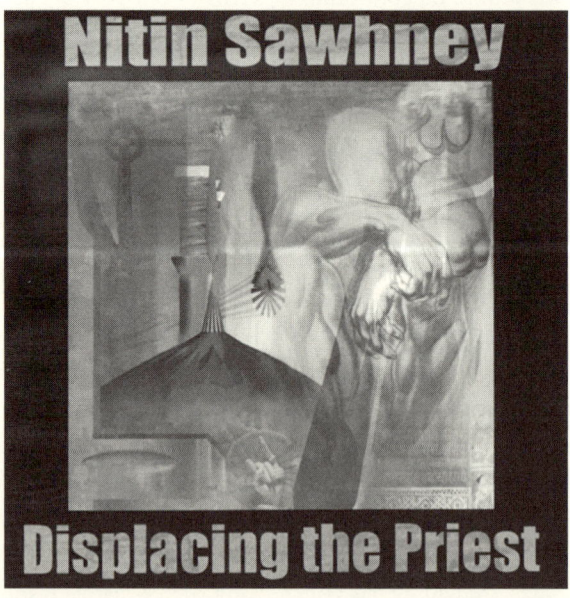

FIGURES 2.1–2.4 Nitin Sawhney's albums: *Migration* (1995), *Displacing the Priest* (1996),

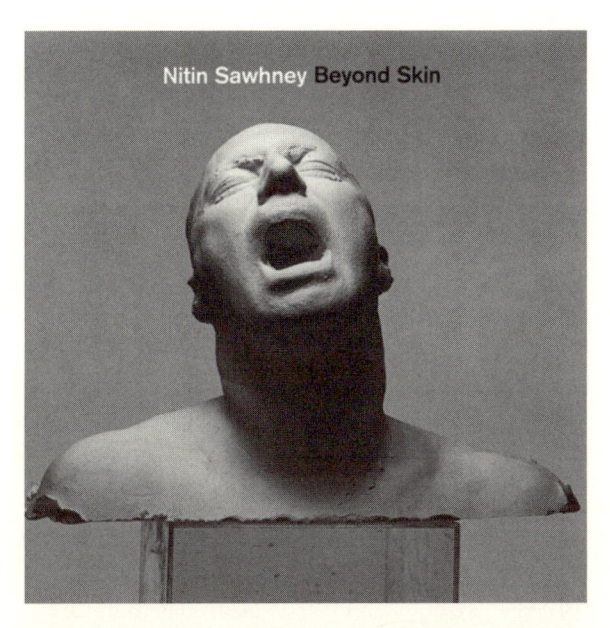

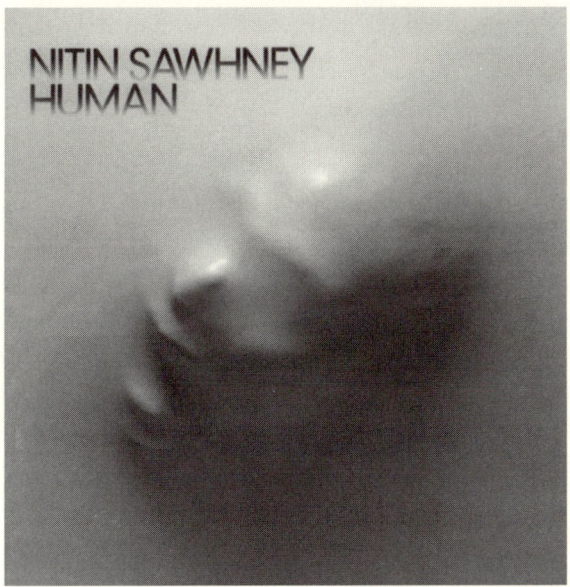

Beyond Skin (1999), and *Human* (2003)

politics, that is, government, inhabited by white men, and, in a show of humility, he also calls into question the protest politics expected of the angry Asian: "I don't wanna preach to people."

While the label British Asian has enabled AU artists to succeed, informing their work and helping them get signed with labels like Outcaste, Sawhney's discussions suggest that it has also been stifling. Partly for these reasons, artists are frustrated by having to discuss their music at all. As Sawhney says, he was reluctant about having to write the liner notes for *Beyond Skin*: "I was asked by Outcaste to actually say what I [felt] when I wrote [the music] . . . and I remember saying, 'Well, the music should say it enough in itself. I don't really want to have to do that, because it's not really my style.' But then they say, 'You've got to say something about what you felt.' So you have to write from your emotions. . . . What I do feel is *very* emotional when I write [music], but . . . *My vocabulary, my language, is music.*" One can therefore understand why AU artists might praise individuality and downplay ethnicity, especially since terms like *artistic freedom* and *artistic uniqueness* ground popular ideas of artistry and are therefore easily available and appealing. Understandably, Sawhney wants to be more than a British Asian symbol, and he has been shaped by and continues to engage with a wide range of musical and cultural genres.

Artists' adoption of liberal humanism is thus multifaceted, not straightforwardly resistant or complicit. In other words, it is inaccurate to assume, on the one hand, that artists' use of this rhetoric simply represents their belief that they transcend the social and are therefore apolitical or not interested in social change. Rather, it is a response to a music industry that is significantly shaped by race. On the other hand, the adoption of liberal humanist rhetoric is also problematic in that its notion of the individual ignores the workings of culture and power. In sum, as Sawhney draws on the sometimes-contradicting discourses of antiracism, essentialism, and liberal humanism to deal with the demands of his diverse audiences, he contests racism. His actions broaden the formulaic notion that political engagement inheres only in protest.

Badmarsh: The Politics of Pleasure

During the height of the AU scene Mohammed Akber Ali, known as Badmarsh (or scoundrel), was a popular artist. Badmarsh is quite different from Sawhney: he's a deejay, not a musician, he doesn't make a point of discussing social inequality in interviews, and he identifies as a practicing

Muslim. But, like Sawhney, he engages in antiracism: his perspectives and practices reveal an interest in social change that impacts how he deals with audiences and industries and how he makes music.

I traveled to Badmarsh's home to interview him in the fall of 1998, after the AU had garnered enough popularity that British Asian activists began leveling public criticisms at it.[48] At the time, Badmarsh was living with his mother and siblings in a modest, yet large house in the East End.[49] He welcomed me, and we settled in a darkish room that seemed to be part studio. Records and audio equipment lay in piles on bookshelves and scattered around the floor. Our conversation, which lasted for more than two hours, was punctuated by knocks on the door from his siblings, informing him about business calls that were coming through.

NEGOTIATING AUDIENCE AND INDUSTRY

As we began the interview, I learned how Badmarsh's experience growing up in the predominantly working-class East End, an area that has long been home to successive waves of new immigrants, impacted his identity. He was born in Yemen of Indian parents but, upon moving to London, was raised in an atmosphere of racist violence perpetuated by the National Front, a right wing, xenophobic political party. Despite the racism his family suffered, his parents were determined to stay in England. Badmarsh said, "My dad always said, 'You will be staying in this country, so the best thing is to contribute something to this society.' . . . We understood what he meant."

Badmarsh moved through the schooling system in the hope of landing a technical job, but a minor disability barred him from pursuing that career option. At the end of his coursework, with no jobs lined up, he turned to the idea of a career in music since listening to records and going clubbing were activities for which he and his friends had developed a strong passion. Badmarsh's first experience of deejaying, which he exuberantly recounts, helped solidify his decision to make a career out of music. As he became more experienced, he began mixing Eastern sounds with Western ones and producing his own tracks. He was soon offered a recording deal with a non-Asian record label, but when Outcaste offered him one, he signed with them instead.

Badmarsh describes how being a British Asian motivated him to include "Asian sounds" in his music. Feeling that something was missing from his deejay sets, he began experimenting with these sounds, an activity which in turn produced his wish to "move Asian culture forward." He states, "When I was experimenting, the fusion of Eastern and Western was so excellent! I thought, yeah, this is the move forward. I'm bringing my own culture forward plus the Western [culture], so I'm bringing two together." When I asked him, "How are you bringing your own culture forward?" he responded, "I think Asian culture in a way is like listening to the Asian sounds—like if I was in India; but I'm not there, I'm here—keeping that alive; cause a lot of British Asians out there are either into rap or bhangra. ... I wanted to bring something else into it—natural, classical Asian sounds."

Badmarsh's story resonates in some ways with Sawhney's. His definition of Asian sounds, for example, privileges classical forms. But, not having had classical training, he narrated his knowledge of this music through the naturalizing metaphor of blood: "Even though I don't understand classical form, some things are in your blood. You *know* that sound. You think, 'Yeah, this is right ... this is what I belong to, I can relate to it.'" While Badmarsh emphasized his affective relationships to Asian music, which he said filled a "lack" in his blood, like Sawhney, he discussed the role of racism in shaping his wish to move Asian culture forward: "All the music that you hear is about my moods, my surroundings, my struggles in this country; it's about me growing up in England. . . . Asian sounds add all the ingredients: emotional struggle, support ... living in London and in a racist society."

As our discussion turned to the topics of audiences and politics, he seemed to contradict his earlier points. Badmarsh distinguished promoting Asian culture from reaching out to Asians themselves, saying he was not particularly interested in whether or not Asians listened to his music: "I never said, 'I want Asians to come forward.' It's just about enjoyment; it's not about pleasing a specific person, region, race; you're not going to please everyone." He also said he didn't want his music to be about politics, differentiating this category from and emphasizing his interest in pleasure: "I want music to be the way I started, as enjoyment, as a passion."

Linking politics to a series of other terms he finds negative, he said, "I would never put a political statement, or anything from religion to say, 'Oh, this is what I feel.' . . . I don't need statements to portray my music; my music will speak for itself. . . . After listening, interview me and ask me about it rather than [assuming], 'Oh you're this kind of person, you don't like this color, you don't like that color, you're about this race, you hate this person.' I'm not about that. I'm not about hating people. I'm not about putting people down. It's about me, enjoying music, playing music; but if you want to know what I'm about, interview me, and I'll tell you what I'm about." For Badmarsh, politics means making political or religious "statements" in music that of necessity entail overt expressions of identity or hate or both. He also associates politics with race, especially with audiences making assumptions about who he is on the basis of his color. Like Sawhney, he said his music has its own language; he felt that anyone interested in his identity should ask directly about it, not make assumptions about it from his music. He implied that explicit portrayals in music invite overdetermined readings of racialized artists.

Badmarsh's use of two registers—stating a desire to promote Asian culture, born in part from personal experiences of racism, but expressing little interest in appealing to Asians specifically—was not unique to him. Other artists did the same thing. Those espousing protest politics might interpret this use as straightforwardly capitalist, that is, as the activist Sofia says, trading in being a cultural Asian but not speaking out against the racism that British Asians face. But Badmarsh's position is complex: it follows capitalist logic yet also resists racism. Knowledge of how race structures the mainstream music industry informs Badmarsh's seemingly contradictory positions. The phrase, "brown is the new black," bandied about in the late 1990s, indicates that British Asians have historically not been considered producers of hip popular culture. As AU artists were gaining mainstream popularity, however, Badmarsh and others were wary that such attention was simply a media fad fueled by a commodification of ethnicity ("flavor of the year") and controlled by the powers that be, who were white. My discussion with Badmarsh exemplifies artists' insecurities. Hesitantly calling his feelings "paranoid" (recalling Sawhney's "slight paranoia"), he discussed his sense that outside forces were preventing British Asian artists from truly succeeding: "I feel like we're growing, but we're still being pushed [down].... You get a sense of when you achieve something, somebody's watching you.... Also, myself, colleagues of mine ... we've been doing this since *time*, and just *now* it's growing ... but slowly. *Why* is it going slowly? Are people just opening their minds now? Why weren't they reacting to it before? ... So major labels are jumping on the bandwagon ... and I think, come five years time, are we still going to be there? ... I don't know. It could just be me—just paranoid.... I hate calling it [the Asian Underground].... It makes you feel like you're a little fish.... It's like you're getting pushed back: stay where you are, underground." In a racialized context, then, AU artists can have particularly heightened concerns for the bottom line. When situated within their larger concerns about racism, artists' voicing of disinterest in appealing to Asian audiences can be seen as reflecting their acute awareness that the mainstream music industry is racialized; and, in a sense, longevity in the industry allows for more opportunities for "moving Asian culture forward."

THE AESTHETIC OF ENJOYMENT

In characterizing his music, Badmarsh disavows politics and emphasizes enjoyment. Yet the contrast he draws between the club culture he grew up in and still prefers and that of the AU points to several ways in which his musical aesthetic is politicized. For him, real clubs emphasize a bodily relationship to music, while AU clubs use ethnic visual iconography to such an extent that they are wrongly transformed into pseudo art galleries: "I was listening to a lot of black soul.... I grew up in that environment.... From that, it went to garage, rave, and just carried on.... All my music was dance music; every place I played at was about pure groove, pure dance.... That's what gives me that rush. It's not just about hearing it, but feeling it as well.... When you're in a club, it's got to be a club environment. With the Asian Underground, they have a lot of lights, paintings, so it's not a club anymore. It's like going to a gallery, checking out visuals.... For me it's not about that; it's about dark, loud sounds, and just enjoying yourself.... It's not about burning incense and hanging saris.... It's about pure groove, pure dance." The black music forms, such as soul, that have influenced Badmarsh have what Paul Gilroy calls a "distinctive *public* political character" in that their lyrics, along with the "performance aesthetic which governs them," denounce capitalism.[50] This music challenges the ways in which waged work is "a form of servitude" both in lyrics and in the space of the club, which celebrates the black body as an "instrument of pleasure, rather than an instrument of labour": "This culture ... views the body as itself an important locus of resistance and desire. The body is therefore reclaimed from its subordination to the labor process, recognized as part of the natural world and enjoyed on that basis.... Rather than aim at the conquest of political power or apparatuses, its objective centres on the control of a field of autonomy or independence from the system."[51] Badmarsh's emphasis on "pure groove, pure dance" and the formative influence of soul music on him, a music critical to Gilroy's genealogy of black cultural production, suggests that Badmarsh's aesthetic shares the political character Gilroy describes. Badmarsh's descriptions of club going in the late 1980s also intimate that he was part of what Gilroy calls a "utopian social movement" in which Afro-Caribbeans, Asians, and whites alike enjoyed soul.

Badmarsh's opposition to the visual signifiers of Asianness in AU clubs contests commodified representations of South Asians in Britain. His disapproval connects to his disinterest in using "statements" in his music: both represent his disdain for explicit signifiers of Asianness and, in turn, for politics. In other words, for Badmarsh, being political consists of making explicit statements in music or in clubs that express ethnic or religious identity or feelings of hate that may stem from claiming these identities. While an adherent of protest politics might understand Badmarsh's stance as being apolitical, it is one motivated by interests in social change. By metonymically linking statements, Asians, hate, and politics, his narrative reflects the fact that representations of South Asians in the UK have historically been overdetermined in ways that erase their subjectivities. Read through this frame, Badmarsh's refusal to have certain signifiers in his music is a form of resistance to the racism that renders Asians as easily legible. As such, it also resists the trope of the "angry Asian (man)." By wanting audiences to carefully listen to his music and not jump to conclusions about him, then, Badmarsh is expressing his desire to be understood as a complex person rather than as yet another angry Asian. His statement, "If you want to know what I'm about, interview me," reflects his desire to have control over the hermeneutics of his identity.

Finally, Badmarsh's aesthetic of enjoyment speaks to his identity as a Muslim. Badmarsh describes himself as "very religious" but adds some qualifications. He explains that he is not a "100 percent practicing Muslim" because he cannot pray regularly owing to the demands of his work, but he reads the Koran, fasts, and prays when he can because Islam is an aspect of his identity that he will "never lose." The difficulties he has faced in his line of work include not only having less time to practice rituals, but also facing the prohibition by certain schools of Islam thought to produce music at all. He said, "My mom told me that music is bad.... When you go to pray, you don't hear music ... in Islam, it says not to mix the two together."

Facing difficulties in reconciling his identities as a Muslim and a deejay, Badmarsh produces himself as a good Muslim by emphasizing enjoyment. He dislikes explicit signifiers of identity, including religious ones, in club visuals and music lyrics: "If I were to have a club, I wouldn't have gods, incense, or saris just to say, 'I'm Asian.' ... People can see your color of your skin, that you're not English. You don't have to portray Islam or religion into music." Since Badmarsh associates making lyrical or visual statements with hate, then pleasure is predicated on *not* having religious signifiers in music, and this enables him to be a good Muslim.

Moreover, for Badmarsh, portraying religion in music is not only counter to what music should be, which is its "own language," but is problematic because religion is private. He feels that whereas music expresses the personal, religion is a different kind of personal because it is sacred. In his opinion it shouldn't be used in music or in the space of the club: "Leave religion home. You have that inside you, you don't have to bring that out in music.... I would never go into stuff which I think is personal to me.... Religion should be with yourself: at home, not at clubs." The ways in which non-Muslim deejays, both white and Asian, have appropriated sacred hymns such as *azaan* for use in club music informs Badmarsh's conviction that religion should be left at home.

Badmarsh associates making public statements about religion with expressing divisiveness. His redemption as a Muslim lies not only in avoiding making these statements, but also in intentionally making music that is about enjoyment. He said, "I'm not a bad person; I'm not doing anything bad, not harming anyone. I'm not putting in any statements to say things. I'm just making music, which I believe in and people will enjoy, and that's it." Badmarsh feels that because his music comes from his heart and is made with good intentions, his actions do not violate the tenets of Islam. His belief that his intentions are manifest in his music, evidenced by people's pleasure of it, is critical to his negotiation of Islam. For example, both Badmarsh and his mother feel that his decision to produce music is validated because of his success: "I don't see God saying to me, 'This is wrong.' If this was wrong, I wouldn't be where I am.... Today, [my mom] tells me I've achieved all this because of Allah; be thankful." Thus, while the way in which Badmarsh adheres to Islam leads him to exclude statements from his music, thereby disqualifying him from being considered political according to a protest politics frame, he enacts an antiracist politics in other ways.[52]

Badmarsh, like Sawhney, holds apparently contradictory positions: while he states a desire to promote Asian culture and express his racial struggles, he isn't greatly interested in communicating to strictly Asian audiences, and he vehemently dissociates himself from politics. However, when understood together with his interest in working with black-owned record labels, Badmarsh's perspectives and practices are political: he deals with audience and industry expectations in ways that reflect a contestation of racism, and his musical aesthetic intersects with histories of resistance in black cultural production, challenges ethnic stereotypes that erase subjectivity, and enables him, as a Muslim, to make music.

Joi: We're Now Artists, Not Politicians

Examining how the band Joi reconciled their desires with various burdens of representation is interesting because Joi originated as part of an activist community organization (similar to ADF) but later decided to focus on attaining commercial success. The brothers Haroon and Farook Shamsher, born to a Bangladeshi father and an Indian mother, created Joi in 1983 as part of their involvement with the League of Joi Bangla Youth, an organization whose goal was to promote Bangladeshi culture. Initially calling themselves Joi Bangla, which means "Victory to Bangladesh," they produced East–West remixes, creating lyrics and sounds aimed at generating pride among young Bengalis and countering racism among whites. In 1998, fifteen years after their start, their approach to music seemed to have shifted dramatically: they were signed with a mainstream label, Real World Records, they had changed their name to Joi, which less directly referenced Bengali identity, they were creating mostly nonlyrical electronic dance music such as house, techno, and trance, whose themes were, in their words, harmony and bliss, and their live performances at times included white dancers and musicians. Their trajectory invites the condemnations that adherents of the protest politics model make of selling out. Examining Joi's trajectory closely, however, one can see that their initial desire to combat racism continues to shape their artistry.[53]

I met Haroon and Farook on a cloudy October afternoon at the crowded Bethnal Green tube station in the East End, an area where the brothers grew up and to which they have a strong connection. My time with them confirmed the sense I already had—after seeing their performances, talking to mutual acquaintances, and researching their media profile—that they were somewhat heretical. For example, they often overtly remarked on how the producing of music is necessarily and unfortunately a business game. So, although all interviews are performative acts in which the involved parties attempt to shape the discussion, the brothers engaged in our interview in blatantly staged ways by often shifting registers, that is, giving more or less rehearsed answers and discussing things on and off the record. For instance, as we walked through the narrow streets of Brick Lane looking for a restaurant in which to conduct the interview, Farook joked with me that he decides to take an interviewer to a "grungy" or "posh" place depending on where she or he is from. Alluding to the poverty of the East End and ambivalently to America's then-powerful economic status, Farook said, tongue in cheek, that he wanted to take me to a nice place—he wouldn't want an American to have a terrible impression of the East End. Throughout the interview the brothers made what sounded like practiced statements about themselves but then at various moments ruptured their narrative with a sarcastic and infectious humor. I note their narrative style because it is in many ways emblematic of their oppositional approach to the business of music making.

POLITICIANS

Haroon's and Farook's early musicianship fits squarely into a political protest model. They began remixing Eastern and Western music with two goals in mind: to empower Bangladeshis and to combat racism. The brothers developed an interest in classical South Asian music early in life by working for their father, a traditional flute player. He would help bring classical musicians from Bangladesh to England and then make recordings of their performances to sell in his sari and music shop. Haroon describes his and Farook's enthusiasm in helping their father: "We used to do the recordings, missing school, with headphones on at four in the morning, recording the artist from Bangladesh in the back of the shop."

While growing up, the brothers developed a keen interest in deejaying and in black popular cultural forms such as American hip-hop, break dancing, and soul that were considered quite hip by their black and white peers at school. They said that although racism was "a lot worse back then," their knowledge of this popular culture made them more accepted than their Bengali peers were. Farook states, "They'd say, *'You're* okay, but I don't know about the rest of them,' and 'I can kind of handle *you*' ... because we were into something *they* were into, and we didn't really smell of curry and spices, and we wore a certain Western dress.... But if ... you're all right ... and your cousin isn't, then.... They *haven't* really accepted you. They're not accepting your people, and they're just being really false about it."[54]

The brothers explain that, given the musical influences in their lives, it was natural for them to remix Eastern and Western music. It is clear, however, that they forged this interest in the racialized context of Britain, as they consciously decided to use the new music they produced to further their work with the youth of the League of Joi Bangla. The acute forms of marginalization the Bengali community faced drove the brothers' desire to specifically empower Bengalis. Farook said, "One of the main things was, and it still is now, that among Pakistanis, Indians, and Bengalis, Bengalis are still seen as the lowest caste, and they're still seen as a very new kind of

Asian culture to the country.... The role of Joi Bangla was to give Bengalis a sense of pride." Farook reported that they started performing at family events as well as at lectures and art exhibitions on Bangladesh to empower youth by making sure they "acknowledged their culture."[55]

Describing how they created tracks, Farook said, "We'd get Michael Jackson's "Billie Jean" record, and we'd mix in a traditional Bengali record—as traditional as it comes—a guy called Amir Uddin, ... We'd roll "Billie Jean," so everyone would think, 'Yeah, "Billie Jean"'s in.' ... And slowly you put out this traditional [track] ... and they'd have it."[56] Switching from particularist to universalist language, Haroon and Farook claimed that music is a powerful tool to combat racism because it appeals to all people on a sensory level (it is an "international language"); it can inspire intellectual curiosity and political solidarity. As Farook noted, "The only way to combat racism ... was through music.... If it appeals to you, if the music has a sensation that it does to you, it's done its trick already.... You give them a bit of a break beat, and you put a traditional Asian kind of vocal in it, and someone really likes that break beat or the drum and bass, and they want to find out what this Asian music's about."

In addition to remixing other artists' songs, the brothers produced their own explicitly political tracks. One of the four singles they released before signing on with Real World Records, a rap from the early 1980s called "Funky Asian," illustrates their creative use of lyrics and melodies.[57] "Funky Asian" begins with a *dhol* beat and a South Asian melody and then incorporates a sample from a rap song (which repeats throughout the track) in which a black male artist sings, "All right!" Lyrically, the song starts with Haroon, the lead singer, "upping" himself in classic hip-hop fashion: "I'm KMD, the man to lead, you've got to listen to me, because I'm making history. I'm the top of the town, the king of the beat, you see I rock this mike, with the greatest of ease."[58] Soon after, he introduces the notion of East–West fusion, claiming ownership of it—it's about where "I come from" and "it's my sound"—and declaring it has the ability to impact the mind and body:

> I thought I'd let you know where *I* come from ...
> East/west hip-hop ... it's going to blow your brain ...
> And when I cut my own mix, and you'll discover ... it's like no other
> It's truly unique, and it's my sound
> So get down party people, get down real low
> Because the east/west mix is really good to go.

The song then showcases its Eastern aspect by featuring a classical Bengali flute instrumental. Immediately afterward, Haroon hails his audience as being in need of this music ("beggin' for more"), curious about its origins ("wondering where it's coming from"), and cognizant that it is, in fact, "number one." The climax of the song, "across the nation, everybody's talking about, the funky Asian," attempts to counter stereotypes of Asians as unhip. The rhyming of "Asian" and "nation" points to British Asians' struggles for full citizenship. After another melodic break that includes South Asian music and singing by a black vocalist, Haroon breaks into a chorus in Bangla. The use of Bangla not only introduces South Asian language into the song but also situates Bengalis in Britain within a transnational frame by linking their struggles to Bengalis in Bangladesh:

naam naam aamar KMD
porichoi mor Bangali
amra shobai bechara
tai gaan hobey, "Joi Bangla"
joi joi joi Bangla!

[my name is KMD
my identity is Bengali
we are all wretched/deprived/exploited folks
that's why the song is "Joi Bangla"
Victory to Bangladesh][59]

After making these declarations, Haroon assures his audience, "This is me, KMD, eternally, so feel easy, feel easy, feel, feel, feel easy," suggesting that Joi was trying to ameliorate what they perceive as the potentially alienating effects of introducing South Asian lyrics to non-Asian audiences.

ARTISTS

After a few years of being Joi Bangla, Haroon and Farook decided to focus solely on producing music, letting go of much of their involvement with the League of Joi Bangla Youth. To reflect their new interest, they changed their name to Joi, but their reasons for doing so seemed somewhat contradictory. On the one hand, they seemed to hold on to their original desire to empower Asian communities by claiming that Joi reflected their new desires in promoting the general British Asian community, not just Bengalis: "Joi Bangla just meant strictly "Victory to Bangladesh." ... [T]he reason we had to change is because the Asian scene that we were fighting for wasn't just for Bengalis." Their decision to change their name was informed by their attentiveness to how all South Asians are racialized; as Haroon said, it was a "racial thing . . . not just Bengali." Their name change was also the result of their being repeatedly identified as Joi Bhangra by the media, evidence of the conflation of Asians with bhangra and of how the AU scene continued to be haunted by its specter.

On the other hand, Joi indicated that their interest in becoming artists, reflected in their new name, meant that they needed to lose their focus on community. Farook juxtaposed art, which he described as an expression of individuality, to community activism or to being politicians. In this sense, his discussion reproduced the liberal humanism in Sawhney's and Badmarsh's accounts:

> We had to appeal to a bigger audience. Making an album is not just about trying to defend or promote your community. You've got to understand, we've been doing this over ten to fifteen years. . . . So now is the time for us to say, "Right, this is art—this is what we feel." . . . And to English people they don't say, "So what do you think about your English culture?" Or to Americans, they don't say to Madonna, so what about all of this? . . . She's an artist, as an individual, people like her for her music. . . . [Y]ou still stick to these community things, but you lose them in a way, because you're trying to give people an impression of what you're trying to create, of art, music.

But in juxtaposing art and politics, Farook leaves room for both to happen at the same time. He implies that creating an album involves engaging in activism along with other things—"making an album is not *just* about trying"—and that one can also "stick" to activism even while losing some aspect of it. In this way he suggests that Joi has struggled to hold on to activism in spite of feeling the need to move away from it to make an album.

Although Joi's explanations for changing their focus appear to be contradictory, that is, wanting to empower Asians but also wanting to deemphasize activism, I suggest that Joi changed their name, music, and performances in ways that enable them to be artists and yet also engage in social change. First, the name Joi signifies a South Asian identity and politics, as its spelling refers to the Bengali word for "victory." At the same time, *Joi* is more legible to white audiences than *Joi Bangla*, as it can readily be heard as *joy*. The fact that their name changed when they first signed with a record label, Rhythm King Records, implies that the shift had to do with becoming more accessible to whites.

Second, Joi's first album, *One and One Is One*, which consists of the nonlyrical electronica most associated with the AU, engages in antiracism, but in ways that are arguably safe. The album, which is framed by themes of harmony, unity, and bliss, represents the South Asian musical influences that Joi has long drawn on, such as Baul music, whose major themes are unity and love.[60] By including, in Sawhney's words, an Asian angle, it arguably represents Joi's earlier goal of empowering Asians. One can also read the album as calling attention to race relations by stressing the need for unity. Yet by not attending to the workings of racial power, it can also be seen as a muted protest that works in a corporate context.

Farook's description of Joi's approach to the album makes clear that Joi was in fact no longer interested in lyrically commenting on social inequality in their music. His references to how their music should speak for itself recall the narratives of Sawhney and Badmarsh that construct politics as art's other:

> You can't just be fundamental about it.... The album's called *One and One Is One*, so it's all just about total unification. It's one of Rabindranath Tagore's poems about metaphysics, bliss, total harmony. ... It's all been a natural kind of progression. It's not like we should be fighting for Asians or for Bengalis or trying to speak for the Islamic world. Now me and Haroon have to say, "Right, we have to deliver this album, and then let the music speak for us," and hope that the impact that we've made throughout the years will still be working, and the album and the music will have that energy ... where people will ... feel a sense of pride ... and if you grab one of [the people who love to hate it], and they convert, it was worth doing the album.[61]

Farook gives conflicting reasons, however, for why Joi shouldn't have to produce protest music, showing an ambivalent desire to empower Asians even as he insists that Joi has no obligation to do so. For example, the brothers state that politics is not the right strategy to combat racism ("you can't just be fundamental about it") and that they have "naturally evolved" from doing politics to doing art: it's a "natural kind of progression." They also hope that, despite their new approach to music, the impact of their prior work will continue—"we ... hope that the impact we've made throughout the years will still be working"—and that Asian audiences will be empowered and racist people will change their views.

This ambivalence, I believe, shapes some of their aesthetic choices. Joi decided not to include lyrics in their first album because they believed, as did Badmarsh, that doing so would mean participating in a protest politics and would leave little possibility of audiences reading them as anything other than "dictator[s]" or "politicians." Farook said, "As soon as you put a word in a track, it changes someone's perception.... And you don't want to be a dictator on your record and give people a headache. It's all right in interviews, but... they've got to listen to [your record] again and again.... You might as well just become politicians and dictate to people and have everything worked out." Farook also implied that including lyrics is not good for sales insofar as it may narrow the meaning of the music: "The first album we want to leave a lot more open, because it is the first album, and it's about this harmonious, one-on-one thing." But despite these stances, the brothers had not abandoned their interest in empowering Bengalis. Farook said they incorporated Bengali rhythms in all of their tracks in order to enable Bengalis to develop selfhood: "We could do a complete Western track, [but we] put our traditional Bengali rhythm in, and there are a lot of Bengalis that recognize that rhythm ... and it gives them a sense of identity.... We always do it ... on the album, there are lots of hooks that people recognize and go, 'Ah, I remember that as a kid. I remember that hook from that movie.'"

Third, Joi uses white women dancers in their stage performances, but their reasons for doing so are conflicting. Farook said:

We don't have to just use our own people.... We did that five or ten years ago. Now we have to move forward.

We use talented artists, musicians, and our dancer is one of the best classical dancers I've come across.... And she's been classically trained.... She's a Hari Krishna all right ... but she's ... been devoting herself to the spirits of dance.... It's her profession. I'm going to use her—not because she's white or black or green or blue, but because she's beautiful and exquisite in her movements.

If I just use an Asian then ... we may be stereotyped as just this kind of Asian-y bhangra band.... [W]e see ourselves flowing into the future, where it is about fusion.

I've already done it five years ago by using ... just Bengalis. That's all we'd use because we'd be trying to fight a certain thing. Now it's more harmonious, and it's more united, and it's more about talent and look. These are people who you should try to be like, and if she can convert, so can you. And not even convert—if she can devote her life, soul, and spirit towards a certain culture and a race and everything else, so can you. [And] Joi can [employ a white woman]. A new band couldn't ... because we've been [performing] for fifteen years or so.

On the one hand, Farook highlights the need to combat racism by expressing a desire to "convert" whites: "if she can convert, so can you." They also acknowledge the existence of racism within the music industry—"we may be stereotyped"—and the problematic ways in which whites have appropriated South Asian cultural forms: "She's a Hari Krishna ... but she's ... been devoting herself to the spirits of dance." On the other hand, they imply that racial struggles are over—"now it's more harmonious"—and that they can therefore focus on the quality of their performances, their "talent and look," rather than on fighting "a certain thing." Here, their notions of quality rely on color-blind discourse: "She's simply the best"; "I'm going to use her—not because she's white or black or green or blue, but because she's beautiful and exquisite in her movements." They use a narrative of progress as well—"we have to move forward," "the future is about fusion"—one through which they situate the use of Asian performers and of so-called traditional forms like bhangra in the past, much in the way colonial narratives construct Asians and their traditions.

Certainly, the presence of these dancers on stage can communicate a kind of racial harmony. The fact that they have trained in a South Asian classical form contests the restrictive, essentialist notions of culture that conservative political discourse often relies on. The inclusion of the dancers, however, can also be critiqued for celebrating a racial harmony that does not exist. Moreover, as Farook insinuates, it can reinforce the long, problematic history of white appropriation of South Asian forms, especially female ones.[62] Although Joi claims that using Asian performers would subject them to being stereotyped as an "Asian-y bhangra band," substituting white performers capitulates to those stereotypes rather than challenging them.

Farook's account also reflects Joi's ambivalence about community activism, particularly in the idea that they feel that *they* can employ white women, but other new bands cannot. When I asked how he'd respond to criticisms that Joi was just being trendy, Farook responded by invoking Joi's prior community work to justify their current musical practices. Their use of the touchstone of "we used to do that" to legitimate their current artistry means they continue to feel that there are important political values and that there is, perhaps, such a thing as selling out. At the same time, employing a teleology of the individual, they disavow the importance of activism in their emphasis that having done this work has enabled them to "move on."

THE BIZ

One can interpret Joi's trajectory as one of trying both to achieve commercial success and to empower community. Yet, to return to the notion of heresy that I opened with, they have in more direct ways defied corporate control of the music industry. Joi has engaged in production and performance practices that work against the capitalist ethos of profit making. In the eight years before they signed with Real World they officially released only four singles because they prized creating tracks that could be heard only at the clubs, a practice that is central to the way black expressive cultures, such as those of reggae, soul, and dancehall, have historically resisted coming under corporate control.[63] This decision by Joi is both about retaining control over production and about valuing the space of the club—in a vein similar to that of Badmarsh—a space in which "pure groove" can become a site of resistance. Although their decision is arguably a strategy to generate more profits from club nights, since audiences could not otherwise listen to the music, Joi has a long history of running club nights in which they charged club-goers next to nothing. Haroon said, "We used to get the best guest deejays, and they'd all come and play for nothing because the club was really cheap—it was two pounds. That's another policy we have—our people come first . . . they should be able to come and see you free. . . . You should avoid promoters and all this other stuff." That Joi's focus was not on profit making is evidenced by the fact that they often operated at a loss. As Haroon said to me laughingly in describing one evening, "I left the club with twelve pound fifty, and the cab cost me ten pounds, and so it really hit me. When I got home I said, 'I've just done all that for two pounds fifty.'"

Haroon and Farook also contest media racism by expressing their solidarity with other British Asian artists. Joi, like other artists in the AU scene, was being subjected to its internal politics. Yet they refused to speak badly about other artists since, in their view, the media had contributed to these politics by sensationalizing conflicts. The brothers were quicker to mention their annoyance with white bands that appropriate South Asian religious iconography and music. As Farook said of one band, "Just because they're English, white, rich mother and father . . . the whole of the industry accepts them, and they go about speaking on behalf of a certain cultural community of which they know nothing about whatsoever. . . . They're just . . . English, rich, kid hippies. *That* annoys." The brothers also expressed frustration at what they saw as the backbiting among AU artists, calling on artists to help each other out: "Some people . . . are by putting other people down when they could be . . . more sensitive to the media to help us all out."

In sum, Joi's discussions of their name change, music, and performances show that they have a kind of double consciousness in which they constantly avow and disavow the importance of combating racism through art even as they struggle to reconcile their prior identities as activists within a liberal humanist frame of artistry. But their new artistic choices enact an antiracist politics, even if they don't accord with a protest politics model.

Resisting Racism, Reproducing Masculine Privilege

Sawhney, Badmarsh, and Joi have highly diverse musical styles. Yet they've all been identified as AU artists and have had to negotiate an incitement to discourse that asks them to bear particular burdens of representation. These expectations are shaped by masculinist tropes like that of the angry Asian, which simultaneously offers them entrée and erasure as artists. Like many minority artists, each of these performers is annoyed about having to talk about their ethnic identities at all, an annoyance they frequently express in their claims that they are artists and that music is their language. But no one will simply take them at their word and listen to their music, so they must find other strategies to talk about themselves in a terrain structured by certain norms. In particular, they dance around identity, using liberal humanist language to stress their individuality and at the same time locate themselves within an Asian community. In this regard, Sawhney's statement, "I am a British Asian. I happen to be one," resonates with Badmarsh's claim that he's an individual but wants to move Asian culture forward and with Joi's shuttling between claims to individuality and the desire to empower their ethnic communities.

All of these artists refuse the political protest script of the angry Asian (and additionally, in Sawhney's case, bhangra fans' and Outcaste Record's scripts of the cultural representative), yet they all resist racism nevertheless. First, they link their musical style to their desire to subvert stereotypes, empower Asians, and combat racism among whites. For example, they incorporate South Asian instrumentation, what Sawhney calls an Asian angle, in all of their music to signify Asian identity as being strong (Sawhney), "bring-[ing] Asian culture forward" (Badmarsh), and "giv[ing] Bengalis a sense of identity" (Joi). Some, like Sawhney, incorporate a range of South Asian musical forms to call into question restrictive notions of Asian culture. In addition, they contest the racism of the music industry, including the threat that they themselves might be short-term ethnic commodities for the mainstream, by signing with British Asian record labels (Sawhney and Badmarsh), working to retain control over the production of their music (Joi), cultivating bonds with other artists in light of internal industry conflicts (Badmarsh and Joi), and exercising caution in dealing with the mainstream media (Badmarsh and Joi).

The strongest thread running through all four artists' stories is the stress they place on their individuality as artists, a liberal humanist approach. One of the primary reasons artists try to distance themselves from Asianness and politics is to secure their credentials as artists. Given the racialized context in which artists are working, their use of liberal humanism is not simply a desire for transcendence; rather, race strongly informs it. Moreover, although these artists' insistence that they are artists, not Asian artists, can reinscribe ethnic identity as static and limiting, this strategy can also enact political resistance: because they reject the labels Asian and political, the effects of their music in bringing about social change are perhaps not as readily recognized and therefore their music is not easily dismissed (recall how NME's review of ADF's "Rafi's Revenge" uses the descriptor "political" to ridicule the album).

Sawhney, Badmarsh, and Joi exhibit a variety of the ways in which AU artists who don't engage in protest politics nonetheless contest racist nationalism. Indeed, their concerns with social justice inform both their disinterest in using lyrics or literal statements in their music and their interest in such themes as enjoyment (Badmarsh) and harmony (Joi). By subverting stereotypes (Badmarsh and Joi), celebrating the body as an "instrument of pleasure" (Badmarsh), producing themselves as devout (Badmarsh), promoting racial unity (Joi), and contesting essentialist notions of culture (Sawhney and Joi), they move beyond the boundaries of a protest model that sees artists as combating social inequality strictly in overt lyrics and militant performances.

At the same time, while they don't personally espouse patriarchal ideas, some of their approaches to resisting the masculinist expectations they face likewise takes gendered forms, at times reproducing the heteropatriarchal logics of national belonging. These approaches do so by replacing the tropes that interpellate artists with others that likewise rely on masculinist norms. For example, in the moments when artists position themselves as a part of their ethnic communities, they adopt subject positions—the bullied boy, craftsman, devout Muslim, funky Asian, fraternity member—that recenter the male subject as the agent of politics and the subject of the nation.

For example, while honoring Sawhney's personal story and the real battles he has fought, one can also read his and other male musicians' deployment of being racially attacked as a way of protecting themselves from several sets of accusations: of embodying neither the ethnic representative, or lad, that many bhangra fans want nor the anticolonial, angry Asian man that many activists and scholars want. And this protection is masculinist: though Sawhney says that whites generally saw Asians as being weak, his stories specifically refer to the history of white men beating brown men. Such stories also connote working-class status, even though Sawhney himself may have experienced these attacks in a different class context. In that Sawhney was a victim of such violence, his mobilizing of the figure of the bullied boy can thus authenticate him as a real British Asian male subject and inoculate him against charges of selling out and not adopting the stance of the angry Asian or the bhangra lad. Sawhney's critiques of white and Asian elites similarly work to authenticate him as one of the nonelite. (Indeed, in my interview with him, Talvin Singh was quick to call attention to Sawhney's experience as an accountant to cast him as middle class and therefore a sellout and to position himself as the authentic working-class artist.) In instances in which Sawhney countered the demands of bhangra fans by arguing that only classically trained musicians are truly authentic, he's arguably referring to an elite, male genealogy of musicianship. So, while at times he contrasts himself to the upper-class brown doctor, he situates himself in another genealogy of male elites as a kind of craftsman, thereby retaining the notion that men have the requisite agency to lead the public.

Badmarsh excludes lyrical statements as a way of producing himself as a good Muslim, but it's not clear that this choice would be available to a female Muslim artist. His ability to decide to leave religion to the private sphere is thus predicated on norms of masculinity that enable him to be an individual in the public sphere, shorn of the markers of ethnicity. Badmarsh's production of himself as a devout Muslim arguably recenters the masculine subject.

Masculine norms shape Joi's adoption of the subject positions of activist and artist. In their early years Joi confronted racism through a kind of protest politics, but their ability to do so was predicated on male privilege. Joi's journey into protest politics—their origin story, as it were—began with them working in their father's shop and getting access to late-night musical gatherings, sites to which their sisters did not have entrée. They became interested in using music to gain ethnic empowerment through their access to a hip-hop and deejay scene dominated by men. Their eventual adoption of the mantle of spokesperson was accordingly shaped by and thereby reproduced a patriarchal anticolonial script; indeed, the funky Asian is normatively male. The few women involved in Joi Bangla, for example, worked mostly on what Joi called the management side.

Gender shapes both Badmarsh's and Joi's discussions of the music industry. Badmarsh and others were exasperated by some of the conflicts between AU producers and the labels. In response, they struggled to retain a form of solidarity with each other as artists: "Outcaste has signed a few artists now, and we all get on so well together as a family.... We know there's politics, it's always around us, but we try to ignore that, and do what we can do." On the one hand, this call to solidarity counters the script of masculine competition. But, on the other hand, Badmarsh uses the metaphor of family, not recognizing that the family he refers to is in fact a fraternity. In their discussions of the music industry, Joi likewise rejects a competitive male script. But given the relative absence of women artists in the AU scene, their calls for solidarity also run the risk of invoking a fraternity.

Joi is an interesting case because in spite of changing their name, music, and performances in order to move from being spokespersons or politicians to being artists, they did so, I argued, in ways that enabled them to be both. But these two subject positions depend on masculinist notions of art and politics. For example, although they changed their name from Joi Bangla to Joi, the latter holds on to the angry Asian man and their interest in empowerment but also deracinates (or reracinates) the brothers by aspiring to whiteness. In that sense, Joi sits between a patriarchal anticolonialism, whose subject is the British Asian man, and liberalism, whose subject is the white man.[64]

Moreover, the musical and aesthetic performance of bliss that Joi used to enact antiracism in their new identity as artists trades in gendered Orientalist signifiers of South Asia that risk reproducing the South Asian woman as culture bearer. For their debut album, Joi brought Susheela Raman in as a vocalist on four tracks, "Fingers," "Asian Vibes," "Oh My People," and "Heartbeat." Her singing on these tracks, though occasionally lyrical, sounds mostly discordant to the Western ear, as she extends notes in ways that signify the East. These songs thus use gendered signifiers of exotica to express harmony and bliss, deploying the South Asian woman as the site of tradition. Joi's use of white women dancers in their performances not only further marginalizes South Asian women, whose presence in the AU scene is already minimal, but also keeps them tied to tradition by suggesting that they are perhaps too evidently burdened with Asian culture for them to represent an embrace of whites. As such, Joi's aesthetic of bliss reproduces cultural nationalist norms that associate South Asian women with tradition and the private sphere and South Asian men with modernity and the public sphere.

Finally, artists' recourse to liberal individualism, like the tropes they mobilize when acting as community members, centers the male subject. Liberal humanism, in its atomistic and individualist view of the subject, is masculinist: "While in theory all *men* are equal, men and women are not symmetrically defined. Man, the centre and hero of liberal humanism, was produced in contradistinction to the objects of his knowledge, and in terms of the relations of power in the economy and the state. Woman was produced in contradistinction to man, and in terms of the relations of power in the family."[65]

Although one can interpret these artists' deployment of individualism as an antiracist politics of representation, it problematically resurrects the male subject. In addition, it may resist a patriarchal anticolonial script to speak militantly on behalf of the people, yet its recourse to an unmarked individualist position restores a different one in which men remain the agents of politics and the subjects of the nation. Indeed, as the legibly male figures on the covers of *Beyond Skin* and *Human* confirm, liberal humanism is not, in fact, beyond gender.

Here, class enters into their narratives. Liberal humanist ideologies claim that the individual functions best outside of collectives: "The *liberalism* of liberal humanism consists in its assuming the existence of a relatively free and autonomous self, a self that has rights vis-à-vis the larger community. It is assumed that the self, even as it is formed in and by society, will function at its best if it is determined to remain relatively autonomous and resist absorption into larger collectives."[66] One of the main collective identities it seeks to distance itself from is that of class, thereby protecting upper-class advantages and interests: "Liberal humanism, laying claim to be both natural and universal, was produced in the interests of the bourgeois class."[67] Artists' use of liberal humanism, in other words, not only centers a male subject but also risks reinscribing an upper-class one.

The mainstream success of AU artists in Britain is neither straightforwardly apolitical nor political. By uncovering the gendered logic that undergirds this binary, one can see how the demand to be political is itself patriarchal. By exploring the practices of so-called apolitical artist, one can see as well how they resist racism. But as they counter the masculinist tropes that plague them, by positioning themselves as members of their ethnic communities and as individuals outside of community, they produce other tropes that reproduce male privilege and potentially class privilege. And as in the case of the bhangra industry, artists' strategies of negotiating the mainstream run the risk of excluding women from the nation altogether.

PART II. **The Club Cultures of Consumption**

Chapter Three

The Troubling Subject of Wayward Asian Girls
Working-Class Women and Bhangra Club Going

Scene 1: "The Naughty Ones"

On one of the many nights I attended Masala, the longest standing and most popular weekly bhangra club night in London, I looked forward to meeting with the head security guard, Nick. The police had shut down most bhangra nights because of recurring violence between young British Asian men, but Masala was able to stay open, in part because of Nick's leadership. As we talked, he offered his opinions about why violence occurred and described how his security company had managed it. But because he normatively understood violence to be clashes between men, he elided men's harassment of women, which also regularly occurred in club spaces. When I asked Nick about how he dealt with this form of violence he began by dividing the young women who attended Masala into two types, good and bad:

> The girls that come through here fall into two categories . . . a reasonable percentage of the girls that come here are the naughty ones. They're the ones that have got away from their parents, and they're enjoying the buzz of it all inside there. And they can be a little bit wayward—because they've got out, they tend to be the ones that are slightly wayward anyway, and they cause a lot of trouble. They've had a drink, and they just wind up different guys, including their boyfriend.[1] And they're running around 'cause they're a bit wild,

'cause I think they're off of the edge.... [W]here their parents wouldn't believe what they're getting up to.... And the other group of girls that we got coming here have come out because there's nothing else to do midweek. They're generally just trying to enjoy themselves. And they sometimes [feel] intimidated.

Nick is white, but his framing was one I heard repeatedly in conversations with a wide range of people, including British Asian youth and their elders as well as the white, black, and British Asian men who manage bhangra clubs.

Scene 2: "We're Good Girls, Really"

I was on my way to the Islington Complex to attend a daytime bhangra event, a "daytimer," only to find out, when I got there, that the hosts had relocated the event to a venue called EC1. As I reentered the Farringdon tube station to make my way to the new venue, I saw a group of eight young British Asian women dressed in various combinations of black attire about to exit. Suspecting they were going to the daytimer, I informed them that the venue had been changed. As they reversed direction, one of the women, whose name I later learned was Yasmin, asked me, "Are you going alone? Aren't you with someone?" I explained that I was doing research on the event and was going by myself. She immediately told me that it was dangerous to attend alone and insisted that I join them. Aware of the violence that often erupted at bhangra club nights, I told her I didn't expect there to be any problems at this event since it was being held during the day. But she cautioned me, "It's worse, because you get the guys who are not allowed to go out at night, and they think that they can do whatever they want to girls."

So, we headed off to EC1 together. During the journey we exchanged information about our backgrounds: Yasmin and her friends were around seventeen years old, were studying business at a college, and had traveled for over an hour to get to central London from Croydon, London's southernmost borough. They joked with each other that they were on a school trip, an ironic reference to the fact that they were skipping classes to attend the event.

We arrived at EC1 at one o'clock. When we walked in, the sound system was blaring mixes of bhangra and R&B. There were already about fifty people there, roughly 70 percent of whom were young men. Yasmin and her friends found places to set down their coats and purses and moved to the dance floor. At the outset, they became annoyed with a young man who was sporting a hip-hop look, which included a puffy red jacket, a baseball hat, and a whistle around his neck that he kept blowing. They glared at him to get him to stop, but this only prompted him to blow the whistle more loudly, to direct the noise at them, and even to follow some of them around the club. While Yasmin and her friends continued to fend off several men over the course of the event, they flirted with others. They also took great pleasure in simply dancing among themselves.

By four most of the women had to return home: they had lied to their parents about where they were going, telling them they were attending an "open day" at a university.[2] Yasmin and her friend Jaspreet, however, were able to stay a bit longer, so we decided to get a bite to eat at a nearby fast-food place. As we sat down, they began asking me what my research was about. When I explained that part of it involved exploring the difficulties that British Asian women face, they immediately exclaimed, "Oh, we can tell you about that!" Comparing their lives to those of their brothers, they said, "They can get away with anything."

As we discussed the daytimer we had just attended, they evaluated its pros and cons. I asked them if they had ever been to a similar kind of event, and they told me they had gone once to a "wicked" Valentine's Day event at a venue called Zenith. Then Jaspreet said in earnest yet with a hint of playfulness, "We're good girls, really."

IN 1989 GURINDER CHADHA released *I'm British But . . .* , the first film portrayal of British Asian music. In a promotion for the movie, Chadha explains that she wanted to document the significance of two forms of music in particular, British bhangra and Bangla,[3] to British Asian identity: "The evolution of British Bhangra and Bangla music marks the beginning of the end of British national chauvinism for those of us who have been born and brought up here. It has helped us define ourselves as a displaced community with a musical language of our own, created for us, but open for enjoyment for all. We cannot be fully British until the idea of British acknowledges redefinition from other cultures. Only then will it be fit for ours and other Black use. Until then we live in Britain but belong to the diaspora."[4] In one of the film's scenes, British Asian women and men, some of whom are dressed in South Asian clothing, are happily dancing to bhangra music in a club. The film narrates this moment as a kind of coming out story in which youth are expressing their identities to a xenophobic Britain that is thereby forced to incorporate their racial difference. This attention focuses on bhangra music as being liberatory, and it implicitly suggests that sites of consumption, such as bhangra clubs, are likewise so. Chadha made this film in 1989, at the outset of the bhangra scene, but as the scene grew in the ensuing decades much of the attention scholars and commentators gave it echoed the utopian frame she used. Scholars liken clubs to "diasporic public spheres" whose resistance to the time–space of the nation and to xenophobic nationalism lies in the fact that they "link producers and audiences across national boundaries."[5]

As my encounters with Nick, Yasmin, and Yasmin's friends indicate, however, a number of gendered problematics structure women's frequenting of these club nights, rendering utopian narratives suspect. Yasmin and her friends are interested in meeting men at bhangra events, yet guard themselves against what they see as dangerous forms of male harassment. They sense that they are being bad girls for skipping school, lying to their parents, and going to a club to meet men, a hegemonic discourse of femininity exemplified by Nick's discussion of wayward club-going women. Yet Yasmin and her friends protest that they are good girls. At the same time, they criticize the unequal treatment of boys and girls, a potential indictment of the bad versus good girl framework that they otherwise seem to uphold.

Concerned about public representations of club-going women as bad and about the elisions of gendered power dynamics in utopian discourse about bhangra, I explored women's clubbing practices at the weekly nights at Masala.[6] I attended several daytimers and large-scale, one-off events as well, but I focused my research on regularly scheduled evening events, which made it easier for me to become familiar with avid club-goers.[7] The women who attended these events were from both middle- and working-class backgrounds; the more regular club-goers I met, however, were all working class.

On a typical club night at Masala, which differs to some extent from a daytimer, the evening officially begins at nine, by which point fifty or so club-goers will have lined up to enter the club. Because of escalating violence at bhangra clubs, the security checks are usually quite thorough, especially with regard to young men. During the first hour or so the deejays have begun to play bhangra remixes on the main dance floor, but there's not much energy there; instead, there is lots of drinking and talking among groups of friends. Many women take the opportunity to check their make-up and hair in the restroom. Mimicking the successful dual music policy of Bombay Jungle (a policy noted in this book's introduction), the deejays on the smaller, downstairs floor set up to start playing hip-hop. The club gets its heaviest number of visitors between ten and eleven, by which time the club is so packed that it is difficult to move around, especially for the women, whom the men constantly touch or call out to. By this time the dancing is in full force, club-goers displaying their expertise in a range of dance styles and flirting with one another on the dance floor. The mix of music usually depends on the deejays, most of whom are resident ones, although the club sometimes features new deejays or emcees. Usually they play a range of commercially popular R&B, hip-hop, and two-step tracks along with bhangra remixes, at times displaying creative license by mixing in multiple tracks at once. Downstairs, the deejays focus on hip-hop music, such as hardcore, with its lyrics about the harshness of the street, to please a clientele that prides itself on not being invested in lighter forms that focus on such themes as partying. Here, one might hear music by artists like Notorious B.I.G., the Wu-Tang Clan, DMX, and Outkast.

By midnight the club has usually hit its peak, after which some folks start to call it a night. But the club remains crowded, and around one fights between men typically begin. Nick says the security staff call it the one o'clock syndrome, by which time "people would have drunk enough ... and we can expect there to start being some sort of crackup inside there." Security is usually able to manage the conflicts, and the dancing continues until the club closes at two. But sometimes a fight that started inside the club spills out onto the street, and, depending on its severity, the local Metropolitan police step in. Meanwhile, most young women and men are figuring out whether they want to continue the night with the new people they've met or go home. Among those deciding to call it a night, the competition is on to hail a taxi. Those who can't afford one make their way to Trafalgar Square, where they may have to wait up to an hour for a Night Bus home.

Drawing on ethnographic observations of these nights as well as on young women's narratives and experiences, I found that bhangra clubs were not racial utopias but spaces shaped by racialized heteronormativity and gendered violence, some forms of which the authorities sanction. Women club-goers, like many other British Asian women, face the cultural nationalist demand to be good Asian girls by marrying the appropriate South Asian men. For the club-goers I met, being working class further constrains their options to exercise control over their lives and thereby exacerbates this demand. These young women attend clubs both to "have a laugh" with their friends and to find men on their own, and thus to exercise agency in a landscape that is nonetheless limiting. But, as I learned about their club-going practices—which involved relationships with young white women, with young black men and women and certain black expressive styles, and with other young Asians—a complicated and contradictory story of agency emerged. Women who attend clubs are crafting their identities as South Asian working-class women who inhabit the world in conditions that are incredibly restricting. In doing so, they perform two kinds of femininity, bad girl and good girl, in ways that sometimes challenge cultural nationalism and at other times reproduce it. Upon closer analysis of these performances, bhangra clubs surface not only as diasporic public spheres but also as complexly private and public spheres in which women grapple with raced and classed femininities in the service of a larger project of cultural nationalism, itself structured by several forms of violence. The contradictions that emerge in the ways young women engage in bhangra club going highlight the complex ways in which British Asians negotiate ethnic, racial, and national belonging in Britain. As women's experiences show, gender and class profoundly shape these negotiations.

My analysis brings into dialogue three generally distinct realms of scholarship: discussions of bad girl femininity in club cultures and in girl gangs and discussions of cultural nationalism in diaspora. Scholarship on club cultures in Britain tends to focus on rave music and its white audiences, paying little attention to questions of gender and race. As in the case of work on youth subculture, feminist scholars have redressed the lack of gender analysis by analyzing the experiences of white women.[8] They show that (white) club-going women are seen as bad girls, that is, as sexually promiscuous. But by not examining the experiences of club-going women of color, they elide the ways in which race and class might alter the impact of that construct on women's lives. In contrast, recent scholarship on the girl gangs formed by young working-class women of color highlights race and class: it demonstrates that in being bad, these women risk being seen as whores, but performing the tough part of bad girl femininity by engaging in violence is a protective strategy they use to defend their status as respectable in a context in which few other resources to do so exist.[9] Yet this work undertheorizes the full implications of race by omitting the ways in which, in many communities of color, being a bad girl means being seen as ethnically traitorous.[10] While feminist scholarship on the South Asian diaspora underscores this latter point, in its emphasis on the hegemonic norm of good girl femininity, it pays less attention to class differences that affect how women might face and, in turn, manage this norm. In other words, it tends to ignore working-class women's performances of both good and bad femininity. I explore that underexamined territory, using an intersectional analysis to examine how young working-class women deploy bad girl behavior in the service of good girl norms.

The narratives of four avid club-goers—Leena and Alisha, who are sisters, and Jess and Sukh, who are best friends—exemplify recurring themes in my discussions with other women. I met Leena, who was twenty-nine at the time, and Alisha, who was eighteen, one evening while waiting in line for Masala to open; all three of us had arrived a bit too early. As we struck up a conversation they invited me to join them. I came to know them over the following year, as I often attended Masala with them, which they had been frequenting for nearly two years, and visited them on several occasions at their home in South London. During the time I knew them Alisha was working part time as a cashier at McDonalds, going to school, and regularly attending bhangra clubs. Leena was managing single motherhood while working in an administrative job and taking evening courses to help her transition into a more professional career. A few years after Leena's marriage ended, she started going clubbing with Alisha, and the two siblings had a noticeably close relationship.

I met Jess and Sukh, both of whom were sixteen at the time, at a bhangra club night at Zenith. Both had grown up in Southall, a borough in West London that is one of the largest areas of South Asian settlement in the Western world and has a predominantly working-class population. When I met them, Jess and Sukh spent most of their time at school, save for part-time jobs they held at a fast-food place at Heathrow Airport. They had been close friends for five years and, as they explained, are often mistaken for sisters because they spend so much time with one another. Jess and Sukh characterized themselves as keen bhangra club-goers. Sukh said, "We go out the most out of all the Asian girls. . . . Everyone else's home by nine or ten!" Jess told me that Sukh was the rebel and the instigator of their frequent club going, as she had been dying to attend clubs ever since she was twelve years old. Although Jess was hesitant, she agreed to go with Sukh to their first daytimer, and after that they were hooked.

Each of these four young women came from families who moved to Britain as economic migrants but who experienced barriers to upward mobility. Leena's and Alisha's two elder brothers were cab drivers, their mother never worked outside the home, and they were unclear about their father's work. They knew he had owned a business, but he never made any money from it, was a "big spender," and left for Pakistan after his divorce to manage his mother's inheritance there. Leena and Alisha moved around a lot because of problems at home, which included the extreme violence perpetrated by their father. At the time I met them, Alisha was living with her mother in council housing, but Leena had managed to find an apartment of her own, also as part of council housing. Jess's mother worked part-time in customer service at a grocery store and full-time as an administrator in social services; her father was a bus driver at Heathrow Airport. Sukh's mother worked in hotel housekeeping, and she said her father was a chauffeur, although she was not entirely sure what he did because her parents had divorced six years earlier, and she no longer talked to him. Jess's family lived in council housing, and Sukh lived with her grandfather and mother in a modest two-bedroom home in Southall.

I show here how race and class exacerbate the demand that young women face to marry appropriate men. In their search for men at clubs they construct themselves as good Asian girls (contrasting themselves from bad white girls). But, in defiance of family and peer norms, they also construct themselves as black British subjects, in alliance with young black women and men. They also use certain black expressive styles to produce themselves as heterosexual Asian subjects, a practice that families police. Their dual relationships to club-going Asian men and women reveal further complexities: while they pursue the men they desire, they also fight with the ones who harass them. And while they bond with safe Asian women, they fight with the ones they consider "tarts." By juxtaposing their relationships to these men and women, I illustrate the tenuous position female clubgoers hold and how they both resist and reinscribe cultural nationalism.

Marriage as the Way Out

A main familial and community demand that many British Asian women face is to be good Asian girls, that is, to practice sexually virtuous behavior and to marry and create families with appropriate South Asian men.[11] The young women I met faced this demand in fairly intense ways, not only receiving verbal messages from their family members but also risking violence if they did not follow certain norms. As Leena said, her mother prioritized marriage and devalued education. Referring to what she experienced when she was sixteen years old, the age at which British students must decide whether to leave school or attend university, she said, "My mom didn't want me to have an education.... She just wanted me to ... get married, wash the dishes, and be tied to the kitchen sink.... She never wanted me to study, and she still doesn't want me to study now because she thinks that, basically, I should just be with a man, a husband." Leena described being beaten by her two elder brothers on a number of occasions when they felt she had damaged their family's *izzat*, or honor. They intensified their attacks after she left a marriage her mother had arranged for her; in one instance they and her mother beat her so severely that she ended up in the hospital. Although Leena's experiences were more extreme than most, all of the club-goers I met had contentious relationships with family members who attempted to keep them within the confines of cultural tradition.

The race and class locations young women occupied intensified the demands they faced to marry. In particular, they curtailed women's desires to take up a career that would give them economic freedom and perhaps lessen their dependence on marriage. A conversation I had one day with Jess and Sukh poignantly illustrated this point. Sukh was flitting about her bedroom in an attempt to tidy it up while Jess and I lay casually on Sukh's bed. As we discussed a number of topics, at one point they began to disparage Southall, which then led to a discussion of their aspirations:

JESS: I hate telling people I'm from Southall!
SUKH: It's embarrassing!
FALU: Why?
JESS: I hate Southall full stop!
SUKH: People automatically assume you're one of those Southall trashy, slags 'init, init' sort of people.[12]
FALU: Does it have that kind of reputation?
SUKH: Yeah. Today, we had to stand up in college and say where you're from . . . and I was like, "I'm from Southall" [said in a rushed, soft tone]. . . . And they were like, "Where are you from, sorry?" and I was like, "Southall." And they were like, "Okay then . . ." It was so bloody embarrassing!
JESS: I hate it though. It's such a trash. . . . I swear to God, if I won the lottery, the first thing I'd do is sort this place out. I hate it.
FALU: Oh, so you wouldn't move out? You'd sort this place out.
JESS: I'm only joking. No, I'd move out, actually. [Laughs]
SUKH: I wouldn't want to move out.
FALU: Where would you want to move in London, if you could move anywhere?
JESS: Umm, just down the road, by Osterley or something.[13] Something a bit more civilized.

SUKH: I couldn't live with all those white people.

JESS: It's just—it's so filthy out here.

SUKH: I like being loud, *Indian* sort of thing. It's like you can do anything here, it don't matter. You're all *apne* [one] at the end of the day—you're all one—sort of thing. They'd probably turn around and call the police for fuckin' noise pollution!

JESS: I'd like to live in the city, though [central London].

SUKH: I wouldn't. [There are] weird people there.

JESS: Not totally *in* the city, but a part of London with nice studio flats and stuff in it.

SUKH: [London's] all right to visit during the day.

JESS: I don't know, I've got this big image in my head thinking, when I grow up, I want to wear one of those nice suits—a short little skirt with a big briefcase—walking down to really nice, posh places, going to my office, putting my legs up, going "Hello, yes, send the next person in," sort of thing. [Laughing a bit]

FALU: And you?

SUKH: I don't know. I ain't got no visions. Just a fit bloke.

Jess's and Sukh's characterizations of Southall as being trashy and their sense that because they lived there others saw them as "trashy slags" demonstrate that they feel humiliated by their working-class status and that gender powerfully shapes that humiliation. Race also structures their notion of trash, given the long history of racial disenfranchisement of South Asians in Britain, one that has played a significant role in the formation of Southall itself.

Notably, Jess and Sukh imagine different routes out of their predicament. Jess pictures a future in which she attains middle-class status and has access to racialized and sexualized power: she imagines living in a "civilized" (arguably white) area of central London and having a glamorous corporate lifestyle that allows her to wear short skirts and "put her legs up" while she orders others around. Sukh, however, cannot imagine leaving Southall, as becoming middle class raises the specter of having to live among whites who would police and silence her. She instead fashions her escape through finding a "fit bloke" and says that, unlike Jess, she has "no visions."

Although they imagine their futures differently, Sukh's vision, even as she claims she has none, wins out. Later in our discussion both young women emphasized their need to marry by the age of twenty-six. They explained that despite the fact that the average age at which women get married is twenty, those who attend universities, as they planned to do, can get married a little bit later without being stigmatized. Sukh said, "If she's got an education and stuff, then they don't expect [her] to get married til [she's] twenty-four or something. But then after that they're getting a bit past it, aren't they?" Jess added, "Yeah, if you're twenty-six and you're not married, they think there's something wrong with you." As we continued to discuss marriage, they seemed somewhat critical of the community's expectations but ultimately appeared to adopt them, as they said that they definitely wanted to settle down, by which they meant getting married and having "a couple of kids and stuff," before the age of twenty-six. Although they planned on enrolling in university at the end of their school year, neither of them considered that to be more than a ticket to freedom from parental supervision: their "freedom outbreak." They said they would rather leave school than quit their current jobs at the fast-food restaurant.

Jess and Sukh see upward class mobility as a fantasy beyond their reach and riddled with the problems of race: Jess is unable to construct an actual plan for attaining her imagined career, in the way, for example, a young middle-class person might strategize to enter college; to Sukh, the path to middle-class success would lead her into an alienating racial lifeworld. Faced with race and class barriers to mobility as well as with pressures to get married, young women like Jess and Sukh may regard marriage as a viable route from "slag" status to legitimacy.

As a woman in her late twenties who had already been married, Leena is an atypical club-goer (most were between sixteen and eighteen years old). Nonetheless, her experiences were emblematic of how race and class inequalities hindered the efforts of women who, unlike younger ones, actively tried to pursue a professional career to survive financially outside of marriage. Leena was deeply ambivalent about marriage. She had witnessed her mother endure abuse at the hands of her husband and leave him as a result. Although Leena ended up getting married, in part owing to family pressure, she left her husband because like her father he turned out to be abusive. In light of her failed marriage Leena wanted to carve out a life for herself and gain financial independence through a professional career. To this end she had enrolled in courses to obtain a psychology degree and become a mental health practitioner.

Leena was facing a number of obstacles to pursuing her career goals.

First, as a single, working-class mother, she dealt with financial stress and found it extremely difficult to manage the demands on her time, which included raising her child, working at a low-income job, attending classes, and completing her homework. Second, when Leena *was* able to carve out time for coursework, she found it hard to complete. Expressing her exasperation, she said, "Today, I was sitting there all day, I wrote about five lines of work, and that's not much, is it? . . . I'm really slow." The frustration she felt about her schoolwork mirrored the way she discussed her job performance: "Everywhere I worked, I [had] problems. I even have problems now. . . . I don't know why, I just get nervous from people, and I end up doing my work wrong." Nearly starting to cry, she continued, "I don't know . . . it's upsetting talking about it."

Leena's account implies a strong connection between her past experiences of schooling, during which she was plagued by gender violence at home and racial violence at school, and the insecurities she experienced at present. Discussing her home life, she said, "I think I was unstable at home, which affected me in school, but I didn't know at the time. I realize it now, but the thing is . . . I still find [studying] hard." Recounting racism at school, she said, "I always got picked on in school . . . we suffered a lot." These prior experiences no doubt continued to trouble her as, at the time I knew her, she was going to school and working in largely white environments.

In addition to these difficulties, Leena dealt with the stigma attached to being a single mother and faced pressures to remarry. She was in fact generally unashamed of her status and carried a photo of her daughter in her jacket pocket. But she was keenly aware that elders in her community construed her as a "bad example on their daughters." Moreover, although she managed to stop her brothers from inflicting violence on her for not remarrying, she felt pressure from her family in other ways. She had recently discovered, for example, that her mother had offered Leena's ex-husband a good sum of money to remarry her.

Although Leena continued to resist getting remarried, the race, class, and gender conditions of her life made advancing in a career very difficult and made marriage an attractive option. While she sometimes expressed her desire to have a partner in romantic terms, practical reasons remained prominent: "I need help . . . if I get back with [my ex-husband], he might help me with the kid, and then I'll be able to get [through] my studies, and then . . . leave him." Leena's desire to marry was thus powerfully tied to her need to share household labor and child rearing in her quest for financial security and an identity outside of marriage.

Club-Going Identities: Whites and Blacks

Many British Asians feel parental pressure to accept an arranged marriage. In defiance, they use club spaces to enact modern scripts of sex and romance, that is, companionate marriage. Young women's desire to meet men was one of the main reasons they went clubbing, as British Asians created these spaces partly to enable women and men to meet outside the purview of their families. To be sure, with the emergence of regular bhangra nights, British Asians were excited about having spaces in which they felt they could express ethnic identities they experienced as private in a public club. The discourse of expression, however, elides the ways in which these identities are regulated and disciplined.[14] Norms of heterosexuality, for example, shape the dynamics of bhangra clubs. Moreover, the clubs do not simply represent public sites of racial liberation; rather, they are private sites insofar as British Asians used them to engage in heterosexual relations with one another. Here, I draw on Ananya Bhattacharjee's rethinking of conventional notions of public as being the state and private as being domestic. Immigrants define home in a number of ways, one of which includes the ethnic community itself. South Asian immigrants in the United States, she says, "see their community as an extended 'family,' separate and distinct from other ethnic communities. The immigrant community sees itself, in all its specific ethnicity, as a private space, within which it must guard its own national heritage against intervention from mainstream U.S. cultural practices."[15] Given that British Asian club-goers and promoters largely neither wanted nor cared much to see bhangra clubs become mainstream—the opposite of their dreams for bhangra *music* to cross over—instead using them as places to meet plausible partners, the clubs arguably represented private spaces.

Social relations within and outside of clubs reinforced their private nature. In the context of the historical alliances between blacks and Asians in Britain, as well as the "coolness" attributed to blacks in youth culture, bhangra clubs were informally open to blacks but not to whites. The bouncers at Masala, who were typically black and white, bolstered this informal policy by dissuading whites from entering. As one bouncer said, they made an effort to warn whites, especially white tourists, about the night by explaining that it was Asian.

In an effort to exercise agency in a landscape that nonetheless limits them, women attended bhangra clubs to meet plausible partners on their own terms. But this strategy was inherently contradictory: while their goal of meeting men whom they might marry accorded with the ideals of being a good girl, attending bhangra clubs subjected them to the stigma of being a bad girl. How did they resolve this contradiction? One way they did so was by constructing club-going identities that protected their status as good girls. But notably, these identities also resisted antiblack racism. One can see this approach in their relationships to white women, blacks, and black expressive styles.

"THEY ARE PROPER SLAGS, THE WHITE GIRLS"

In one of my discussions with Jess and Sukh about their interest in the bhangra club scene, I asked them if they would ever attend a predominantly white dance club. Jess replied, without hesitation, "There's no point because you're not gonna get with a white man." Sukh followed by saying, with slight disgust in her voice, "I ain't gonna get with a white man." She and Sukh then began describing their interactions with whites at their local college, revealing the intense anger they felt as a result of the racism they regularly experienced. Emphasizing that others made them feel as if they were outsiders in Britain, Sukh, mocking the queen's English to make her point, explained, "You feel that you have to speak *standard* English with *good vo-ca-bu-lary* and prove that you're nothing less than they are 'cause they look at you as second-class citizens, as in, *you* came to *our* country, and *we* know the language better." Jess and Sukh in fact often felt insecure. Describing how jarring and displacing it felt for her to face her mostly white classes, Jess said, "I walked into my lesson late today . . . [and] all I saw was blond heads, white faces. I was like 'Oh my god, I walked into the wrong bloody country or something!' . . . I put my name down and stuff, and when I looked up, all eyes were on me, and I was thinking, 'Oh, shit!'"

Although Jess's and Sukh's responses reflect their experiences of growing up in a racially segregated area, their feelings resonated with those of other club-goers I spoke with, some of whom had been victims of racial violence. For example, Leena and Alisha described living in Glasgow: "White people are very racist . . . although [Asians] are a big community there, we suffered a lot. . . . [I]f there's a black person or Chinese person seen on the street, there'd be violence." Remembering an incident involving her brother, Alisha said, "My oldest brother got chained by these white people. . . . [He] was only ten at that time . . . he was just playing football on the field, init?" Such experiences strongly direct young women's desires to socialize in nonwhite spaces. Sukh said, "There's so many white people [at college]. . . . [When] we see each other, it's like 'Oh, my God, *finally!*' sort of thing.... It's *so* good to get home ... but still ... there's all these white people in Southall, and it's like 'fuckin' get out of my face, you fuckin' honkies!'"

If experiences of racism are a main reason British Asians prefer clubbing in their own spaces, female bhangra club-goers in addition drew distinctions between themselves and white women, whom they criticized for being promiscuous and immoral. Alisha explained that she used to have white friends when she was sixteen but no longer did because, despite their pretense of moral superiority, "white women are slags." Describing one of these former friends, Lisa, she said, "Me and her used to come up [to the] west end ... and this guy [went], "Do you want to come around my place tonight?" and she was like "yeah." [laughing] They are proper slags, the white girls. Then I [went] home, and then, the next day, I go to Lisa, "Did you ... ?," you know, like that [signaling that she asked Lisa if she had sex with him]. She goes, "No, not on the first date." And I go, "What do you mean not on the first date?" She goes, oh, she done it the next morning! [laughing] Do you get me? Trying to make herself out to be all superior!" In order to underscore her own proper conduct, Alisha went on to describe how she and Lisa dealt with two men they met at the movies who were blatantly "after it": although Alisha told the man who approached her to "piss off," Lisa went home with the other man ("a total stranger!"). Alisha also contended that white women are immature: "After clubbing, she [came] around to my house ... [and] she pissed herself in my sofa bed.... That was disgusting because that was adult piss, do you get me? It was sick!" Leena then interjected her own observations of the white women she knew at work: "All they did was go to pubs and get drunk, and they talked about men, sex, drugs ... things like that."

Stories like these, which denounce white women for not having the attributes they claim to have, such as propriety, morality, and maturity, reveal that gender and sexuality play a major role in how female club-goers contest racism and construct club-going identities. White oppressor groups often disparage the sexuality of racialized women to legitimate nationalism, colonialism, and racism.[16] In response, "racialized immigrants claim through gender the power denied by racism," using female morality to "construct the dominant group as other and themselves as superior." To this end, they contrast their own ideal woman with the figure of the immoral white woman: "She is everything that they are not: she is sexually modest and dedicated to her family; they are sexually promiscuous and uncaring." Read through the lens of racial marginalization, then, criticisms of white women's morality serve as "a strategy of resistance—a means of asserting a morally superior public face to the dominant society."[17]

In Britain whites have used Orientalist stereotypes to characterize South Asian women as being overly sexualized or as victims of "barbaric traditions" that unduly constrain them.[18] These portrayals historically fueled colonial rule and continue to inform perceptions of and juridical decisions pertaining to South Asians residing in Britain.[19] In this broader context one can read club-goers' condemnations of white women as countering the gendered racism that afflicts them and their communities. Their use of such terms as *slag*, which can connote working-class identity, is arguably a way of healing their class injuries. The other side of the coin is that, in adopting such discourse, women are constructing sexualized racial identities that sustain the power of cultural nationalism in their lives. That is, they are not bad white girls but good Asian girls who tell inappropriate men to "piss off." Indeed, Jess's and Sukh's avoidance of white men and their desire to partner with Asian men accords with the gendered and heteronormative demands of cultural nationalism.

While young women often leveled their rebukes of white women stridently, at times they did so ambivalently, revealing the tensions they feel in inhabiting good girl status. When I asked Jess and Sukh if they had any white friends, for example, they both replied with an emphatic "No!" and went on to explain:

> SUKH: It's cause we can't really relate to them . . . they've got more freedom and everything. They don't relate to how our families are and our background. . . . So it's like you're only gonna get into trouble with them all.
> JESS: I think they act a lot more maturer than we do as well.
> SUKH: They act like women!
> JESS: They've grown up a lot quicker than we have.
> SUKH: It's cause their parents allow them to.

As other club-going women did, Jess and Sukh pointed to white women's sexuality as a marker of racial difference. Sexual freedom signifies the crux of that difference, as they indicate in their references to white women being "more mature" or more sexually practiced because they "grow up a lot quicker." Unlike Leena and Alisha, however, who forcefully denounce it, Jess and Sukh are ambivalent about this freedom. On the one hand, Sukh's intimation that white women grow up too fast represents a cultural nationalist argument that lauds supposedly pure South Asian culture over supposedly corrupt Western culture. On the other hand, Sukh seems envious when she says, "Their parents allow them to," where her use of "allow" and her overall tone reveal both her judgment and her jealousy. Their comment that white women are more mature contradicts their other statements holding that these women are immature (as noted earlier), further evidence of the ambivalence they feel about the sexual freedom they believe white women have access to. For club-going women, consequently, the figure of the bad white girl as the antithesis of the good Asian girl can mark the constraints of having to be good and the frustrations they feel as a result.

"PEOPLE WOULD THINK I'M A RUDE GIRL"

Young women discussed their relationships to blacks in ways that differed dramatically from how they discussed whites. In light of their experiences of racism, perhaps it is not surprising that the club-goers I met tended to have black and Asian friends and enjoyed socializing with them at bhangra clubs. Alisha, for example, saw Masala less as a nightclub than as a gathering place: "A lot of people I know go there—it's more like a youth club." Women characterized club outings with friends as "having a laugh," that is, having a good time by poking fun at themselves and at others. Their friendships with blacks, however, posed a problem for some of their Asian peers at school who held racist views and who judged them as a result. Some of Alisha's schoolmates would make statements about her such as, "She doesn't even know she's Asian," suggesting that her having black friends made her ethnically inauthentic. Others made a point of speaking to her in Urdu whenever she was with her black friends: "If I'm introducing my Asian friends to a black person . . . they'll be like 'Oh, yeah, whatever, hi.' Then they'll talk to me in Urdu so the other person can't understand." Alisha's peers used Urdu to interpellate Alisha as an Asian and to thereby strengthen their construction of her as a traitor to the Asian community. Since cultural nationalist discourse sees women as ethnically inauthentic if they become intimate with men from a different ethnic or racial background, these examples also indicate that women's peers saw them as violating norms of Asian femininity. In a seemingly offhand comment, for example, Alisha's schoolmates said of her, "She's even wearing trousers," as if by having black friends Alisha had become simultaneously less Asian and less feminine.

Gender is central to the mistreatment young women experienced vis-à-vis their families for their friendships with blacks. The fact that Jess and Sukh had close friends who were black, such as their manager at work, made their mothers highly anxious. Jess said, "My mom thinks, 'What's your obsession with black people?'" Sukh reasoned that their mothers' anxieties are based on long-standing stereotypes of black criminality: "They still associate black people with *crime*, going out, doing this, doing that. It's like they have the stereotypical view, don't they?" However, there was clearly more at stake. Sukh continued, "My mom said to me, 'You're going out with him, aren't you? That's why you come home at one in the morning from doing a shift which finishes at ten!'" Describing what she called her mother's paranoid reactions at the prospect that she might be actually dating her manager, Sukh said that whenever her manager called her, her mother would nervously start asking her, "Why he was ringing you for? Why you was on the phone to him for?" As Sukh finished telling me these stories, Jess said, "I don't think there's nothin' wrong with goin' out with black people. I've been out with one." Sukh then interjected, "[Yeah, but] our parents would shit!" The fact that Jess's and Sukh's mothers tolerated their daughters' black friends (even if they didn't fully approve of it), but wouldn't allow them to date black men reveals their anxieties about their daughters' sexuality. Given that parents expect their daughters to reproduce South Asian culture by marrying and producing families with British Asian men, they saw their partnering with any other men as a problem. The persistent association of black men with hypersexuality in racist discourse renders them especially problematic:[20] parents see them as a greater threat to the cultural nationalist norms that dictate that sexual relationships should be contained within sanctioned forms of marriage and should fulfill the ends of biological and cultural reproduction.

Despite the frequency and intensity with which young women encountered antiblack racism, they consistently confronted it. In some cases they tacitly critiqued the gendered terms of that racism, as when Jess said, "There's nothin' wrong with goin' out with black people." In most cases, however, they invoked the experiences of race and class disenfranchisement that blacks and Asians share in Britain, stressing the need for political solidarity. Alisha said that when she went to a school that had a mostly white and black student population, she befriended the black students in part for politicized reasons: "Most of the white people were racist against the black people, so, I used to be more . . . [with black people]. . . . Asians and blacks together, init?"

Read through the lens of the difficulties young women faced in enjoying friendships with blacks, their attending bhangra clubs to have a laugh with them merits further analysis. Paul Willis theorizes the "laff" as "a multifaceted implement of extraordinary importance in the counter-school culture," one which is used to "defeat boredom and fear, to overcome hardship and problems—as a way out of almost anything."[21] In this case, women's efforts at having a laugh, that is, not being serious, being mischievous with people, and "causing trouble," the main point of which is humor, serve as a way to not only escape but also resist the pressures they face at school and at home.

Young women's stories point toward a general dynamic in their everyday lives of discipline and resistance regarding their having black friends, and gender is central to that dynamic. But blackness shaped their participation in the bhangra scene in other ways. As they became avid club-goers, they drew on certain black music forms and youth styles to produce themselves as heterosexualized Asian subjects. Although this led their families to discipline them for falling outside the standards of ideal Asian femininity, the women themselves steered clear of making those judgments.

Alisha's narrative is a case study in this nuanced resistance. Alisha began the story of how she became a regular club-goer as if she were about to narrate how a good Asian girl became bad. Using normative language to describe what she was like before she attended clubs, she said, "Up until the age of fifteen, I used to just be normal. I used to come home from school. I used to be a good girl. My reports were good." Although she was attending a predominantly black and white school at the time, she was a fan of Hindi film music, a fact that she repeated several times and that seemed central to her self-description as good. When she turned sixteen and was poised to take her final exams for the General Certificate of Secondary Education, her mother and elder brothers left for Pakistan. Seemingly blaming them for how she acted in their absence, and thereby implicating them in her turn toward the bad, she said, "They left at the wrong time." She "naturally" started exploring the club scene in central London with her best friend, Simone, an Afro-Caribbean woman, became hooked, and subsequently failed all of her exams.

As Alisha continued her account, however, she abandoned any hint that she was acting like a bad girl. She began recalling her truant behavior in a humorous way: "I used to go home [straight after being at a club], put on my uniform, and then my friends used to give me a lift to school.... I was mad [crazy]... it was a laugh." She started describing excitedly how club going gave her opportunities to explore romantic and sexual relationships with men. She said of her first club outing, "That's when the first bloke ever chatted me up ... in my *life*. I thought 'wow!'" So, while an ideological framework that distinguished good girls from bad ones impacted her sense of self, she didn't wholly judge her actions by the yardstick of morality inherent in this framework.

As she discovered bhangra clubs, it was as if she were rediscovering South Asian identity itself. She referred to bhangra club events as Asian nights, eliding how these events entail specific performances of British Asian identity and are not, for example, expressions of a preexisting, homogenous British Asianness. Describing her reaction to her first night at a bhangra club, Masala, she laughingly told me that she and Leena were scared to enter the club because they "weren't used to Asian people." Alisha, expressing her shock, exclaimed, "I never ever saw so many Asian people *in my life*, I swear!" As evidenced from her descriptions, entering the club made her curious and uncomfortable. But in spite of these initial reactions, bhangra clubs quickly became a site of belonging for her: "They're like a youth club."

As with most club-goers, Alisha drew on certain forms of black music and style to construct an Asian club-going identity: she developed a strong interest in the swing, or R&B, music played at bhangra clubs, which took the place of the South Asian music she had customarily listened to before. Because the clubs welcomed blacks Simone was able to accompany her.

Alisha's story took a slightly different turn as she described her initial forays into the bhangra club scene. Telling me a story of regret about her sexual behavior and her adoption of a black, rude girl style, a style originating with young street-corner gangsters in Jamaica in the late 1960s, she said, "Between the age of sixteen and seventeen, that's when I experienced a lot of things, like finding out what guys are really like, and you have to be careful and all that. You know, when you just learn, and then you look back and think of all the stupid things you done ... when you just start regretting what you've done. . . . Because before, I did think that I was acting all, you know, *kali* [black]. . . . The way I used to dress was . . . people would think I was a rude girl. . . . Because I used to like gel my hair . . . wear trousers and rings . . . [I didn't think I was a rude girl], but that's what people stereotyped me as. But . . . you just learn, init? . . . Because Asian people used to take the piss out of me [laughs]. . . . I started acting like a black, like a rude girl." Here, it seems that she didn't think she was trying to act black but others did, and she came to accept this description.

Although Alisha links her presumably bad sexuality to her performance of the black subcultural style of rude girl (although the exact relationship between the two is unclear), in her self-critique she decouples the two.

While a racist discourse might blame her bad sexual behavior on her performance of blackness, her own criticism is not racialized: she focuses on her ignorance and on men's behavior as the real problems. She does not evaluate herself in terms of cultural nationalism, that is, she doesn't refer to herself as a bad girl or view her behavior as morally problematic. Though Alisha could have been protecting herself, the language she uses still stands in marked contrast to how she differentiates herself from white women. Likewise, her censure of acting black is desexualized. She instead uses a discourse of racial authenticity, suggesting that she was performing the wrong racial identity. And again, although the language of ethnic authenticity her family and schoolmates use to discipline her is gendered, her own use of that discourse is not. Thus while she links her behaving in ways that don't accord with the ideals of the good Asian girl to her adoption of rude girl style, she does not discuss her behavior in gendered or moral terms. Furthermore, she does not censure black style, women, or sexuality at all, let alone in cultural nationalist terms.

When Alisha's brothers returned from Pakistan, Alisha's new identity as well as her ongoing friendship with Simone enraged them. They had always tried to discipline Alisha (and Leena), but now they became increasingly racist in a violent way toward her and her friends. Her brother Faizal, for example, began hurling racist insults at Simone. Describing the events of one afternoon when Simone was visiting her, Alisha said, "I went to the toilet, and my brother went into my room . . . and he goes [to Simone], 'You nigger! You nigger!' Do you get me? What for?! . . . She was just crying . . . I was mad; that *really* upset me."

Music played a central role in her brothers' attempts to discipline her. Faizal would demand that Alisha listen to Indian music, expecting that by doing so she would retain her Asian identity. In a dramatic storytelling moment, Alisha enacted him waving his finger at her, telling her "Culture, culture." Music forms such as R&B and hip-hop signified to him especially corrupting force. Alisha said that one afternoon she had come home from school with a headache, so she sat on the sofa and didn't say anything. But because she often listened to popular R&B, her brother assumed she was high on drugs and immediately reported her to their mother. In one particularly violent incident, Alisha went clubbing at Masala and came home to find that Faizal had broken her stereo, smashed her speakers, and destroyed over two hundred pounds' worth of her CDs, many of which had been loaned to her by friends. He made a special effort to destroy an album by TLC, an all-women R&B group, titled *CrazySexyCool*, which arguably signified to him black female sexuality.[22] Alisha said, "He really went mad at TLC." Alisha was so upset by his actions that she spent the entire night crying and shortly afterward tried to kill herself by overdosing on pills. At the time I knew Alisha, she had still not spoken to her brother. As Alisha concluded her story, Leena added that Alisha was lucky because their brothers had never physically abused her as they had Leena. To this, Alisha replied, "I'd rather get beaten up than him doing that to the CDs," indicating not only the extreme harm she felt her brother's actions caused but how highly she valued the music and the friendships associated with it.

In addition to the political solidarities and genuine friendships they had with blacks, perhaps young women don't adopt their families' disapproval of their use of black styles because it has cachet as cool in popular culture. Jess and Sukh, for example, admit that the popularity of certain forms of black music is part of their appeal. They draw a line, however, between being interested in black music and what they call acting black:

FALU: Have you ever heard people criticize young Asians for trying to "act black"?
JESS: Yeah.
SUKH: You know those people who act it—who look it—like Kiran. That was a wannabe black, that is.

SUKH: It's just that . . . hip-hop is so *in* now, and it's like if it's in . . . you tend to listen to it. But if you look to us, we don't think we try to *be* black, where there are some girls that are like "yeah, we say, we, we" this and that. They try to speak—they're talking black. And then it's like, they're lookin' it as well. So they're tryin' to buy all these designers and stuff. And you can tell the difference between them.
FALU: Between them and people like?
JESS: Like us.
SUKH: It's like we listen to it, but we wouldn't walk around tryin' to look like them or do our hair like them or whatever.

These women construct notions of what it means to try to be black, which they disapprove of, and what it means to engage appropriately in black expressive forms, which they purportedly do. Furthermore, they not only sanction some forms of engagement but also normalize them ("of course we're into it because it's in"). It thus appears that the combination of a political and a commercial relationship to black identity works to trump the sexual criticism of blackness that is prominent in public discourse.

Alisha's account implies that club-going women adopt certain black expressive styles to perform a heterosexual Asian identity; it gives her an entrée into the clubs and to meeting British Asian men. Although she formally rejects rude girl style because her peers see it as racially inauthentic, having black friends and enjoying certain black music and styles continue to shape her performance of Asianness in and out of clubs. Consequently, blackness is part and parcel of how young women produce themselves as what they see as Asian. Through the actions of Alisha's brothers, one also sees how women's use of black expressive culture can become the occasion for heightened family discipline. Thus, instead of there being a categorically political bond between all blacks and South Asians in Britain, South Asians can not only adopt racist views but also draw on them to discipline women. Women are not simply victims of this treatment, however, as they don't interpret their behavior through a racist or cultural nationalist lens and attend bhangra clubs despite the resistance they meet. Moreover, they actively construct black British identities; that is, they consider black and Asian to be distinct racial identities but at the same time exhibit an allied racial politics.

To revisit my earlier question, how did young women deal with the contradictions of attending bhangra clubs to meet men to marry—in other words, of being labeled bad girl while trying to attain good girl status? One sees them playing out this dilemma differently in their stances toward white women and in their relationships with black people and expressive forms. Although they used cultural nationalist discourse to condemn white women and to portray themselves as good Asian girls, they drew on race and class alliances to forge friendships with blacks. They constructed themselves as black British subjects in defiance of their families and schoolmates, denouncing the racism within South Asian communities at large. Moreover, while they adopted certain kinds of black style, within normative limits, to craft heterosexualized Asian identities, in contrast to their families they didn't resort to cultural nationalism to evaluate this behavior —even as their parents and the media regularly expose them to stereotypes of black sexuality as being excessive and immoral. The ways in which they navigate relationships with whites and blacks simultaneously protect their status as good Asian girls, resist racism in Britain, and enable them to take part in bhangra club culture, in which heterosexuality and black expressive cultures play a constitutive role.

Fit Blokes and Perverts

> FALU: What do you dislike the most about clubbing?
>
> JESS: This is gonna sound *so* stupid . . . we already said that one thing we like are the blokes. But the thing I hate the most is the blokes—all the perverted blokes!

Just as young women's practice of attending clubs to meet men is a contradictory one, their relationships to club-going men are rife with contradictions. As private spaces that enable British Asian women and men to meet, bhangra clubs were aggressively masculine, in part because of the kind of music played there. Not only is much bhangra patriarchal (see chapter 1), but as young people took it up they often remixed it with commercial hip-hop music, much of which is misogynist.[23] The club nights that played this music attracted clientele invested in those gender norms. Although promoters were dismayed by recurring violence between men, as this threatened their ability to hold bhangra nights in the first place, they nevertheless patterned their clubs on typical mainstream clubs in which the emphasis is on heterosexualized dynamics and music.[24]

The fact that these clubs were for British Asians and were aggressively masculinist was in various ways attractive *and* unattractive to avid club-going women who, as many of them said, both loved and hated going to them. Women described a host of reasons for frequenting bhangra clubs, but the most prominent one was their desire to meet British Asian men. They had great ambivalence about these men, however, encapsulated in their oft-repeated statements that men are "the best things about the clubs and the worst." As I learned more about this dichotomy, it became clear that it is a sexualized one: the "best things" are the men they call fit and whom they desire for partnership and marriage. In contrast, "the worst" things are the "perverted blokes" that harass them. Fit and pervert are not opposite categories, however; their distinction lies not so much in men's behavior, in that both categories of men could taunt women, but in women's desire. As women searched for fit men and fought the harassing ones, they performed bad girl femininity by being tough. In doing so, they unevenly dealt with the demands of cultural nationalism.

"SHE'S CONSTANTLY ON THE MOVE TO FIND THAT ONE PERFECT PERSON"

Certainly women's desire for men is a complex subject given the imbrications of politics with pleasure. During one night at Masala, for example, Leena described to me the "buzz" she felt at clubs but then puzzled about how much she also hated being at them: "You just get this buzz from Asian gigs.... I feel attractive; I am attractive. There's nothing wrong with me, do you know what I mean? And it makes you feel good about yourself when you go out. Even if the guys are ugly, or are the ones you don't like, at least you still pull, and that makes you feel good about yourself. It boosts your confidence.... you just get this buzz from Asian gigs ... but I don't know what it is. I hate them. I hate the people!" Here, in classic Foucauldian fashion, pleasure is tied to the conditions of constraint that produce it: Leena gains pleasure from what can be read as a conventional form of gender, namely, women being admired for their beauty. This pleasure is arguably amplified given the difficulties that young women like her face in their everyday lives. At the same time, seeking it ties her to a specifically Asian social scene about which she has an unnamable critique.

Leaving aside the thorny question of how pleasure enters into young women's pursuit of men, the fact remains that they still needed to attain good girl status through marriage. By pursuing men in clubs they were attempting to take control over the process of marrying in that they felt free to meet men without their family's interference. My discussions with them confirmed that they were looking for long-term partners rather than short-term "hookups." When I asked Sukh if she went to clubs to find someone to settle down with, she said, "Yeah, I'm always trying to find someone." Jess, commenting on Sukh's answer, confirmed, "She's constantly on the move to find that one perfect person. And if she can't find him, then she's like 'fuck you!'" Although I met Jess and Sukh at a bhangra nightclub, they actually preferred daytimers because the people who attend them are similar to them in age, making the possibility of meeting a long-term partner more likely. As Sukh said about meeting older men, "You can't make a relationship out of it, can you?"

In pursuing men, women adopted a tough comportment, mobilizing bad girl femininity to ultimately achieve good girl status. In language laced with sexual bravado Sukh described to me the techniques she uses to find men, which included actively surveying and approaching them:

SUKH: Upstairs you just eye people out . . . and see who you're gonna go bang downstairs.

JESS: Yeah, *that one, that one!*

SUKH: Yeah, and then you go on downstairs and then you go dance with them. . . .

FALU: What do you do when you see a guy that you want to go for?

SUKH: Lately, I just go and jump them . . . you get the message. If you're dancin' near a bloke, and he moves away, then you understand, init? And if they come jump you, then that's a different matter!

FALU: You mean go down, and you just dance next to them?

SUKH: Yeah. You're just dancing near someone and then you look; you catch their eye or something. Then, I don't know, just funny things happen.

Although there is some contrast between the language Jess and Sukh use ("bang," "jump") and their actions (dance next to), what is key is that women performed tough identities.[25] In trying to exercise agency within the constraints they faced to marry, then, women deployed bad girl means to attain a good girl goal.

MISGUIDED MEN AND PROACTIVE SECURITY

The story of women meeting men becomes more complicated when one examines the ways in which men harassed women, how security managed this, and how women dealt with the consequences. But, to contextualize these practices, one must understand how security dealt with violence between men. Within a few years of their creation bhangra nights began to close down, as frequent clashes between men began to entail exorbitant security costs. By the late 1990s a few clubs with effective security systems had managed to survive, but they still had to contend with recurring violence, violence not only between men but also by men against women.

Although researching the causes of violence was outside the scope of my research, I explored how violence was understood and punished by those whose job it was to control it, specifically, the security staff at Masala, as noted, one of the few remaining bhangra nights in London. Through my discussions with Nick, the head of Securon, the security company in charge at Masala, I found that particular notions of race, class, and gender played a central role in how security managed young men.[26] Nick began by describing the demographics at club nights and told me that young Asian men are a majority of the audience, sometimes as much as 85 percent (an observation that was consistent with my own estimates). Young women are not as likely to attend, Nick said, because of "strict parents."

When I asked Nick why the men engage in violence against one another, he said that factors such as excessive alcohol use and religious communalism played a role. But he said the primary reason was that young men had "mistakenly" adopted a black identity: "Asian people are losing their identity." "Everyone seems to be acting like Jamaican yardies as opposed to an Asian person." For Nick this included "talking like" and "taking on the culture of" a black person. When I suggested that young people may form identities in complex ways, he extended his argument, saying that men had adopted a "hard psychology" that was black. Moreover, they wrongly used this psychology against one another in religious conflicts and more generally in combating racism, a needless effort since "racism has ended."

Two aspects of Nick's account are problematic. First, he locates violence in the so-called pathological personalities of British Asian men. He thereby discounts both the long histories and the contemporary realities of race and class oppression in Britain, disarticulating club violence from structural factors. Second, he uses blackness to construct men as mindlessly violent, drawing on long-standing stereotypes of black masculinity. As Claire Alexander reports, in the mid- to late 1990s (pre–9/11), the British media increasingly used racist ideas of blackness to characterize an alleged rise in "Asian gangs." For example, a story from the Sunday *Times* states, "Police and community groups are increasingly alarmed by an upsurge in inner-city violence, led by traditionally well-behaved Asian youths. Detectives blame the disturbing rise in crime on the disintegration of family life in Asian homes as children refuse to obey their elders. . . . The gangs . . . take their inspiration from Afro-American cultures. Mimicking gangs in L.A., they wear hooded jackets and baggy jeans and listen to rap and ragga music. An increase in drug taking and dealing among young Asians has happened in tandem" (August 21, 1994). Nick is extending these racist portrayals of Asian gangs to bhangra boys.

Such racialized and gendered ideas of British Asian men's criminality, along with cultural ideas about how men engage in violence, underpin the proactive, or preemptive, approach that Securon uses to manage men. To begin with, they employ more staff than usual on bhangra nights to help locate problems before they occur. Nick said that having more security staff helps contain violence because Asian men often fight in groups of eight or more, which Nick identifies as a cultural trait. Having the same team run bhangra nights helps identify troublemakers, as Securon's policies are especially strict on those evenings: once someone is kicked out of the club, he is "barred for life." In addition, Nick believes that having the same team provides a cultural advantage by helping the staff to "build rapport" with young men, a crucial factor in mediating conflict. Male staff members attempt to establish a connection by using masculine forms of sociality such as "having 'a laugh' with the guys." The staff will also enjoy the music: "The guys'll have a laugh and join in. They won't totally integrate with it ... because you can't really understand some of the bhangra music, but you'll see the guys tapping their feet, 'cause they just got used to it."

Securon deploys a number of security strategies at the entrance to the club, such as using video cameras to detect and then bar men who may have had too much to drink, a judgment that is up to the security's discretion. Staff also ban men who are wearing clothing that might indicate religious identification: "We know what to look for on religious celebrations or occasions." They further exclude those wearing "casual clothing" because, as Nick said, "most people will actually prefer to have a fight in a track suit than they would do in their best shirt and trousers." This exclusion can also keep out working-class men, who can't afford higher-line apparel. At the entrance all club-goers undergo an exhaustive search, but for men it is especially intensive as it involves the removal of religious objects as well as ordinary ones that can be used in fights: "Everything, including religious items like bangles and knives and daggers are taken away."[27] Before the audience arrives, the staff removes items from the nightclub itself, such as glassware and heavy metal ashtrays, that could be used as weapons.

Once men are inside the venue, Securon staff rely on supposed cultural procedures to bolster security. For example, they look to the British Asian deejays to help them understand whether an action is really aggressive or not so as to avoid confusing dance steps with fights. (Most traditional dance moves mimic body movements related to harvesting. Young people have incorporated these moves with those of hip-hop and other dance styles.) Nick said, "The dancing ... can be quite aggressive; soon as bhangra music comes on, people start pushing and shoving. ... [B]ut providing that a fight hasn't broken out, there isn't a problem ... if you're not used to it, you could actually see that as being a little bit unruly. Other security might go in there and jump on a situation that isn't really a situation, but we rely on our [Asian] deejays. ... [They] will call for us."

Finally, throughout the evening the staff maintains close communication with the police, which gives them access to strong measures of "crowd control." Nick said, "If we rang outside there, they'd put out the large riot wagons; we'll have two of those out there and probably two units with dogs." Nick explained that bhangra clubs are a top priority of police because officers perceive violence between men to be political in nature: "The police intelligence that follow the scene around are quite concerned because it is a lot of politics involved.... [A]ll the local authorities ... are concerned with the situation." By *politics*, Nick clarified that he and the police are concerned about the possibility of a race riot erupting. That is, they do everything they can to contain club conflicts because they fear that if they let the men onto the streets and they continue to fight, the police would have to get involved, which could then spark riots throughout the country. (These worries are a testimony to ongoing racial tensions in Britain.) Because of these anxieties security forces, including mounted police and special units with video cameras, have become a regular part of the landscape wherever bhangra music is played publicly in Britain, for example, at Asian *melas*, or festivals. The disciplining of bhangra boys is thus not simply about promoting safety in clubs but also involves broader questions of national security.

WAYWARD WOMEN AND REACTIVE SECURITY

While racialized and gendered beliefs about criminality inform the proactive measures Securon uses to discipline young men, their approach to young women, which is quite different, draws on other ideas of race and gender. Owing to Britain's imperial legacy, its inhabitants often construe Asian culture as backward and mired in tradition, ideas that, in turn, presume grave consequences for women. Stories regularly appear in the British media, for example, that focus on the "barbaric" practice of arranged marriage, the plight of runaway brides, and the domestic abuse that occurs at the hands of Asian men. Generally portraying women as victims, these stories draw their force from colonial discourses that portray Anglo-British men as saving Asian women from the savage traditions that uncivilized Asian men perpetuate.[28] With the rising visibility of perceived Asian gangs, the media have shifted some of their focus from a supposed concern about the lives of women to anxiety about the activities of young men.[29] Bhangra youth cultures, however, have produced a new category, wayward Asian girls, around which a less visible set of "moral panic[s]" has congealed.[30]

Nick's statement that few young women attend bhangra clubs because of the parental strictures placed on them as well as his use of a framework of the good versus the bad girl points to the idea that authorities see the women who attend clubs as having escaped "containment," in both the literal (home) and figurative (tradition) sense of the term. They therefore regard them as being wayward, that is, outside the norms of public morality. Staff members thus view them as being complicit in the harassment they face and therefore not worth "saving." The result is they don't regard men's violence toward women nearly as seriously as they do the clashes between men.

This lack of attention manifests itself in several ways. To begin with, Securon employs gendered notions of what constitutes real violence. When I asked Nick how often he sees cases of men inflicting violence on women, he mentioned that men who have been issued a warrant for domestic violence occasionally enter the club. His notion of violence seems to be restricted to formally policed cases, ignoring the routine harassment young women face in the form of unwarranted touching, name calling, verbal threats, and cornering in a club. Jess described her experience of being mistreated: "After this one time, I didn't even go back on that dance floor. It was me and Shazia (the other girl), and we was dancing, and there was a couple of blokes from school with us as well, but they drifted that way slightly. And this bloke started dancing with Shazia. So his friend thought, 'Oh, it's all right now, I'll go and dance with her friend.' And I was like, 'Na man, fuck you, get away from me,' and then you know what he started? He started twirling me, and he twirled me into this big perverted circle. And it was like, 'Oh, my god!' And you know what it is? I felt like *meat*. All hands were comin' in, yeah, from all places. I was like 'Fuck you!'"

Second, Securon approaches women's complaints in much less clearly specified terms than they do violence between men. According to Nick, if women state a concern about misconduct, the staff will "listen to both sides of the story" and also "warn the guys." But Nick also invoked, for the first time, the "rules and regulations" that prevent him from fully intervening and that also seemed to allow inordinate room for personal discretion:

> You have to remain impartial—same as the police. If you've got two people making a complaint, you can only listen to both sides and make an assumption. Now you could be wrong, you may be right. It might have been better to boot the guy; it might have been better to boot the girl. You can't really say; you have to make a decision there and then.

As head of security here, that's a decision that will fall on my lap. That is part of our rules and regulations. Once I've assessed the situation, and generally I think I'm fair, then I would then analyze what I think is the problem.

And it's not to say I can't be wrong, because you could leave the guy inside there, and he might go and hit the girl. But he is a paying customer, and she is a paying customer. As far as I'm concerned, they've not broken any terms and conditions of the entry to the club.

Now, if this is a serious allegation, i.e., that the guy is molesting the girl in a serious fashion, then we give her the option to call the police. We will retain the guy, 'cause that is a criminal offense. But we will still remain impartial because I haven't seen it. Then I would phone the police, and the police will deal with it.

Giving young women the option to call the police, rather than mandating women do so, or better, doing it themselves, further renders the violence as personal and less of an official interest.

Third, Securon is not only cautious about women's accusations but often finds them suspicious. Nick said, "You can't always take for granted that the woman is right and the guy is wrong, can you? There might be ulterior reasons." As Nick and I discussed the violence toward club-going women, he cast the entire bhangra scene as an adolescent one, a language he did not use when we discussed conflicts between men:

FALU: When they're having a particular problem with a guy and tell you, do you then send somebody to watch him?
NICK: Yeah, we keep an eye on the situation. If the girl comes back a second time and says, "Well, you know, I'm really trying to keep out of this guy's way, but . . ." then we'll look at it further, and then we might put the guy out. But we do have ex-girlfriends . . . because the guy's with another girl or something like that, that are causing the problem.

You got to remember the age group . . . which is between eighteen and nineteen years old, and that is very typical. Unfortunately, they think they know everything, but they don't know very much at all 'cause they're still living with their parents, and they don't have to pay bills yet. So it means that they might think that they know a hell of a lot about life, but they don't really. And it is very childish; a lot of the psychology behind these evenings is childish.

By linking young women's concerns to "childish" behavior, Nick cast men's harassment of women as not being worthy of attention, unlike the political causes he sees as the greater context of men's conflicts.

In all, Securon uses a reactive rather than proactive approach to men's violence toward women. That is, they wait until complaints occur, then deal with these to the limited extent that the rules and regulations, their personal discretion, and their suspicion of women allows. Given that the policing roles are shared between staff and the state, despite the fact that British Asians see the bhangra club as a private kind of public space in which men and women can meet, it is also very much a public site insofar as it is the locus of anxiety and intervention for local and state authorities concerned with the behavior of British Asian men. But even this dual construction of it as an insider space and as a site of clashes between men that are of public concern elides the regular violence that occurs against women.

"THERE'S ENOUGH ABUSE THAT A BLOKE CAN TAKE"

Because security routinely focused on conflicts between young men, the mistreatment of young women, which often took place in micropractices, went unnoticed by them and was thereby normalized. This had consequences for women club-goers: while many whom I met complained about this wrongdoing (recall Jess's descriptions of the "perverts"), they did so in ways that were outraged but also somewhat subdued. For example, they rarely expressed a desire to have access to larger recourse to address their concerns. They also spoke about men's actions in the later parts of interviews, almost as addendums. It was as if facing some violence from men was a necessary evil of club going.

Nevertheless, these women did not simply accept violence but took control in managing it themselves. Most often they would enlist a backup or a group of men friends who would fight in their defense if they were at risk. Jess, continuing her story about being twirled into a group of men (with Sukh interjecting), said that her backup saved her:

> SUKH: I would've turned around and gone "Whoosh"! [Motioning that she would have hit them].
>
> JESS: And then this one bloke ... it was like he was helping me. I'm not even joking. He came and started going, "Leave the girl alone!" [But then] *he* tried to have his piece as well! I thought "What the fuck?!" There was not one decent bloke at that night!

SUKH: Simon is decent.

JESS: Then, one of my mates just grabbed my arm, and he just pulled me out, and he goes, "Don't fucking touch the girl!" to the boys. And do you know what? While I was being pushed out . . . they were making noises. They were going "Aaahhhh." They started coming behind me. I swear—that was so sick. After that day, I don't know, man. And I just went out there, and then I was like "fuck this man." I told everyone. We had another friend with us. He's pretty big. And he's like, "Show me who they are cause I'm gonna bust them."

SUKH: You could've showed *me* them!

JESS: I just didn't want to go back in there. I didn't go on the dance floor after that, and that was like one o'clock. . . . That's [all] in one night. I'm not even joking—*in one night.* I haven't been so harassed in the whole time I've been clubbing!

In addition to getting a backup, as Sukh's interjections in Jess's story show, women at times adopted the same tough comportment they used to pursue men to fight harassment. At other times they'd evaluate whether or not they needed to use their own tactics in conjunction with support from men. For example, Jess and Sukh described another incident in which they verbally attacked their abusers, but only because they were confident about their backup:

SUKH: The men will turn around and say, "Bitch, I'll fuckin' rape you when you get outside!". . . . But at the end of the day, we got backup. . . . We had enough backup at that gig.

JESS: That day, we had so many people looking out for us!

SUKH: Just general boys we know. Everyone was like, "If it happens, you come and tell us." . . . When you know you're insecure at the gig, you won't make as many comments—[you] just turn around, move out of the way, you'll be good. But when you know you've got the backup there . . . that day, we knew that if we could start anything—they'd finish it off for us.

Occasionally, women did take on their abusers even when they lacked support from their men friends. Once when I was on the dance floor with a young woman, Pumi, and her friend Suma a young man kept coming up behind Suma in an attempt to dance with her. Pumi took her cigarette and started waving it around her friend to carve out a space for her to dance and to threaten to burn this man if he came any closer. Women also verbally confronted men on their own. When I asked Sukh if she had ever had to use her backup, she said, "We do it ourselves! . . . 'You don't fuckin' touch us! I'll fuckin' kill you bastards!' . . . They back off then. At the end of the day, there's *enough* abuse that a bloke can take.[31] Once you pass the limit, they ain't gonna come back."

These examples illustrate that the approaches young women used varied in relation to how much they relied on and therefore reproduced the patriarchal structuring of club space. But in using them, women adopted the comportment of a tough bad girl, a comportment that resists the cultural nationalist ideal of the good girl. As I learned more about women's lives outside of the clubs, it became clear that they crafted this self-presentation and their strategies against abusers partly as a response to the violence they faced in their everyday lives. This violence occurred across the spaces of home and street. In a poignant story Leena told me about her attempt to mock her family's disciplining of her, she explains how she learned to use violence to defend herself. About a year earlier she had introduced a potential male partner to her family. Although she was, in her words, desperate to marry someone, she was actually not very interested in this man, but she wanted to witness her family's reaction to him. Leena and Alisha both recounted her lack of interest humorously. Alisha added laughingly, "He was such an idiot, you couldn't tell where his stomach and where his legs were!" Leena, also laughing, confirmed. "He was really ugly man!" Shocked at Leena's boldness, her brothers proceeded to attack her physically and verbally: "They told me, 'How dare you bring a man here!'" Faizal started threatening to kill her, citing the family's izzat. Then her other brother started physically attacking her. In a moment of rage, Leena fought back: "I started punching him, and I picked up a knife, and I said, 'If anyone touches me, I swear to God, I'll kill them! No one's going to touch me now! Those days are gone!' And my brother goes, 'What's wrong with her? She's a psycho case!' The thing is, I've had it in the past *so* much. I just picked the knife up, I said 'Come on then, touch me, and I'll kill you!' If any of them come for me now, I just pick up a weapon. My daughter sat there crying and everything."

While Leena suffered physical violence at the hands of her family, Jess and Sukh discussed how the violence they experienced and their contestation of it occurred in such everyday activities as walking down the road, waiting for a bus, and going shopping:

FALU: So, where do you get harassed the most?

JESS and SUKH: Walkin' down the road.

SUKH: Whatever time I go and drop her off at the bus stop, men'll go past horning or go "whooo," or whistle at us; this always happens—everyday.... We just swear it off.

JESS: But sometimes, like the other day, I nearly got run over cause they thought it was funny. They were going at such a high, fast speed, and I was just about to cross the road, so I just stood at the side thinking, Wait for the car to go. They put the brakes on the casket and everything, and they thought it was funny, but I thought You bastards! You just only, nearly killed me! Sometimes they take it too far.

SUKH: Yeah, but it's not just people that are drivin' past in cars. The bus drivers are like that now. People who work in shops are like that. It's like everywhere you go people are like that, especially around here. But we respond to it in a different way [from other girls] though, don't we? It's like, if he's fit, then we're like "oh yeah, sort it out" sort of thing. If he's not, [then] it's like "fuck you, get out of my face!"

JESS: I reckon we're pretty loud, though, like when we was at McDonald's, we saw these really nice blokes. We went "Whoa, whoa...!"

SUKH: Yeah, lately we've gotten real loud, haven't we?

JESS: Yeah, we don't give a shit anymore. Blokes can do it; we can do it!

Jess and Sukh have developed tactics to counter everyday violence akin to what they use in bhangra clubs, such as "swearing it off." Moreover, they pride themselves on not being passive victims and, even better, having the power to ascertain whether a man who is troubling them is fit and worth aggressively pursuing or not fit and therefore worthy of abuse. In an arguably greater transgression of good girl behavior, they try to change the terms of their violent encounters with men so that instead of men objectifying them, they get to objectify the men ("blokes can do it; we can do it!").

Safe Women and Stupid Tarts

The dual relationship club-going women had with so-called fit versus perverted British Asian men mirrored the relationships they had with other women club-goers, who, for them, tended to fall into two categories: they were either safe women with whom they identified or they were women with whom they had antagonistic relationships. Club-goers made these distinctions on the basis of how the distance between themselves and others closed: if uncompetitively, then women were safe but if competitively, they were not.

A central theme in their friendships with other young women was their ability to relate to each other because they shared dilemmas. Their troubles were not simply about dealing with strict parental norms (as Yasmin and Jaspreet indicate in complaints about their brothers' freedom). Rather, many of them had violated the norms of being dutiful daughters, for example, by having had unsuccessful marriages and multiple partners, and therefore dealt with dominant perceptions of them as bad girls. This struggle manifested itself in a kind of double consciousness: they would reject claims that they were bad, but at the same time indict their actions. Leena, for example, felt she had made the right decision in leaving her abusive husband. But she also experienced self-doubt that was exacerbated by elders who felt she was a bad influence on their daughters. She said, "I get on with the new generation . . . people my age. . . . I just can't get on with the older generation because they seem to think badly of me." She laughed and said, "'Bad example' on their daughters," in a way that was sarcastic yet revealed her pain. In light of their battles, women took solace in being able to connect with one another. Leena continued, "A lot of girls talk to me about their problems: they're being forced into arranged marriages, they're not allowed to go to college. That's why I think they can relate to other Asians. We have a lot more to talk about." Women felt a sense of community with those with whom they could share difficulties. Leena said, "They come from the same cultures; they all have the same problems, mostly." Bhangra clubs were spaces in which women could forge such friendships. They in fact made many friends by going to the club: they recognized up to a quarter of the people there, what Jess called "familiar faces." Sukh confirmed, "It's like the same crowd, it's like 'all right, how are you' sort of thing."

On the other hand, conflicts between young women at bhangra events were common. In my discussions with club-goers, they spoke frequently about clashes with others, often raising these issues before discussing the harassment they faced from men and speaking about them more emphatically. Fights in clubs often begin because of the ways women glance at one another; in fact the look is commonly the pivotal factor in women's battles. If a woman perceives the look to be a cut, or a put-down, this becomes an instigation to attack. Women's fights also take place in a way similar to those between men: if one woman starts something, her girlfriends will help finish it:

SUKH: Every time I go, I nearly get into a fight!
JESS: The thing is right, the girls . . .
SUKH: Silly slags!
JESS: They're all into themselves, and they just look at you and they just . . .
SUKH: They think they're all that and more.
JESS: The girls have a lot of confidence.
SUKH: We see all these hos there, and out of us lot, I always get into the fights first, but then we all jump in together.[32] I'll stand there cuttin' a bird out, and these lot [her friends] are like "Just forget it!"[33] And then afterwards, they all back me up anyway, it's like we all jump into it together . . .
FALU: Why do you start it?
JESS: If she doesn't like the look of someone, [then] she looks at them. But there's always the way *they* look at her as well.
FALU: So it's not a good idea to look at anyone in the women's loo or wherever?[34]
JESS: I don't think so; unless—it depends.
SUKH: If you turn around and look at someone, if there's any friction, then you know you all are going to jump each other when you get outside; but if you turn around, and the woman's [nice] . . . then it's a different matter.
JESS: Yeah, it depends on the way *they* look at you first. Cause, we don't go out there and deliberately give people daggers or cut them out. But it's what the *other* person does, and then *we* think, all right, fuck you now! *or* okay [it's all right].
FALU: Why do they give you looks like that?
SUKH: Cause they're stupid little tarts. It's like "fuck you, stupid ho!"
JESS: They're really blatant they are, when they do it. It's like they're up there, and they just look at you like you're shit. It's really bad.

Wayward Asian Girls **153**

Although Jess and Sukh said that other women are to blame, for example, that the possibility of a fight depends on how others look at them first, it is unclear which party actually first commits wrongdoing, making the energy between women extremely charged. It is possible for women club-goers to form friendships with one another, for example, if two of them deem each other to be okay. But if either party sees the distance between them as competitive in any way, this forecloses all possibility of friendship. The line between those who are safe and those who are not is fragile, and women can easily cross it if they don't guard it carefully.

Both the foregoing and following stories show that club-goers generally used sexist language to describe other women, for example, as *slags* or *hos*, and portrayed themselves as individuals who can fight these women and, more important, can win:

> FALU: Have you ever had a physical fight with anyone?
> SUKH: Yeah! We've beaten up a lot of girls.... One time I had a fight right on South Road with a girl and her sister. A week later, we followed her home, and we jumped her in the alley, me and my friends.
> JESS: I fractured my hand beatin' 'em up.
> SUKH: We jumped her, and we beat the *shit* out of her.
> FALU: Why?
> SUKH: I had friction with her.... You know what it was, she walked past, and I cut her out, and she was with her sister, and I swore at her—"fat slag"—or whatever. [Then] she turned around and swore at me. Then her sister says to me, "You don't curse my sister." I went, "I do what I fuckin' wanna do." She spat at me, but it missed me. Then I spat back at her . . . and it spread all over her face. Then me and her got into a punch-up.... And then her sister jumped in, and then I dealt with that matter, and then that's it.
> JESS: She beat two girls up at the same time!

The ideologies of cultural nationalism and class-based models of achieving respect help situate these women's antagonistic relationships toward one another. These conflicts are a vehicle through which they negotiate the notions of morality embedded in the ideal of the good girl. As noted, in that the framework of bad versus good girl interpellates British Asian women and that female club goers are seen as bad, bhangra clubs are difficult for young women to frequent, even if, in doing so, they are pursuing the good goal of finding an appropriate marriage partner. Moreover, many of the regulars had, in fact, violated cultural nationalist norms by having unsuccessful marriages, children out of wedlock, or the "wrong" partners. In this context, club-goers' regular use of such misogynist terms as *slags, tarts,* and *hos* to distinguish other women from themselves enables them to retain a sense of self-identity as morally good. In other words, given that the space of the bhangra club "contaminates" them, they reassert their moral standing in conflicts with one another.[35]

But class is also important here: part of being a good girl is being respectable, which means appearing and behaving in ways that are sexually modest. Because the class backgrounds of working-class women position them as inherently less honorable, they can have pronounced concerns with respectability.[36] For working-class girls of color, such concerns often appear in the attention they pay to appearance and conduct.[37]

One can detect the strength of cultural nationalist notions of morality as well as the emphasis on behavior and appearance in women's disparagements of one another. Jess and Sukh, for example, made intense efforts to differentiate themselves from other club-goers, referring to clothing styles, makeup, and actions to demarcate lines of morality and to deflect being potentially seen as bad girls:

SUKH: The other girls are like hos. They just go around and bang anyone—like Nadia and Mini and them lot are solid hos.
JESS: The thing is . . . the clothes we wear—this is it—we dress casually, init?
SUKH: They dress like they're going clubbing every day.
JESS: Their faces are *packed* with makeup.
FALU: Do you think that someone might call you tarts if you're going clubbing all the time? Has anyone called you that?
JESS: The thing is, everyone always sees us like this. They can't call us tarts or whatever. . . . If they see us on a regular basis when we go clubbin', they might think oh yeah, look at them. They changed now, haven't they? Makeover time or *what*?!
FALU: Then how do you differentiate yourself from them?
SUKH: They actually go around bangin' the blokes. . . . Those fucking hos just jump into bed.
JESS: We go clubbing, but we don't go out telling everyone, "Oh yeah, we did this that day. This happened to me, this happened to me."
SUKH: Or "I met this bloke, and I did this with him."
JESS: And they, they [tell us].

FALU: Even though you might?
SUKH: No, we don't though.
JESS: We don't tell them like that.
SUKH: We don't do it, love!
JESS: *We* might not, but *she* definitely does! (lots of laughter)
SUKH: Shut up! I have not had sex with anyone; thank you very much!
JESS: No, not sex, not sex! I tell you that much. We're not like that. We haven't gone that far. We've got that much respect for ourselves.
SUKH: And for our parents.
JESS: Yeah.
FALU: For your parents?
(laughter)
SUKH: No, for myself!

In this dialogue Jess and Sukh repeatedly referred to other women as "hos" because of the way they dressed. Yet when I tried to understand how they viewed themselves given that others could also see them as dressing provocatively when they attend clubs, they distinguished themselves by referring to their clothing and sexual behavior. They stressed that they, at least, dress casually during the day, and they do not have sex with men (or at least, they don't talk about it).

Class can also be a factor in the violence of young women's conflicts. While respectability involves performing good girl femininity through proper appearance and conduct, for working-class women it can also mean defending oneself. As Karen Joe Laidler and Geoffrey Hunt write in their study of young female gang members who are both working-class and women of color, "The meaning of 'respectability' goes beyond middle class notions of the term.... Given their embeddedness in street life culture... respectability also means being aware and being able to stand up for yourself."[38] This sentiment is evident in a discussion I had with another clubgoer, Saba. When I asked her what young women usually fight about, she said, "It's attitude, basically.... A lot of the girls.... have got a lot of attitude. They'll barge you, they'll do something—deliberately drop a drink on you, something stupid, and you can't stand there with all your friends and take it, 'cause your friends will think, What? You're taking it? What's wrong with you? You know? Then obviously, you're going to have to hit her or you'll be left out."

Examining club-goers' relationships with other British Asian women as a whole, the latter seem to act as a mirror. On the one hand, club-goers have safe women friends to whom they relate because of their shared struggles as bad girls. Bonding in this way challenges the force of cultural nationalism in their lives because in the very act of recognizing it and helping each other ameliorate their feelings they resist it. On the other hand, they adopt a tough bad girl comportment to fight other young women. While such comportment challenges good girl femininity, women's goals are to ultimately assert their status as good girls, thereby reproducing cultural nationalist norms. Women's agency is thus fraught: it entails their behaving in ways that invite judgment and then challenging the judgments that are made of them by leveling them against other women, ultimately reinforcing the legitimacy of the judgments themselves.

Conclusion

An intersectional approach to young women's bhangra club-going experiences demonstrates that clubs are not racial utopias. Neither are they simply "diasporic public spheres." Rather, they are private and public and shaped by racialized heteronormativity and gendered violence, some forms of which are sanctioned locally and by the state. Moreover, women participate in clubs in ways that both resist and reinscribe cultural nationalism. One can map onto a grid the strategies women club-goers employ vis-à-vis other British Asian women and men that they like and dislike (although there's a third category of men, their "mates," women focused on the fit ones and the perverts):

	British Asian women	British Asian men
like	bond with "bad girls"	pursue "fit" men
dislike	fight "tarts"	fight harassment

The ways women contest and reproduce cultural nationalism can be read in the lines that cross this grid. They challenge it insofar as they bond with other bad women, a bond that can loosen the stranglehold of cultural nationalism in their lives. They also confront it when they join together to fight sexual misconduct, calling out male dominance and using a tough comportment that counters norms of proper femininity. Their social bonding in these instances and in the earlier examples of friendships with black women is identifiable as a challenge to the discourse that sees bhangra clubs as strictly a public sphere. Writing about working-class Chicana girls in all-female gangs, Marie Keta Miranda shows how they "utilize forms of unity and solidarity borrowed from the domestic sphere, reworking them to consolidate a feminine culture in the public space," thereby engaging in a "domesticization" of the public and a "publicization" of the private.[39] Similarly, the ties between British Asian women who attend bhangra clubs are often based on friendships formed through emotional bonding, trust, and intimacy, that is, characteristic ways in which working-class girls create their own culture.[40] By reworking these forms in the space of the club and employing them, as the girls in Miranda's study do, "as a survival tactic in patriarchy," they are "translating a form of solidarity characteristic of the domestic sphere into a new public space."[41] Consequently, their bonding also represents "an interstitial or liminal space before the actualization of the gendered 'compulsive heterosexual' ... social roles."[42]

Yet in their fights with other British Asian women over respectability and in their search for a male partner they use bad girl means, fighting and pursuing, to achieve good girl ends, thereby reinforcing the norms of cultural nationalism. The difference between the safe women and the women they dislike is not about the people per se; rather, it is about the social dynamic in which they engage: when this dynamic activates the question of respectability, the way they bond with friends becomes the very thing they brutally judge in the case of their enemies.

As young women pursue good girl ends, often through bad girl means, they inhabit a tenuous and constantly negotiated position. Because of their class location some of the only means they have to achieve respectability position them on the line between being bad and good, depending on whether one is evaluating their actions through a working-class or middle-class lens. Indeed, Yasmin indicated this tenuous position when she told me playfully, "We're good girls, really." But women constructed a *kind* of good girl-ness: their concern seemed not so much about reproducing tradition as about the partly instrumental, class-related goal of getting married.

As the experiences of these young, bhangra-club-going women illustrate, utopian discourses that assume British Asians express preconstituted, "hybrid" identities in the space of the bhangra club, itself assumed to be liberatory, are deeply flawed. Such static representations elide the ways in which race, class, gender, and sexuality intersect in the lives of British Asians, in the music they enjoy, and in the spaces in which they enjoy that music.

IN THE LARGELY working-class milieu of the bhangra club scene, the constraints of class and expectations of cultural nationalism combine to create an environment in which the good girl/bad girl dichotomy becomes salient for women club-goers. In contrast, the largely middle-class character of the AU club scene makes for an altogether different set of negotiations for the women who take part in it.

Chapter Four

Roomful of Asha
Middle-Class Women and Asian Underground Club Going

Although it was a cold Monday night in Hoxton Square, my friends and I joined the eager club-goers who began queuing to enter the Blue Note an hour before it was to open. Hoxton, located in the East End and home to a predominantly working-class Bangladeshi community, was being gentrified. Sleek cafes, warehouse lofts, and renovated nightclubs were gradually transforming it. The Blue Note, a historic jazz club, had itself received a face-lift, and Talvin Singh, a young British Asian musician, cleverly chose it as the venue for his new weekly club night Anokha, which he opened in late 1995 and which featured Asian Underground music.[1]

The term *Asian Underground* (AU) suggests that Anokha was a strictly British Asian nightclub, but the people in line included whites, Asians, and blacks. As we all waited patiently to get in, a few journalists asked club-goers about the new interest in Asian music. When we finally made it into the warmth of the club, with minimal security checks, we found ourselves in the midst of a kind of commodified Asian interior adorned with iconography signifying South Asia. We entered on what turned out to be an upper floor, where the walls were glimmering with South Asian fabrics and art. The word *Anokha* was written on the main wall in stylized South Asian lettering. The deejays on this floor played down-tempo, South Asian–infused lounge music that we could listen to while enjoying a drink and relaxing on the welcoming couches. To "chill out" even more, we could purchase *chai, papad, bhajia,* and other South Asian foods at a snack bar.

We could even enjoy a half-hour massage on the long table strategically positioned near one of the walls. When we ventured downstairs, we discovered the main floor, where people were dancing to a range of electronica, such as drum 'n' bass, infused with South Asian instrumentation and, occasionally, vocals. To provide a South Asian feel to this space, a large video screen hung above the dance floor, looping segments from popular Hindi films from the 1960s and 1970s. The main segments being shown, moreover, were those of women dancing and singing in the melodramatic contexts of these films, which invited a reading of them as gender parody and promoted a near-camp aesthetic. In an extension of this aesthetic and of a general counterculture vibe, one of the deejays, Bobby Friction, had marked his forehead with decorative *bindis* like a South Asian bride in a wedding ceremony.

As the night went on, the upstairs floor remained a chill out space, a place to hang out with friends and recollect oneself after dancing. Downstairs, however, the activity became increasingly energetic, with folks often enjoying the music so much that they danced on their own. As I continued to attend Anokha I found that in addition to playing the usual record music, on certain nights Singh himself would perform for an eager crowd on tabla on the small stage downstairs. As the press coverage grew, luminaries began to visit Anokha. One night I found myself standing two feet away from Björk as we watched Singh perform. As this night wound down, as with other nights, those who had to work early Tuesday morning made their way home. For those who didn't, the evening continued, the mission to replenish calories being accomplished at the nearby Brick Lane Beigel Bake or the local curry houses.

Two tracks that the deejays at Anokha often played and that later became anthems of the AU scene were State of Bengal's "Flight IC 408" and Singh's "Jaan." These songs have a few elements in common: they are forms of drum 'n' bass, and they use tabla, synthesizers, and South Asian women as vocalists. Other than that, however, they differ. "Jaan," which is six minutes long, uses minimal instrumentation and vocals: it features tabla, synthesizers, ambient sounds, and vocals by Amar, a British Asian woman who sings on the track in both Hindi and English. There is also little variation in the track: it slowly introduces layers in its buildup to a fast tempo, has a break midway, and then continues its fast pace. The track begins with a background tabla beat along with an atmospheric synth that provides a trance-like, ambient sound.[2] Twenty seconds in, Amar sings the song's chorus in Hindi: "Oh mere jaan e jaan, ankho se door na ho," which means, "Oh my love, don't stray too far from my eyes." She repeats this phrase several times as the music, which introduces additional layers of synthesizers and percussion, begins to pick up tempo. After another minute comes a faster tabla beat, interlaced with a synthesized drum 'n' bass beat. The chorus, however, continues its slow, melodic pace, contrasting with the faster tempo of the music, letting audiences engage in the song at two speeds. Midway through, when the tempo, instrumentation, and tabla are in an established pattern, Amar starts to sing in English: "Don't move out of sight, things are getting stronger," repeating this chorus several times in the same melodic, slow fashion. Then, at what could be interpreted as a climactic break in the song, the music stops, save for the tabla and ambient background sound, to focus on the vocalist, who returns to her Hindi chorus, extending it with the phrase, "utar jayega," which means "the intoxication [of love] will leave me," repeating this twice. As she extends the words, "ankho se" (from my eyes), the track returns to its fast pace, after which she continues to sing, alternating her lines in English and Hindi, until the track winds down.

"IC 408," which is over seven minutes long, is a more straightforwardly drum 'n' bass track with more variation in instrumentation and vocals and in its general journey. Compared to "Jaan," it has more distinctive Western features, such as its instrumentation, which includes guitar. It starts with a static-filled recording of an airport lobby, and then a South Asian man states three times over an intercom, "Your attention, please." After this, he says, "Indian airlines announces the departure of the flight IC 408 to Calcutta. Passengers are requested to proceed to the aircraft." Over the sounds of an engine revving up, a sampled tabla beat is looped to create a unique drum melody. Over this, a South Asian woman flight attendant announces, "Good evening. Ladies and gentlemen, on behalf of Indian airlines and Captain Das Gupta, we welcome you on board our flight, IC 408. We're about to take off for Calcutta. Will you kindly fasten your seatbelts, keep your seats upright, and refrain from smoking while the 'no-smoking' sign is switched on. We hope you enjoy your flight. Thank you." After this, there are brief new synthesized instrumentation, the sampled tabla loops, and pronounced percussion. This stops momentarily, and the woman repeats, "Flight IC 408" as one hears the sounds of a plane taking off. At this point the track becomes more solidly drum 'n' bass, with the earlier melody of the tabla being repeated by synthesizers and coupled with tabla beats and other percussion. Gradually layered over these is the sampling of a South Asian woman's voice, which sounds broken up because it is in the form of an echo, and the words she's uttering are unintelligible. About halfway through, all of this stops, and a syncopated guitar plays a funk-inspired riff, coupled with synthesized music, over which the sounds of a plane taking off can be heard. Here, the earlier tabla loops are brought in periodically to punctuate the guitar melody and make it even funkier. At three minutes and forty seconds in, there's a melodic break, in which a guitar, playing a single line rather than chords, is made to sound like sitar. It produces a sound that is a bit 1970s and *Hawaii Five-O* over the ongoing drum and bass percussion. Tabla is brought in a couple of times to punctuate the flow. Then the song breaks again, after which, layered in turn, come the woman's broken voice, percussion, the flight attendant saying, "Flight IC 408," and the sounds of planes taking off. After a few repetitions of this pattern, it returns to the guitar melody. Then a break occurs to focus on the percussion, punctuated by the twang of the sampled tabla loops. The track ends by returning to the sitar-like, guitar-produced melody, with the woman's broken voice layered on top.

ONE NIGHT I overheard the main club promoter, Sweety Kapoor, state that Anokha was not an "Asian-only" club, but it was meant to "feel Asian" and to do so in a way that could appeal to a broad population. This use of an Asian aesthetic was akin to the strategies used by the AU record label Outcaste. As I noted in chapter 2, because it was interested in achieving mainstream success Outcaste preferred artists who created music that was more open, that is, more accessible to whites, than, for example, bhangra and overtly politicized forms like rap. As in the case of Outcaste, the strategies Anokha's promoters used proved to be successful: the club attracted a wide audience, achieving unprecedented crossover success.

In general press coverage of the club night, one can find stories in which British Asians claimed that frequenting it helped them resolve the "identity crises" they experience as being a part of "two different worlds." Krishnendu Majumdar's testimony is exemplary (see introduction). A young journalist and fan of AU music, Majumdar described his experiences of going to Anokha in an elaborate essay he posted on the Internet, part of which read, "It was the first time I . . . felt truly proud of my heritage: it was incredible. The clash of cultures in me—born in Wales with a western education at school, entwined with a Bengali upbringing at home—was no longer a force pulling me apart. I was glowing and felt that this is where I belonged."[3] While his essay reinforced the discourse of culture clash often used to describe the issues that British Asians face (and which scholars have widely critiqued), it did make a powerful claim: that club going helps one heal the injuries of cultural alienation born of coming of age in a society that sees British and Asian as absolutist, mutually exclusive categories. Such claims raise the question of what attending clubs like Anokha meant to its British Asian audiences. Yet scholars have largely focused on AU music itself, ignoring club going altogether.[4]

Moreover, while there is some public and scholarly commentary about gender dynamics at bhangra clubs (see chapter 3), there is no such commentary on AU clubs. Indeed, AU clubs come across as gender neutral: unlike bhangra clubs, AU clubs were frequented by men and women in roughly equal numbers and experienced no fights between men, regular harassment of women, or policing. It seems that gender is not a problematic issue in regard to AU clubs, let alone a category worthy of analysis. And, in fact, in light of the evidence of gender parody and camp at Anokha, it appears to be a space that might contest the heteronormativity so constituent of bhangra clubs like Masala. With the emergence of the AU club scene, then, had youth of South Asian descent, in all of their difference, fully arrived in Britain?

As I came to know women club-goers, utopian narratives about the AU scene became untenable. Not only racial inequality but also gender norms and class difference played a role in their club-going practices. Unlike the women who avidly attended bhangra clubs, these women were mostly middle class, which raised distinct challenges for them. The working-class women who went to bhangra clubs did so as a way of negotiating the challenge of becoming good girls under constraining conditions; in those conditions, deploying bad girl femininity was simultaneously a form of exercising agency and a practice that resituated them as not good. In contrast, the middle-class background of the women who frequented AU clubs often meant they came of age in non-Asian areas. As a result, they had grown up with a sense of being ethnically inauthentic, a doubly difficult feeling given that, as women, they were tasked with reproducing culture. Club going, for them, was thus in part a way to legitimate and thereby produce themselves as British and Asian.

To analyze this process, I focus here on the narratives of fifteen women who regularly went to Anokha and similar clubs.[5] There were several commonalities in their backgrounds. All but one were in their twenties and all were middle class: ten grew up middle class, and the five who had been working class experienced upward mobility. Although one-half grew up in working-class Asian areas, the women who grew up there either were or later became middle class. Each of the women had pursued education beyond high school and were employed, and all but two held jobs that were not part of the traditional career path of British Asian youth, let alone of British Asian women. (Two women were in financial investment and medicine, and the rest pursued careers in the arts or as activists: they were filmmakers, television producers, aspiring musicians, singers, music promoters, visual artists, activists, or nonprofit workers.) Each of the women was single and had never married, and two of them identified as lesbian. They differed in ethnicity, being Pakistani, Punjabi, Gujarati, and Bangladeshi, and in religious background, being Hindus, Muslims, and Sikhs, but these differences had no significant bearing on their narratives.

How did these women use AU music and club going to produce themselves as ethnically authentic and with what consequences? They constructed identities and imagined communities in four ways, ways that contest essentialist and gendered ideologies of Asianness. First, they found in the AU ways to denounce narrow notions of ethnic identity espoused by folks they call typical Asians. Second, the emergence of AU music and clubs enabled these women to call into question the gendered ideas of ethnic identity that emerged in the bhangra scene, in which, in their experience, being Asian was equated to enduring sexual harassment. Third, women enjoyed the relaxed ethos of AU clubs; while many club-goers touted that aspect, it had specifically gendered meanings for the women who attended. Fourth, they drew on the racial diversity of the scene to produce themselves as Asian vis-à-vis non-Asians and Asians alike, in the process contesting cultural nationalism.

Women's practices, however, risked naturalizing class privilege and, unlike the bhangra club-goers, showed little evidence of a broader black British politics. Further, despite examples of gender parody and gender bending in the AU club scene, it remained heteronormative. Finally, the commercialism of the AU scene circumscribed women's efforts to legitimate themselves as Asian, threatening to reinscribe race, class, and gender inequalities. The complex ways in which women drew on AU music and club going to produce themselves as truly Asian highlights the varied ways in which British Asians negotiated ethnic and national belonging in Britain in this period. As in the case of the bhangra and AU producers as well as of bhangra club-going women, these negotiations were not simply about race and nation; rather, they were profoundly shaped by gender inequalities, class differences, and dominant discourses of sexuality.

A Refuge from Bhangra and Typical Asians

The men and women who attended AU clubs largely understood the bhangra scene to be populated by "typical Asians," a concept that reflects both their contempt and envy of this community. These club-goers were in fact drawn to the AU scene because it was interested in advancing nontypical ethnic representations. However, the women in the AU scene, who because of their gender have often grown up dealing with accusations from "typical Asians" that they are not really Asian, found in the AU a way to authenticate themselves and in turn criticize ethnic essentialism.

In my conversations with British Asians from a range of backgrounds, I was struck by how often they used the phrase *typical Asian* to categorize identity. They usually used the term in a disparaging way to refer to someone who embodies the negative characteristics they associated with older and more so-called traditional Asians. These include being closed-minded and conformist, socializing only within one's ethnic group, upholding conservative gender roles, and following a teleology of identity that consists of being, according to one young man, "married, mortgaged, and bored." When young people invoked this term, they usually did so to condemn these others and thereby distance themselves from them.

In addition to claiming that typical Asians were conservative, the largely middle-class fans of the AU who didn't feel so typical often associated them with the working class. For example, Imran Khan, the editor of the glossy magazine *2nd Generation*, which covered the AU, situated typical Asians in a broader, classed narrative about the three different types of Asians in Britain:

> There are three sets of Asian people in Britain. You have your typical Asian people, who really don't care about the wider Britain. They're just happy being insular, being successful within their own communities, and they're predominantly the working class Asian kids who are just happy with religion, with arranged marriages, etc. And then you have the English Asians who are the professionals, who have made their money, who have left, and basically don't want to be judged by the color of their skin or their culture. As far as they're concerned, they're just British people in the wider sense of the word. And then we have people like me: we're never one or the other. A lot of us grew up with conflicts within our own communities, who didn't feel British, who didn't feel Asian, who didn't feel part of their town and all of the normal things that make you who you are.

Notwithstanding the stereotypical representations that appear in this story, it reveals that a binary of being *either* Asian *or* British—a binary further underwritten by class (Asian is seen as working class and British as middle or upper class)—is a dominant framework with which many middle-class British Asians grapple as they come of age in Britain.

Despite the negative connotations of *typical Asian*, however, the fact that young middle-class people use the term reproachfully indicates its power, that is, it represents a kind of genuine Asianness whose perceived lack can produce feelings of guilt and nostalgia. *Typical Asian* is thus doubly valenced: while it evokes the conceit of modernity triumphing over tradition (I'm not typical or backward-looking like you), it can tacitly express the guilt and longing surrounding the absence of tradition (I'm not authentic). These young people experience this lack because they feel both literally and figuratively distant from Asian culture, often because they have come of age in non-Asian areas. This lack stings because the desire to be more Asian than British is not merely a cultural one but also often a political one: it's born of the wish to maintain cultural sovereignty in the face of a dominant, frequently racist Anglo-British culture. And because women bear the burden of reproducing tradition, their position is a tough one: a woman who becomes too British risks being seen by her community as not only inauthentic but also traitorous.

Many middle-class British Asians link the construct of typical Asian to the geographic concentrations of South Asians that exist throughout Britain, patterns created in part by racist housing policies.[6] Asians and others widely refer to these areas as little India, little Pakistan, or little Bangladesh. Describing their social dynamics, Nadia, who grew up in the East End, said, "I don't know what Asian communities are like in the U.S., but in Britain, they're very closed. They are almost like their own little world—you need never leave. You need never have any black friends or white friends." Within these areas, various subcultures of youth have emerged, among which bhangra is prominent. Though some AU club-goers had lived in these areas, using a chain of signification that links typical Asians with bhangra fans, all of them defined themselves against what they perceived as bhangra's insularity.

As middle-class British Asians, women who frequented AU clubs often came of age outside of Asian-dominated neighborhoods, schools, and communities and therefore often felt, as did their male counterparts, ethnically illegitimate. But, as women, the demands they experienced to reproduce Asian culture made their feelings of illegitimacy doubly difficult.

During their time at school, for example, their peers' use of racial epithets such as "coconut," a long-standing insult used to characterize a South Asian person, reinforced their sense of being ethnic outsiders. Many grew up haunted by the feeling that perhaps they are "too white." Anju, for example, said, "The only actual overt racial stuff I got was from Asians of the 'you're not a proper Asian' type stuff." Saba, Nadia's older sister, who also grew up in an Asian neighborhood, was subjected to racial epithets as well. Though careful not to indict Asian communities alone for having what she calls a "sheep mentality," she nonetheless drew attention to the consequences she experienced from such an attitude: "I never, ever had a real sense of just being *wholly* Asian.... I never used to hang around with Asian kids at college. And I used to be called a coconut when I was at college... and I was like, *why*?! And I always used to think... basically, I don't have that mentality. And that kind of sheep mentality actually takes place not only within the Asian community, it takes place in all kinds of groups.... where you have people following a similar thing, and there's a few people that don't, and because they don't... they get [called out].... In fact, most of my friends at university were white or black."

These women appropriated AU music and clubs to validate their Asianness, in the process belittling typical Asians and the bhangra music scene. Women often used the construct of typical Asian and the associated sheep mentality to denigrate what they perceived as rampant conformity among other Asian youth and to instead stress their individuality. For example, Anju, who is Gujarati and grew up in an upscale, mostly white area of West London, repeatedly said that she found young Asians in London to be incredibly narrow-minded and conformist: "They dress the same, talk the same, like the same music, same places. It's a real sheep mentality.... [There's] no scope for individuality at all." During her early years of schooling, her Asian peers criticized her for not regularly socializing with them. Later, her experience of dating a white man crystallized her sentiments about typical Asians. Her younger sister's predominantly Asian friends found it difficult to communicate with her boyfriend, a fact that, for her, was only further testimony of their closed-mindedness, a quality that she implies is absent from her own group of close friends. Similarly, Mina, who is also Gujarati and middle class but grew up in northwest London in the heart of a Gujarati community, chose not to associate with her university's Asian society because she felt the members were all conformists: "All Asian youth seem to be typical: they look the same, dress, speak the same, listen to the same music, go to the same clubs.... They are intelligent people, but it is the whole sheep attitude. They all have mobiles, listen to R&B.... They are proud of who they are, but don't embrace anything else."[7]

Nadia explains how bhangra music came to represent typical Asians and how she turned to other forms of music in order to express her own distinctive identity: "I normally don't listen to as much Asian music; it's normally cheesy bhangra stuff that I hate. Because of the whole culture associated with it, and because I grew up in an Asian area, it was one of those things I wanted to get away from. So, you know, the norm was to listen to bhangra music and all the Hindi film music and be into all the film stars, so I went totally the opposite way and got into the Smiths, and that sort of indie music. I think that was sort of a rebellion thing." Nadia's experiences resonate with those of several other women who, in remembering their past, describe their experiences of being rebels in school and their interest in musical forms other than that of bhangra in order to express that rebellion.

Despite women's rebukes of Asian communities, typical Asians, and Asian culture, however, none of them rejected the idea of being Asian. They held instead to a more ambivalent identification. Situating herself between the Asians who only hung out with one another versus those who associated with whites, Nadia said, "There were quite a few Asian people at university, but they either tended to be the sort that would immediately join the Indian and Pakistan societies and stick among similar sorts of people or totally reject it and mix with exclusively white people. Or people like me who—because my course was an Arabic course, it was kind of a mix; it was kind of ethnic anyway, so I had kind of both. I mean the whole Asian thing isn't something that I'd run away from.... I feel comfortable in it; but then again it's not something that I would choose to surround myself with twenty-four hours a day." These women were distancing themselves from typical Asians, yet trying to find a way to be authentically Asian. As I show later, AU clubs, as spaces that felt Asian but weren't only for Asians, enabled them to produce themselves as such.

Critiquing Gender Politics

Women who attended AU clubs condemned typical Asians as a way of dealing with their middle-class and hence supposed ethnic outsider status. But they also used this construct to call into question the sexist aspects of the bhangra scene and, more broadly, of gendered power relations within Asian communities. For example, Swati had enthusiastically responded to a sign I had posted in Anokha requesting interviews with club-goers. We decided to meet at one of her favorite cafés in central London. Accompanying her was her friend Parmjeet, who, by the end of the interview, was an active participant. At the outset Swati made several emphatic statements about music: gesturing to her position as a racialized diasporic subject and to her sense of having a fractured identity, she claimed that music has the ability to mark and map people. And here she identified AU music as a form that made her feel "whole":

> SWATI: We still go through racism, but it's very different to the racism that our parents have. . . . We have to constantly rehistoricize to find who we really are. Just going back to tellin' stories and listening to stories. . . . So that's why I think that music is important because it's global, it's accessible, and it's something that marks us as people—it puts us on the map more or less.
>
> FALU: Why are you particularly drawn to Asian Underground music?
>
> SWATI: It's like a sense of belonging. It's like when you have déjà vu, and you just . . . really feel comfortable. . . . I really relate to it . . . you feel whole because it's everything that you've ever known, all put into one.

It became clear that her personal history powerfully shaped the connections she made to this music. Swati grew up in Manchester as part of a working-class, Hindu Punjabi family that had experienced upward mobility. In addition to the alienation she already felt from her culturally different white neighbors and an overly watchful Asian community, her upward mobility caused her to feel estranged from her working-class Asian friends and her new, predominantly white, middle-class schoolmates. Swati also struggled intensely with her family, particularly with her parents' moral injunctions about good and bad Asian girls. Her description of her father's reaction to discovering she had been dating a Muslim boy dramatizes her predicament: "He was just so horrible about it, he actually called me a whore, you know. And he said, 'I couldn't believe that a daughter of mine would do something like that to shame the family.' . . . It's just such that whole kind of emotional blackmail, and the guilt trip, and he wouldn't only just take it out on me, but he'd take it out on my mum. And the whole family suffered, and my mother then found out that my grandmother had got cancer, and my dad said it was my fault, you know . . . all that kind of thing."

Swati ultimately found herself needing to escape to London, a city that promised anonymity and an opportunity to remake her identity. As a university student she began participating in the rituals of college life, which for many Asians included going to bhangra events. She had grown up listening to bhangra and other Punjabi folk music, and her fluency in Punjabi and Hindi allowed her to enjoy what she called the *masthi*, or playfulness, invoked in the lyrics of bhangra tracks along with a host of cultural references to which she could relate. After attending some events, however, she stopped listening to bhangra: not only was it no longer as "rootsy," but, more significant, she discovered that bhangra was now part of a club scene in which she felt incredibly uncomfortable because of the violence that occurred there between men and men's harassment of women: "I didn't like the atmosphere. It was a whole group of Asians locked in one room, with too much adrenaline, starting fights. It was really childish.... It's as if they were *so* repressed that when they saw any female that looked half decent, they'd want to, not just look, but it was like *real attack*—it was touchin' and 'how are you doing, darlin'?' It was so blatant that I just couldn't handle it." In an indictment of gender roles that Swati extended to her community, she explained that women like her found themselves caught between patriarchal notions of tradition and modernity that circumscribe women's behavior: "Women [are] accepted as long as they don't talk to too many men at the same time. They can be 'modern,' and they can enjoy music and dance, but as long as they stick to their boundaries. And if somebody's girlfriend chats to another guy, that's a real no-no, because in my culture . . . it is machoistic, and it's all about having possessions, and a woman is a possession, and nobody else touches her." Parmjeet and other club-going women shared Swati's sentiments: they enjoyed listening to bhangra (especially since, for some, it held an important role in family rituals), yet they were dismayed by the ways in which clubs sanctioned misconduct toward women.

In their criticisms Swati and Parmjeet were not reacting simply to their experiences of bhangra club going. A historical framework informed their perspectives: they said that in the 1980s young people found bhangra to be politically important, as it provided them with a kind of self-representation. Despite the fact that young British Asians were obtaining educational credentials and jobs, they still felt culturally alienated, and that alienation played out in a constant battle between their families and Anglo-British communities. Parmjeet said, "Young British Asians needed an answer. They needed something that could say, 'This is *us*, this is *ours*, and up yours!'"

As a form of self-representation, however, bhangra failed many of its female fans. Women like Swati and Parmjeet not only found the gender politics of the bhangra club scene problematic, but also objected to men's use of bhangra to justify the mistreatment of women by equating enjoying it with being authentically Asian. Parmjeet said she was accused of not being Asian because she disliked going to bhangra clubs: "I went to one bhangra gig, and I will never go again. These guys had a bet between them regarding whether I'd go. They kept accusing me of being a 'wannabe' Asian. I said I'd go to prove something to them, but I left by midnight. It was that bad. I *hated* it."

Through their engagement with AU music and clubs, women constructed new forms of ethnic identity and community. In light of their experiences, for example, Swati and Parmjeet felt that the emergence of AU music was politically important. For Swati, this music represented the diversity of British Asian experience: "This music wasn't just us saying, 'Hey, we're Asians, we exist.' It was saying, 'We're Asians, we've been brought up in Britain, we've been brought up in all different parts of Britain, and we have very different experiences.' Some of us come from very working-class families, some upper-class, some filthy rich, but we still need something to identify with . . . to represent us . . . that draws in all of the influences that we've grown up with." Parmjeet, who likewise felt she could relate to AU music, emphasized the need for a new politics of representation given her sense of being stuck between racist whites and closed-minded Asians: "I think what was quite important was for people who didn't actually like bhangra, there had to be an alternative form of music because you were . . . called a coconut. . . . I think the problem is that we get stereotyped by the white community, which is hard enough to deal with. . . . And if you don't conform to their stereotypes, then when you talk to the Asian community, you then get stereotyped—'You don't like bhangra? Don't you think you're one of us?' And it's like you can't be anything but those two things. And it pisses me off . . . and it's only until someone like Talvin's stuff came along, and I thought, yes, I relate to that . . . that's everything I've been wanting to say for so many years." As Parmjeet indicates in her comment, "You can't be anything but those two things," that is, either a proper Asian who is into bhangra or a coconut, constructing and claiming a British Asian identity meant, to her and to other women, struggling with Anglo-British *and* South Asian communities. Given that they experienced bhangra clubs as spaces that equated being Asian to enduring gendered strictures and harassment, many of them found bhangra music and clubs to be problematic sites through which to represent or, really, produce themselves as Asian people. In contrast, these women embraced AU music and clubs, which, by providing them with another kind of representation, enabled them to denounce violently gendered notions of what constitutes true Asianness and, at the same time, produce themselves as authentic.

The AU Club as a Safe Space

In their attempts to stage an Asian aesthetic, AU club promoters tried to create a "chill vibe." These efforts were successful, as the ambience of AU clubs became one of their major selling points. Asians and non-Asians alike roundly extolled social interactions in clubs, which they characterized as being friendly, chatty, nonjudgmental, and a welcome break from other clubs in London in which the dominant ethos was about being seen and having attitude. They felt that one could go to Anokha just for a drink or to enjoy the music, something that was impossible at mainstream clubs.

While the "chill" meme arguably represents a social interactional style that is middle or upper class, the image and forms of sociality of AU clubs held different meanings for their racially diverse audiences. For some of its white participants, the clubs instantiated a familiar and appealing image of South Asia as a site of spirituality, an image that accords with a colonial imaginary still present in Britain.[8] For much of its Asian audience, however, given the long history of racism in which whites prohibited Asians from entering dance clubs or inflicted violence on them once inside, AU clubs provided a feeling of relative safety and a sense of belonging. The clubs also afforded a space in which alienated youth—in Khan's words, youth "too British for Asians, and too Asian for the British"—felt a sense of comfort and freedom.

For British Asian women, however, the ethos of these clubs held an additional set of meanings: Swati, Parmjeet, and other avid club-goers said they enjoyed AU clubs because the focus was on the music or on being at ease rather than on an aggressive sexual attention to their bodies (the harassment of women was in fact rare). More subtly, they didn't feel judged by others in these spaces. As noted, having grown up in middle-class homes and therefore outside of concentrated Asian areas, these club-goers felt they weren't genuinely Asian. But as women they experienced acute frustration when others negatively evaluated them. For example, Harsha, who is Gujarati by background and who grew up without having much contact with Asian communities, emphasized, as did many other women, how much she disliked it when other Asians judged her. The content of her narratives and the depth of her discontent show that her feelings are linked not only to her membership in a British Asian community but also to being a *woman* in that community. I excerpt her narrative at length, as it is one of the most elaborate statements of why AU clubs felt like safe spaces to women:

> That was its pulling power for me because of the fact that my parents split up, and I wasn't going to weddings every weekend, and I wasn't going to have an arranged marriage . . . and yet, I'm Indian. . . . You know, I speak Gujarati. . . . It's a very odd situation that I'm in anyway. Like the schools I went to—I didn't go to places where there were lots of Indian people, things like that, so that's why when I came back [to London] from my master's, that's why it was *so* wonderful to be in a space where they didn't ask you what caste you are, what your background is. Nobody *cared* about that kind of shit, right?
>
> Because of the situation . . . we don't have a sense of the Indian community. My mother doesn't have lots of Indian friends.
>
> A lot of my uncles married English women, a lot of my cousins are half English, half Indian, and so, it brings things into an openness. We're not closed in any sense; we're always receptive to being open, and that's what Ma's always taught us. Yet, she's, of course she's an Indian mother. She had an arranged marriage, blah, blah, blah. . . . *all right it didn't work, which is why she's not going to force that on me.* But . . . she said something funny last year; she was saying, "God I just have this feeling you'll probably end up marrying an English person." And I looked at her, I said, "Ma, for the first time in my life I'm actually meeting people who are like me because of this scene."
>
> That's why for me it was amazing, brilliant to come back to London [after college] and have this thing. Suddenly, I was going out and meeting people who were . . . not judgmental. . . . As an Asian woman, I have that in my subconscious from the whole thing that happened to Ma. You know, my mother's gone through that, she's always going to have that element of fear of judgment.
>
> Bumping into the same people everywhere was nice. You actually felt part of something and that was a really good feeling, which is rare in London. Also, for me, not being part of a community as such, it was a really important thing for me.

Gender structures Harsha's feelings of being judged. A note of defensiveness tinges her discussion, evidence of the power over women of hegemonic constructions of Asian identity and the sense of lack they experience when they feel they are not proper Asians. For example, after acknowledging that her parents separated and that she didn't participate in particular rituals, for example, attending weddings or having an arranged marriage, she maintains, "And yet, I'm Indian." As she narrates how her mother's divorce impacted her, she says that her mother's fear of judgment had entered her own subconscious—"as an Asian woman," she is sensitive to the stigma of not having fulfilled the demand that women reproduce culture and community by marrying South Asian men. Gender also appears in her focus on marriage-related signs of Indianness: weddings, divorce, and arranged marriages. Finally, Harsha links her mother's situation, which she again describes defensively as, "She had an arranged marriage . . . all right, it didn't work," to her own, with both of them expressing concern about Harsha's marital fate. Harsha's newfound connection to the AU scene eased her feelings of lack and her awareness of not having lived a properly Asian life: not only did she now feel that she is part of an Asian community, but she was also hopeful of finding an Asian partner, as she was, "for the first time" in her life, meeting British Asians who are "like her."

The AU and Racial Identity

The emergence of the AU generated much racial pride among its British Asian fans, who felt they now had music and spaces that were theirs and not just something typically Asian or another imitation of black or white youth culture. Implicitly referring to the ways in which British bhangra has drawn on such music as dancehall, ragga, and hip-hop, Mina said, "The Asian Underground isn't about Asians borrowing as they have for years and years—it is not just a black thing." Notably, however, club-goers' powerful assertions of racial pride relied on the presence of multiracial audiences in clubs and on the AU's mainstream success. In other words, British Asians' expressions of racial pride crucially depended on the attention of black and white youth who were witnessing them succeed. Consider, for example, Parmjeet's reflection on a moment of recognition she felt all Asians could share: the playing of a popular Hindi track from the classic film *Sholay* (1975), one of the most successful films in Indian film history: "I think what was quite interesting was when we were at Anokha that one night because there would have *never been a time* where you would have heard a song from *Sholay* in a *club* full stop. It was *brilliant*, because as soon as we heard it, all of our faces just lit up, didn't they? And it was this moment where we realized, Hey, this is becoming more mainstream. I mean Anokha's really big now. It's jam-packed every time you go there. And all of us Asians looked up, and knew *exactly* what the song was. That film represented our entire childhood! And it wasn't something that we had to share. That one minute was for us saying, as Asians, all of us here know that song, and nothing can destroy that." Here, Parmjeet's joy is based on a collective recognition between Asians that gains its strength by marking a difference between the insiders (Asians) and outsiders (everyone else).

Although many AU club-goers experienced new pride in claiming an Asian identity, women appropriated club spaces in gendered ways, as they drew on the racial diversity of audiences to produce themselves as legitimate British Asians. For example, the fact that AU clubs had a multiracial character yet were still seen as Asian enabled middle-class women, whose lives traversed black, white, and Asian communities, to bring their non-Asian friends and partners along. Anju said, "Anokha is nice because it has a mixed crowd and different music. I can deal with different music, but the crowd is also really, really important. I bring different friends, and I go really often." By exercising the freedom they felt in clubs to associate with a "mixed crowd," women contested cultural nationalist norms that mandate that women marry and create families exclusively with South Asian men.

Women adopted liberal discourses about the role of this music in a multiracial Britain. Anju said, "It's an advantage to have a mixed crowd because I believe that we're all living together, and there are things that we can take and give to each other as communities. Also, music is something that should bring people together—that's an important thing that art should do. It should allow people to look at all the things that are different about them and that are the same about them." Thus, in complex ways women club-goers drew on the AU scene's racial diversity and its cool cachet to sanction their identities vis-à-vis non-Asians, that is, through a discourse of racial pride like Parmjeet's, and vis-à-vis their Asian peers, that is, by enacting particular forms of sociality and espousing a liberal position about Britain, as Anju's stories show. In other words, women could draw on the fact that AU clubs were mainstream and were enjoyed by different racial groups, yet still considered Asian, to legitimate their Asianness to non-Asians. To Asians, they could justify their mixing with a multiracial crowd as an activity that didn't result in them losing their Asianness.

Because the AU scene could stand for Asian culture itself, women used it to produce themselves as Asian in other ways. For example, it could help them heal the lacunae they felt as a result of being geographically distanced from Asian communities. Having grown up in a predominantly Asian area in London surrounded by her relatives, Mina left for Cardiff to attend a predominantly white college. Soon after she began experiencing "a craving for Indian culture," one she later claims was satisfied by listening to AU music: "You're by yourself.... You are quite alone ... obviously you've got friends and stuff, but.... For some reason, cause you're away from London, you're away from your family. I guess it's a kind of homesickness, isn't it? When you want to have ... I don't know, it just suddenly became cool to be interested in your culture and stuff.... I suddenly found that it was cool to me."

Women's narratives showed that AU music also had a powerful ability to confer Asian identity *on* them. For example, Rubia, whose mother is Anglo-British and whose father is Pakistani, and who grew up in a white suburb, said that as a child she was not aware she was in any way Asian. When I asked if she had ever experienced racism, she said, "I had an easy life; I didn't feel Asian half the time." She recalled that other than once being called black, a comment whose derogatory tone she didn't understand at the time, her teachers and peers were polite to her. She also didn't feel Asian in her upbringing: her father did not emphasize Asian or Pakistani culture beyond insisting on *halal* food. When she moved to central London a few of her new Asian friends, who jokingly call her a pretend Paki, decided to take her along with them to Anokha.[9] There, Rubia became interested in learning about her culture by listening to the music and by socializing with her newfound "Asian brothers and sisters."

Revisiting Liberation Stories

Women's relationships to the bhangra scene and to typical Asians as well as to the forms of sociality and the racial constitution of AU clubs reveal an imagined community they were creating for themselves. One can read the way these women inhabit club spaces as a form of resistance: they denounce essentialist notions of Asianness that see it as only working class as well as sexist and cultural nationalist norms that police women's behavior. In turn, they produce themselves as legitimately Asian. However, their middle-class status, their racial pride, the heteronormativity of club spaces, and the AU's commercial success circumscribed this resistance.

Women's identities as middle-class subjects resurfaced in some of the ways they crafted their identities, particularly in class guilt and in the kinds of cultural capital and discourses of individuality they sometimes used to authenticate themselves. Class guilt impacted AU women in such a way that their efforts to claim that they were genuinely Asian risked resignifying British Asian identity as only middle class; they thereby risked naturalizing class privilege. Despite the efforts of many women to distinguish themselves from the typical Asian, that figure often remained for them a site of nostalgia, guilt, and lack. This imagined other often shaped women's sense of who they are supposed to be, destabilizing their carefully constructed status as authentic. My discussion with Tehmina shows how women struggled with their liminal positions. I met Tehmina at Anokha one night, sitting upstairs in the chill out room of the Blue Note. We struck up a friendly conversation, and she agreed to be interviewed at her house in South Kensington. Upon arriving at the tube station, I was surprised that her family resided in such a wealthy area, one that boasted arty boutiques, well-heeled patrons, terraced white homes, and small sculptured parks. It was rare for an Asian family to reside in one of the most upscale areas of central London, far from the less well-off, densely populated neighborhoods in London's outer zones. Tehmina greeted me cheerfully, and we went into the living room to start the interview.

Before I had a chance to glance at my list of questions, Tehmina started talking about her impressions of a bhangra club called the Limelight. She knew I had come to interview her about the role British Asian music played in her life and began by telling me she found it interesting to think about her experiences as well as what they might represent more broadly. I turned on the tape recorder to signal that we might as well begin the interview. But the idea that her ruminations were now being officially recorded was briefly jarring to her, and her thoughts quickly began shifting around what kind of discourse she should engage in and offer. Her hesitations, which marked the spaces between what she really thought and what she should not think or say, went on to inform the entirety of our discussion.

At the start of the now-official interview Tehmina began describing the youth that frequented bhangra clubs in a disparaging way, one that emphasized how she was different from them. She said, "They're usually working-class kids from Asian neighborhoods who are kind of uneducated and a little bit backwards." But in spite of these initial remarks Tehmina began to admit, in a somewhat embarrassed tone, that she actually enjoyed bhangra nights at the Limelight because the club attracted Asians who made her feel as if she belonged to something. That something was not merely a social scene, since she never actually came to know anyone at the Limelight, but referred to her ethnic identity as an Asian.

The feelings of estrangement and longing that can impact middle-class women's relationship to Asian identity became evident as Tehmina elaborated that she felt as if she did *not*, in fact, belong at the Limelight because the other youth at the club were much more Asian than she was. This realization introduced an anxiety in Tehmina that maybe she was not Asian at all and that she had attended bhangra clubs only because she was trying to be Asian, as some kind of fraud. But Tehmina, not feeling comfortable with this idea, once again shifted positions. This time she recast all of the contests around ethnic authenticity as problematic: "[We'd say,] 'Oh they're really typical.' It was just a stereotype that you had in mind. And for some reason we kind of decided that we weren't *as* typical. But in fact it was all very dodgy because what you perceived as being really Asian was to do with class and education and style."

As Tehmina began discussing her involvement in the AU scene, her ambivalence resurfaced. She said she often frequented clubs like Anokha because she enjoyed the ways in which they were "self-consciously Asian." But she remained suspicious of its commercialism. Referring to its white fans, she said, "You look at the people who go, it's a very middle-class, wannabe trendy crowd. It doesn't feel *real*, really. It's *in* at the moment, and you always think of them as being there because of that." But then she extended her criticism of Anokha's consumers to Asians, hesitantly and uncomfortably implying that maybe *they* were not real: "I think the Asian Underground types *are* very different to the type of people who were going to Limelight. I don't know, because both groups are very into the Asian thing. But I suppose I think of them as being less . . . do you know what I mean? They *are* different." In the next moment, as her ambivalence resurfaced, Tehmina began to lay claim to a legitimate ethnic identity by arguing that the AU scene was, in fact, truly Asian because of the kind of music it drew on. Here, like Mina, she contrasts AU with bhangra, which she sees as black: "It's possible that the Asian Underground types are into the *more* authentic Asian thing cause the ones going to Limelight are listening to hip-hop. And these guys are listening to their *own* thing. So maybe I'm more into it because I think that this is more authentically Asian." Notably, her description elides both the Western beats of AU music and the Asian elements of British bhangra.

Tehmina's narrative highlights the tensions of being a young, middle-class, British Asian woman: ethnic nostalgia powerfully shapes women's cultural identities and sense of belonging. Just as the working-class youth at bhangra clubs represent a more authentic other through which Tehmina experiences a kind of desire and disgust, her middle-class background produces in her a sense of guilt and betrayal that causes her to cast AU youth as not really real. At the same time, she credits the musical sources of AU as being more Asian, not borrowed, not black. While reflecting on her feelings prompts Tehmina to dismiss the idea of ethnic authenticity, she occupies an unstable position in her efforts to simultaneously lay claim to one. Moreover, she does so in a way that privileges her class status. In fact, while she and others extensively commented on the bhangra scene (the music, participants, and club scene), women who went to bhangra clubs either knew nothing about the AU scene or didn't take any interest in it—it wasn't in their orbit. This fact further reveals the circumscribed parameters of their lives in contrast to those of women who attend AU clubs.

Tehmina's narrative suggests that women argue that AU music is more Asian than bhangra in order to authenticate their identities. The narratives of Ritu and Parminder, two club-goers who, like Tehmina and others, were avid music lovers, reveal how middle-class forms of sociality and knowledge shaped women's relationship to music in ways that could recast Asian identity as normatively middle class. Ritu and Parminder said they enjoyed going to AU clubs because the focus was on an appreciation of the music itself. They took particular pleasure in how AU music remixes classical sounds with modern dance music, especially since they could understand and relate to the classical references. Such pleasure, in turn, became a form of cultural competence that they tacitly and sometimes explicitly used to produce themselves as truly Asian.

Another example of women's musical knowledge and tastes being tied to class is Mona, who grew up in wealthy surroundings having little contact with Asian communities and who feels a sense of lack as a result. She said, "Talvin Singh's music draws on references that relate to me directly. I wasn't brought up in a household that watched Indian films all the time. There was a time when we had a restaurant, and of course we played film music, and the waiters all loved it. But we were brought up on classical music. Because of that influence, I could hear Talvin's music on many levels." Many women had sufficient cultural capital, that is, the class-based knowledge, skills, and worldviews that are passed on in families and that provide societal advantages, to enable them to understand the references to classical instrumentation in AU music.[10] They used this knowledge to claim their so-called true

Asian identity, thereby linking their middle-class status to ethnic authenticity. Accordingly, these moments were not simply claims about their own identity but risked naturalizing class privilege within the South Asian community at large.

Finally, the discourse of conformity they sometimes used to disparage typical Asians and the language of individuality they used to describe themselves reinscribe the liberal humanist ideologies that the AU artists perpetuate. These discourses thereby also reproduced class privilege. Recall, for example, Anju's statement, "[Typical Asians dress the same, talk the same, like the same music, same place.... [There's] no scope for individuality at all," and Mina's statement, "All Asian youth ... look the same, dress, speak the same, listen to the same music, go to the same clubs.... They are proud of who they are but don't embrace anything else." These statements resonate with those of AU artists, who stress their individuality as artists. Recall, for example, Sawhney's statement in his liner notes to *Beyond Skin*: "My identity and my history are defined only by myself—beyond politics, beyond nationality, beyond religion, and Beyond Skin." Such liberal humanist narratives not only center a masculine subject but also reinforce class hegemony: they distance themselves from any form of collective identity in society and thus from the forms of power by which these identities arise, such as gender and class (see chapter 2). The views of progress embedded in these narratives sustain class dominance by suggesting that the working class is backward while the middle and upper classes are modern.

The racial pride women exhibited at Anokha was about articulating an Asian identity that is unique from a white or, especially, a black identity. Recall, for example, Mina's statement, "The Asian Underground isn't about Asians borrowing as they have for years and years—it is not just a black thing." Yet such statements elide the ways in which some AU music draws on black expressive forms such as jazz and jungle (a genre that incorporates elements of Jamaican music culture prevalent in London). It also ignores the ways in which bands such as ADF lyrically call attention to the similarities in the colonial and postcolonial struggles of black and Asian communities in Britain. Furthermore, whereas women who frequent both bhangra and AU clubs challenged cultural nationalism by socializing with their black friends in clubs (and, in the case of AU women, with white friends as well), unlike the bhangra women AU women's focus on producing themselves as Asian meant that their narratives rarely evidenced a broader black British politics. Recall, for example, that their assertions of racial pride depended on the attention of black and white youth who were witnessing them succeed; women drew on the multiracial character of the scene and its status as cool to legitimate their identities to non-Asians. This is not to say, however, that these women did not espouse a broader racial politics in other aspects of their lives. The sisters Nadia and Saba, for example, were actively involved in the Stephen Lawrence campaign, which called out institutional racism in the police force and elsewhere. Swati partnered with an Afro-Caribbean man and as a result had to contend with antiblack racism in her family. Yet in terms of club going itself, unlike the case of female bhangra club goers, AU women's focus on producing themselves as Asian tended to elide the influence of black music on the scene and risked reproducing an ethnic absolutist account of Asian identity, the rise of which, in the 1980s, severely undercut black British politics.

Gender inequalities were in some ways challenged at Anokha. For example, there was some evidence of gender play in the visual displays and the club gear, it was not an aggressive heterosexual space in the ways bhangra clubs were, and women didn't feel as bound to the rules of cultural nationalism. Yet the space was nonetheless heteronormative. For example, the two women who identified as lesbian narrated their interest in the scene in largely the same ways that heterosexually identified women did; none of their discussions noted distinct ways in which the scene spoke to them. In fact, the scene offered them less than it did to heterosexual women, as the benefits of attending Anokha didn't extend to their being able to openly express their sexual desires. The alternative forms of desire for sexual partners or spouses and for new ways of articulating Asianness and Asian femininity that the AU scene enabled did not extend beyond heteronormative interests. In contrast, queer clubs like Club Kali, a monthly club that DJ Ritu ran and that played a range of British Asian and non-Asian dance music, were spaces in which British Asian club-goers and others could express nonheteronormative desires even though the club night has historically been male dominated.[11]

Finally, the commercial success of the AU club scene circumscribed women's efforts to produce themselves as Asian. In particular, it troubled the racial pride women felt. Although women were enthusiastic about the scene for the many reasons named above, they felt certain ambivalences about it. In particular, they were highly disparaging of what they called the trendiness of the AU scene, by which they meant its commercialism and thus the precarious balance of power that shaped it. Anju, describing one club, said, "It didn't really feel like an Asian night anymore. Not that an Asian night has to be full of Asians. Maybe it just didn't feel like it was ours."

Gender played a crucial role in women's uneasiness. In the process of staging an Asian aesthetic—in the very act of staking its Asianness—the AU scene heavily relies on popularized Orientalist signifiers of South Asia as a site of spirituality or exotica that are heavily gendered. For example, club décor often consists of saris pinned up on the walls and video monitors that feature women in song and dance sequences from Hindi films. Further, *mehndi* and *bindis* have become popular AU club gear among non-Asians, and AU music often uses women's vocals. These gendered representations could produce a sense of disembodiment among women club-goers, who often felt they were part of the décor of the club to be consumed by others.[12] Tehmina, for example, felt "othered" in a gendered way: "You feel othered at the Blue Note, but it's almost like you're doing it to yourself—in the sense that you're celebrating a lot of things about your otherness—rather than it being thrust upon you. But it would be nice to not feel that it's part of some exotic thing for a mainstream, trendy, white crowd."

Highlighting the gendered aspects of commodification and crossover success, women also took issue with how the representations of South Asian women as exotic manifested in white club-goers' wearing of bindis. Expressing her discomfort with white appropriation, Anju said, "After a while, it was just white hippies with their bindis and their saris, and you don't want to be in that kind of atmosphere." It is in moments such as these that the contradictions of using the AU as a vehicle for ethnic representation, and the ways in which this use is gendered, became most clear. Women objected not only to the ways that bindi-wearing had become a widespread practice in clubs and beyond, but also to how this phenomenon involved them *as* women. That is, the widespread adoption of bindis popularized and naturalized the link between bindis and Asian women at the same time it was appropriated by whites. As Anju complained, "You shouldn't have to stick a bindi on to be accepted by a culture." Women's presence at AU clubs was thus inherently contradictory: while they participated in the scene in ways that challenged hegemonic ideas of Asian and British identity, their presence authenticated the Asianness of the scene to others, reinscribing them as objects of ethnic display.

Conclusion

Women participated in AU clubs in ways that created new ethnic identities and communities. They denounce what they experience as the essentialism and the misogyny of the bhangra scene, legitimating British Asian identities that emerge in middle-class contexts. Women enact these resistances through their participation in the safe spaces of AU clubs—in other words, spaces they see as free of gendered violence and judgment. These clubs enable them to socialize and meet partners in a racially diverse crowd; rather than erase their racialization in the name of a kind of cosmopolitanism, the popularity of these Asian spaces outside the Asian community legitimated the women's own Asianness to Asians and non-Asians alike. But the very vehicles women use to struggles with their outsider status, including liberal ideologies of individualism and progress, and to validate their Asianness, such as cultural capital, can reproduce existing class hierarchies among South Asian communities in Britain. Moreover, the racial hierarchies and commercialism that shape the AU clubs, which position women as exotic signifiers of Asian culture in the eyes of mainstream audiences, circumscribe women's efforts at countering racialized and gendered power relations in Britain at large.

Taking together the practices of women who participate in AU and bhangra club going, one finds that British Asian clubs are not straightforwardly liberating spaces and that gender, race, and class are not, in fact, absent. In both cases, women went to clubs in part to produce themselves as good Asian girls, yet that production takes different class forms and has distinct consequences. For the working-class women at bhangra clubs, class, in conjunction with racism, constrains their life options in such a way that marriage provides the easiest route to respectability. Yet some of their only means of exercising agency positions them on the line between being bad and good. They consequently inhabit a tenuous and constantly negotiated position, sometimes challenging cultural nationalism and at other times reproducing it.

In contrast, the middle-class frequenters of the AU scene must deal with not being considered ethnically authentic in the first place: their middle-class status, which leads to their growing up with, mixing with, and even dating or marrying non-Asians, threatens their identities as Asians. Even worse, as women they risk being considered traitorous for not reproducing their culture. While they use AU clubs to produce themselves as legitimate Asians, in the process challenging cultural nationalist ideals, their class position and the commercialism of the AU scene mean that, even though they enjoy greater agency, they reinscribe class power and are themselves reinscribed as sexualized objects for white consumption.

Women's club going reveals that neither bhangra nor AU clubs are simply "diasporic public spheres." Rather, they are complexly private and public spheres in which women craft identities under the conditions created by a larger project of cultural nationalism. In the case of the bhangra clubs, which are private spaces for Asians to meet and public spaces insofar as authorities discipline only violence between men, gendered violence underpins this project. But the AU club's private and public status as a space that feels Asian but is not only for Asians, a status which has enabled its commercial success, means that commodification shapes women's efforts, at once helping and undermining them.

Conclusion

Bhangra and Asian Underground in the 2000s

Shortly after my sustained period of fieldwork ended in 1999 the cultural politics of British Asian identity shifted. Several events led to the heightened policing of British Asians in general and particularly of Muslim youth. These included the "race riots" that took place in Britain in the summer of 2001 and the events of 9/11 and 7/7. In turn, some youths increasingly identified along religious lines. Perhaps surprisingly these events hardly affected the bhangra and Asian Underground (AU) music scenes: the AU scene was fading by 2001, the central London bhangra club scene ceased because of increasing violence, and bhangra producers became more concerned with industry problems caused by changes in technology and the economy. To the extent these music forms still exist, they continue to be sites through which one can see the ongoing viability and crafting of the identity *British Asian*. As such, they are evidence that British Asians have not wholly abandoned the category of Asian in favor of religious identification. Moreover, while the bhangra and AU scenes changed in the 2000s, many of the themes central to the late 1990s, such as identity, racism, and the mainstream, continue to be central in the new turns and shifts. Yet the celebratory language with which these scenes are described remains largely the same, in scholarship and in public discussions.[1] I sketch here some of the changes in broader cultural politics and in the two scenes and raise questions about recent articulations of British Asianness.

After the Crises

The race riots of the summer of 2001 took place predominantly between young British Asian Muslims and white youth in such cities as Oldham, Bradford, and Leeds. In response to the riots and these new problem areas, the state largely abandoned multicultural policies of tolerating diversity in favor of the project of community cohesion, whose subtext was that Muslim youth lacked core, that is, British, values and needed to assimilate. For example, the government issued a series of reports blaming the riots on the Asian (read: Muslim) community's lack of loyalty to the British state. The main government document, *The Cantle Report*, tied the need for national loyalty to the meaning of British citizenship itself: "A meaningful concept of 'citizenship' needs establishing—and championing—which recognizes (in education programs in particular) the contribution of all cultures to this Nation's development throughout its history, but establishes a clear primary loyalty to this Nation."[2] The report recommended that immigrants swear an oath of allegiance in order to prove their loyalty. Home Secretary David Blunkett supported these proposals and added a few of his own, arguing that applicants for British citizenship should take two exams to enforce respect for "British values, institutions, values, beliefs, and traditions": one that ensures that they speak enough English to be able to maintain an unskilled job and another that tests their knowledge of British history.[3] The report further noted that the reform of young Asians would be central to the future harmony of a multiethnic Britain and urged that they adopt "British norms."

After the riots came the events of 9/11 and 7/7. Horrified that the London bombings were committed by "home-grown terrorists," Britain joined the United States in strengthening its powers in the form of a security state, intensifying its disciplining of Muslims in particular. Collectively, the state's responses to 9/11 and 7/7 bolstered a long-standing Islamophobia in Britain whose prior existence had been evidenced by such events as the Salman Rushdie affair in 1988. The state, however, did not wholly dismiss multicultural discourse as its intensified disciplining of British Asian Muslims and the increased racialization of this group have to some extent been shaped by geography. Because of the histories of immigration, deindustrialization, and institutionalized racism in the areas in which the riots of 2001 occurred, the predominant strife there is between groups understood as being Muslim and white, and the state has focused on policing those areas. In cities such as London, however, there has on the whole been more intermixing and less hostile relationships between ethnic, racial, and religious communities.[4] This is not to say that racial abuse has not increased there, especially for young Muslim men. As Dhiraj Murthy writes about men who live in Bangladeshi neighborhoods in the East End, "A significant number of Banglatown's young British Bangladeshi Muslim men remain ostracized from gainful employment as well as suffer continued physical and verbal abuse."[5] But stereotypes of Asians as terrorists sit alongside discourses of cultural diversity and multiculturalism, which continue to have an active life in London.

For their part, many non-Muslim South Asians responded to 9/11 and 7/7 by identifying less as Asian and more along the lines of religion. As the scholar Arun Kundnani explains, "There was a political mobilization to get rid of the word *Asian* on the part of Hindu and Sikh organizations who wanted to define themselves religiously ... after 9/11. ... Hindus and Sikhs wanted to disassociate themselves from Muslims."[6] This effort led to some bizarre identity claims: in the wake of the attacks of 9/11, Sunrise Radio, a self-defined Asian radio station launched in 1984 and the first independent local radio station to cater to the Asian community in England, was prepared to ban the word *Asian* as a description of its radio station as a result of pressure from its listeners. As Avtar Lit, the chief executive of Sunrise, told Nick Britten, a journalist with the *Telegraph*, in January 2002, "In the last three months, especially, we have received many calls from Indians, Pakistanis, Sri Lankans and Bangladeshis asking us to be more precise when it comes to our news coverage. Hindus and Sikhs feel that Muslims are bringing the Asian community into disrepute in Britain and do not want to be put in the same bracket as them."[7] But while some communities increasingly identified with religion, the bhangra and AU scenes, which underwent many changes in the 2000s, remained sites in which youth crafted British Asian identities.

Whither the Asian Underground?

It's no longer enough to wear your identity or nationality or culture as an emblem. It's not any longer about movements or categories or anything like that.... It's not novel anymore, and the record industry feeds on what is novel.—NITIN SAWHNEY, July 2006

In hindsight one can see that 1999 was in many ways the apex of the AU. That year Talvin Singh won the coveted Mercury Prize and Black Star Liner, another media-defined AU act, was short-listed for it. But then interest in the AU began to wane. As a journalist reports, "For a moment... the 'Asian Underground' stood close to mainstream success. Then Talvin Singh won the 1999 Mercury prize and the public moved on, leaving groups such as Joi to survive out of the spotlight." Over the next several years nearly all of the artists were dropped by their record labels, including the label Outcaste as well as more mainstream ones. The club scene also suffered: while occasional one-off nights feature what is now termed Asian break-beat or Asian drum 'n' bass music, by the early 2000s the vibrant club scene of the 1990s no longer existed. Much AU music continues to have a life, however, albeit in a new context. As Nilanjana Bhattacharjya wrote in 2002, "Although many are struggling to get their latest albums released, their earlier songs are reappearing in an astonishing number of compilation recordings.... British Asian musicians now find new homes for their music among compilations of exotica-tinged lounge music and virtual itineraries for armchair tourists."[8] Such compilations erase aural and cultural distinctions between artists, collapsing them into "an amorphous mélange of 'global ethnic sound,' which they then target to upscale jet-lagged tourists and their aspirants."[9] The musicians and sounds of AU have persisted, then, but largely heard by new audiences.

In the 2000s the enormously successful Nitin Sawhney was the only consistently signed AU artist. Playing to a sold-out crowd at Royal Albert Hall in December 2001 was only the beginning. He has since gone on to complete a wide variety of projects, including producing scores for orchestras, films, theater, dance performances, television programs, ads, and video games.[10] What accounts for the demise of the AU scene and for Sawhney's success? The AU ended for several reasons. Record companies discovered that marketing "movements," such as the AU, had limited profitability and commercial longevity. As Bhattacharjya notes, "The same record stores that once devoted extensive advertising campaigns to British Asian artists in the past now rarely carry any British Asian music albums because 'they don't sell.'"[11] In this sense, the fears of many AU artists were realized. Reflecting in 2006 on the late 1990s, Sawhney, in my interview with him, said the media reduced the cultural change that artists were making to "a fad or fashion," and their music subsequently became "last year's big thing." Audiences became so familiar with the descriptor *East–West fusion*, that it no longer became a feasible way of selling music. Referring to a surge in South Asian–influenced electronica, Sawhney said, "Those sounds have been done to death. The idea of what they call fusing ... music from the East with Western sounds is *no longer* anything new at all.... So if that's all you have, if that's the only string to your bow, then it's very difficult to maintain any longevity.... No one cares what the AU is right now. It's an old term, and it's been and gone. No self-respecting company will look at an artist selling himself that way." Unfortunately, artists strongly associated with the AU, like Singh, have faced a real struggle to remain viable.

Changes in the economic environment of music have exacerbated the problems artists have faced. Because of the massive drop in sales that the music industry as a whole has witnessed because of Internet piracy, companies have become less willing to take risks. As Sawhney explains, "The record companies are thinking differently now.... They're not going back to the next cool thing, they're going back to the next thing that they know consistently sells: white, skinny, indie kids playing guitar ... they're looking for songwriters, they're no longer looking for innovative, clever experimentation."

Outcaste Records, which had once championed AU music, contributed to its downfall. Many of the artists who signed with Outcaste gradually became aware that certain higher-ups were much more interested in profits than in cultivating artists or subverting dominant notions of British Asianness. They discovered that their contracts were exploitative to the point that they were not able to make a living from their work. Sawhney said, "We believed that this was almost like a cooperative situation where we all had a say in what was going to happen. We were very naïve about things." Sawhney entered into a legal battle with Outcaste and was able to leave his contract, and because his album *Beyond Skin* had done so well he was offered a lucrative deal with V2. Others, however, were not so lucky. Eventually, when Outcaste dropped them all, they weren't as commercially viable. Needless to say, some artists became very disillusioned and abandoned the idea of making a career out of music. Other artists, like Shri and Ges-E, who wanted to continue their careers (but not be "slaves to the record companies"), went on to form their own labels. Yet taking that path hasn't been easy. Commenting on Ges-E's label, Nasha, Sawhney said, "Nasha is still making brilliant music" but knew Ges-E was struggling to make a decent living. Other artists, like Joi, have been able to continue work through the world music scene, an arena that many British Asians consider to be outside of the mainstream. And many criticize *world music* for being a catchall category for non-Western music.[12]

Unlike these struggling artists, Sawhney, as noted, has moved on to have a very lucrative career. He attributes this to several proactive steps he took.

From the outset of the AU he did as much as he could to distance himself from the label: "It just didn't feel like it was going to make a lot of sense to stay in something that definitely was going to be last year's big thing." With record labels less prone to taking risks, Sawhney diversified his music and promoted experimentation by working outside the record industry. This was a deliberate strategy stemming from the lessons he learned while with Outcaste: "I never put all my eggs in one basket.... I made absolutely sure after that bad experience with Outcaste that I never allowed my record career to be something of a crutch.... [I]f you want to stay in the music industry, you have to be able to think in lots of different ways." Finally, because Sawhney is a trained musician, as opposed to a deejay, with grounding in piano and guitar and the skills to produce records, he has been able to work in a range of ways.

In looking back at the late 1990s—after 9/11 and 7/7—Sawhney felt that because of the exciting developments in British Asian music and the impact of the Stephen Lawrence campaign confidence grew among Asian artists: "There's always an artistic response now whenever there's injustice towards Asians in this country." At the same time, because of 9/11 there was a shift toward an atmosphere of "incredible paranoia, lying, and racism": "9/11 undermined the credibility of Asians in this country because there is a lot of prejudice and ignorance out there.... [I]t fed into a lot of paranoia, and those people were suddenly able to express themselves, and *that* took a lot of the edge out." This atmosphere had an impact on artists: "There *are* going to be people who want to express themselves artistically against [institutional racism], *but* it's getting harder for them to have a voice or a platform because institutional racism is now *so* accepted ... that it's very difficult to really have any kind of longevity as a real voice against it." Kundnani suggests that in Britain sustained musical responses to 9/11 can be found not in AU music but in hip-hop: "The legacy of the music scene of the 1990s hasn't really dealt with it. Nowadays, the places you'd go as a young Muslim to hear in a musical form some kind of reflection on that whole post 9/11 period would be hip-hop videos that circulate on YouTube."[13]

While it appears that 9/11 and 7/7 have had no serious impact on the AU, and, in turn, that artists have not responded to these events in any sustained way, the identifier *Asian* has an ongoing viability in what can be called post-AU music or Asian electronica. Sawhney, for example, responds to 9/11 as British and Asian, not as a Hindu (a category he has also identified with) and certainly not in a way that fuels Islamophobia. When he played at Royal Albert Hall in December 2001 he made a point of incorporating imagery critical of U.S. president George W. Bush in his performance. In another example, the electronica group Shiva Soundsystem holds an annual Independence Day Mutiny to celebrate India's and Pakistan's independence. Studying this event in the mid-2000s, Murthy writes, "Through the shared musical aesthetic of Asian electronic music, a unique collective bond between ethnically diverse (though it should be said predominantly heterosexual male) British Asians has developed.... British Asians (of Bangladeshi, East-African, Indian, Pakistani and Trinidadian ancestries) from a range of socio-economic and religious backgrounds are identifying with each other through an 'Asian music.'"[14] Furthermore, musicians and attendees considered the event a challenge to "the continuing hegemony of white Britain over its Asian 'others.'"[15]

Bhangra in the 2000s

While the AU scene faded away, the bhangra scene has, perhaps ironically, continued on full force, albeit in different ways than in the 1990s. In the 2000s the popularity of bhangra has grown globally: it is played in nightclubs across Europe, Asia, and the Americas, it has become part of the soundtrack of both Bollywood and Hollywood films, it is used in advertisements, it features in music festivals and exercise videos, and it has become part of an expansive South Asian wedding industry. As one story reports, commenting on its appearance in popular films and global concerts,

> From humble beginnings as the music of poor Punjabi farmers to the Eighties 'Golden Age' and British bands such as Alaap and Heera to today's fusions with hip hop and grime, bhangra has travelled far over the past 30 years. Cast back to the wedding party in *Bend it Like Beckham* when the heroine, Jess Bhamra, tries desperately to slip out of her sari and into football shorts, while the grannies from No. 42 and hunky men in turbans wave their arms in the air and cheer to the rhythms of drummers in gaudy robes and matching turbans: that's bhangra. And at Live8, 2006, when UB40 played with the thunderous drumming of the Dhol Blasters—sinuous female dancers and men in glittering turbans with fan-shaped coxcombs, directed by the leading UK bhangra drummer, Gurcharan Mall: that's bhangra.[16]

A main factor spurring this global popularity was the immense success of Panjabi MC's remix of "Mundian To Bach Ke" with Jay-Z in 2003. But bhangra has had an uneven trajectory in Britain. On the one hand, new artists have emerged, it has become more visible in the public sphere, and new productive relationships have developed; on the other hand, it has yet to attain the mainstream success that the AU did, and the industry continues to struggle for survival.

Britain has seen the rising popularity of what the scholar Rajinder Dudrah has recently called "post-bhangra" artists.[17] As in similar formations, for example, postmodernism and postfeminism, *post* here has a double meaning: many have used post-bhangra to describe artists who became popular chronologically "after" bhangra, that is, AU, rap, and hip-hop artists, but Dudrah uses the term to refer to artists who are influenced or inspired in some way by bhangra music. One example of such an artist is Rishi Rich, who has become a very successful music producer; he has worked with such artists as Jay Sean, a British Asian singer (now signed to Lil Wayne's record label, Cash Money) and his singles have topped R&B charts in the United States. In my interview with Sunni Suri of Metro Music in 2006, he said Rich is "in a league of his own." Sawhney attributes Rich's success to his deep knowledge of music: "He *knows* how to make good beats, he *knows* how to make good records... and he's a musician as well." Sawhney also lauds Rich for giving the bhangra scene more credibility because he knows South Asian as well as Western beats: "You need to be literate in both to cross over."

Bhangra has become more visible in the British public sphere. In 2002 BBC Radio 1 launched a show called "Bobby Friction and Nihal" that featured bhangra and other British Asian music. As a newspaper article reports, this was a critical moment: "The fact that Friction and Nihal's show has a primetime slot on national radio also speaks volumes for the rising profile of British Asian culture. A few years ago it would have been unthinkable to hear a Radio 1 DJ play an unreleased bhangra track to a nationwide audience. Then, in 2003, Panjabi MC's "Mundian To Bach Ke," with its sample from the theme tune to Knight Rider, became a national hit. A huge and vibrant culture, that had hitherto remained isolated, was exposed to the wider world."[18]

Bhangra has also appeared in the worlds of theater and art, which are memorializing it as a part of Britain's history. In the spring of 2010 Theatre Royal Stratford East ran a musical titled *Britain's Got Bhangra*, which "charts the rise of British Bhangra from the sequin clad 80s through to the RNB fusion of the current charts," and marketed it as a family event for all to enjoy, Asians and non-Asians alike. In the world of visual art, the journalist Gurshuran Chana, the scholar Rajinder Kumar Dudrah, and the record label head Punch Ammo have put together an exhibit titled *From Soho Road to the Punjab* that traces the rise of bhangra in Britain, showcasing the stories of individuals who have championed the scene. Composed of press stories, album sleeves, period photography, and promotional art, the exhibit began its tour in 2005 and has traveled throughout Britain to such venues as the Bristol Central Library, the Brunei Gallery in London, and the Art Vinyl Gallery in London. At certain venues there have been accompanying panel discussions and conferences whose aims have been to reflect on the history of bhangra, to build an archive, and to form the pedagogical function of teaching the history of bhangra to younger generations. As Chana said in a panel discussion, "The new generation don't really know history past five years, they don't know what happened in the early seventies."[19]

In addition to the emergence of new artists and music and a higher profile in the public sphere, bhangra has seen productive relationships emerge. For one thing, there are no longer intense debates between the bhangra and AU scenes since the AU no longer exists as a scene. Instead, new institutions have enabled these music forms to be played side by side. One example is the BBC Asian Network, a national radio station launched in October 2002. The BBC describes this network as: "A national digital radio station providing speech and music appealing [to] anyone interested in British Asian lifestyles. The station broadcasts the best in Bollywood and Bhangra music as well as R'n'B & Hip Hop and British Asian Underground. Asian Network also broadcasts news, discussion programme[s], [and] documentaries and reflects British Asian arts and culture."[20]

In January 2006 the BBC significantly boosted its financial commitment to the station in an attempt to mainstream their programming. Friction had joined the network in 2005 and subsequently started a weeknight show called "Friction" dedicated to British Asian music. "Friction" quickly became the flagship show and has won several awards, including the Sony Gold. The Asian Network is very popular in South Asian communities in Britain: in 2010, the BBC's announcement that it might close the network because of a lack of funding galvanized these communities as they engaged in a nationwide as well as a global protest through such social media as Facebook. Another example is Shaanti, a club in Birmingham that features a range of British Asian music. Having deejayed there, Sawhney says, "People are a lot more sussed [aware]. . . . I'll play a load of old Asian Underground stuff, so-called, drum-and-bass and whatever, and there'll be a load of people who will all be into their Bhangra and just as easily dance to [AU music] because they get both."

There are growing transnational connections between bhangra enthusiasts in the diaspora. For example, the exhibit *From Soho Road to the Punjab* traveled to New York City in March 2011. There, it was transformed into *Soho Road: From Five Rivers to Five Boroughs* and included visuals that narrated the impact New York has had on the spread of bhangra, highlighting individuals who have helped further popularize bhangra in the United States. In this new incarnation, the exhibit included items from the personal collection of DJ Rekha, a long-standing deejay named "Ambassador of Bhangra" by the *New York Times* and whose own club, Basement Bhangra, is, as of 2013, in its sixteenth year. The panel discussion accompanying the launch included key figures from both the American and British scenes comparing and contrasting the state of bhangra in each locale, thereby producing a new kind of diasporic conversation.

Notwithstanding all of bhangra's growth, visibility, and travels, its industry faced new challenges in the 2000s. The widespread attention to Panjabi MC's single "Mundian To Bach Ke," as well as to the album *Legalised* on which the track appears, raised many people's hopes that bhangra would cross over into the mainstream. For a while this success represented *the* important moment in British Asian music. As Sawhney said, "Suddenly, everyone was going bonkers about that, and wherever I was being interviewed ... everyone was saying, 'What do you think of Panjabi MC?' And I'm going, Panjabi MC? A while ago you were asking me about Asian Underground. Now it's Panjabi MC." However, the smash hit proved to be a one-off and didn't lead to the sustained presence of bhangra in the mainstream. Indeed, some folks argue that the success of "Mundian To Bach Ke" did not represent the crossover appeal of bhangra at all given that it is primarily a hip-hop track. As Sanjay Sharma argues, "It appears only when Bhangra is mediated through hip-hop for instance does it become properly acceptable for a 'mass' multicultural appeal. (Recall Panjabi MC's track, Mundian To Bache Ke [sic], only being picked up in Britain via the circuitous route of a USA hip-hop DJs remix)."[21]

What transpired was an increased sampling of bhangra and other South Asian music by artists such as Timbaland and Missy Elliot. Bhattacharjya notes, "These days the sampled sound of Indian instruments—a tabla here, a few strums of the sitar there—is so ubiquitous that few people even notice American hip-hop artist Missy Elliot's recent incorporation of a popular contemporary Bhangra song in her latest song, 'Get Your Freak On.'"[22] This sampling led to a round of criticisms about appropriation, as many British Asians and other young diasporic South Asians felt that artists sampled South Asian music without a real understanding of their meanings musically and lyrically. In the hip-hop track "Stomp," on Rich's album of 2006, *The Project*, the singers, who include Juggy D, Jay Sean, and Mr. Phillips, denounce the fact that when non-Asian artists use South Asian samples they become "cool," whereas Asian artists who use them are seen as "typical" and "tacky" and are disregarded by the (Anglo-British) public: "Is it true that they won't play certain music on the radio? / I won't say which one had a problem with this drum / You know the tabla? / The one that Timbaland loves usin', but it's cool in his music / But it's typical and tacky if we use it. . . . Is it true that I really had two top 10 hits? / Yeah! / Any nominations for the Brits? / No! / Any nominations for the Mobos? / No!" In another take, Suri said, "There will never be a mainstream Indian industry, just certain tracks that cross over. . . . People are into Asian-influenced tracks, so technically, it has hit the mainstream. . . . But we should consider when the artists themselves platform as a separate, important thing." In other words, he maintains that because South Asian artists themselves are not being credited, there hasn't really been nor will there be true crossover success.

Suri told me in 2006 that the difficulties facing the industry then, compared to those in the late 1990s, had "only gotten worse." The industry had always struggled: in the words of Ninder Johal, the managing director of the long-established bhangra label Nachural Records, it has always operated as a kind of "cottage industry":[23] it is fragmented and isolated from the mainstream, artists often have limited understanding of contracts, promotion, and management, and there are few centralized institutions governing it. But the problems that have historically troubled the industry have been exacerbated in the 2000s by Internet piracy.

The growth of the Internet, which has made it much easier to distribute and download music freely, has affected music industries globally. But businesses like bhangra, whose sales are small relative to the mainstream, have suffered inordinately. As Suri explains, "Whereas they're selling a million copies of an album, we're just selling one to five thousand . . . so, if 20 percent of sales is piracy, that is a lot of money for us, not for them." Although piracy has always plagued the bhangra industry, Suri said that the problem has expanded tenfold as Internet piracy joins new forms of "old school" piracy. Album duplication is now globalized, and people from countries like India, Pakistan, and China are bringing counterfeited albums into Britain. These new forms of piracy have made regulation nearly impossible.

Because profiting from music sales has become more difficult, record labels have demanded more from their artists, asking them to subsidize the production process as much as possible. As a result, artists have started to form their own labels, releasing their product themselves. Suri argues that this has created another kind of flooding of bad bhangra into the market: the music suffers in quality as the new artist-producer figure now has to reconcile questions of making good music and making profits, a struggle that Suri maintains is inherently conflictual and can lead to the production of poor music. In turn, the market is now flooded with unfamiliar labels, which has led to lower sales because, as Johal said, consumers who historically used familiar labels as a purchasing guide are more discerning because they "know there's crap."[24] Moreover, consumers in South Asian neighborhoods have a hard time finding the music offline at all, as the big music shops like Planet Bollywood have either closed down or, like Metro Music, diversified their inventory. Now, stall keepers, who sell a mix of legal and illegal products, are the main retailers. Thus, while tracks may still gain enormous popularity through clubs and weddings, they do not generate much profit or make the charts because it is nearly impossible to log sales.

In conjunction with the problems posed by Internet piracy and distribution is concern about the deejay/producer figure taking over and the declining emergence of bands. By 2006 the bhangra scene saw the sharp rise of the deejay/producer. Suri explains, "Because it is so lucrative: [a deejay / producer] can hire eight different singers and have really nice tracks for one-third of what a bhangra artist has to do.... And record labels like deejay/producers because there's less money involved in creating a stage identity and presence." The rise of this figure has remained a central issue in the late 2000s, being a focal point of attention in recent panel discussions in the United States and Britain. For example, Shin, the lead singer of DCS, said, "Deejay culture has taken over.... One major factor contributing to this is that bands have grown old, and nobody is stepping into their shoes... then... sampling came in [and the] computer arrived— all contributed to a produced sound versus live sound."[25] It is roundly felt by many of the folks who have now been in the industry for up to twenty-five years that the quality of bhangra music is suffering because of the lack of live bands. As DJ Vips said, "There are a handful of ghost producers, and that's why the industry got boring; the sounds have become very familiar.

... [T]o keep the music live, we have to push the live element."[26] Moreover, the only way current bands have been able to survive is through private functions, weddings above all. Shin explains, "The Asian wedding industry is turning into a multimillion pound business.... Around 85 to 90 percent of my work is private work; it has enabled me to make a career out of it."[27]

Finally, the bhangra club scene in central London has also changed dramatically. While in the late 1990s there was a bhangra club event almost every night, by 2006, Suri said, "it's now really, really gone down." He attributes this to the fact that "fights got so bad that clubs started denying nights." Though there are still one-off events coordinated with college calendars, there are few if any regular weekly nights. Both Suri and Shin indicate that club-goers are more likely to attend an event that plays mostly R&B with a few post-bhangra tracks mixed in. Suri adds, "There's now less interest in going out Monday to Wednesday; back in the day, they were [real] clubbers."

Although the bhangra scene has experienced much change, 9/11 and 7/7 seem to have had little impact on it. Scholars and producers in Britain have had very little or nothing to say about this topic, even when questions have been directly raised in panel discussions. In contrast, Nina Chanpreet Singh's research on bhangra dance competitions in the United States indicates that second-generation Punjabi Sikh men have found in bhangra a way to respond to the phenomena of misidentification both within and outside their communities; *misidentification* refers to turbaned Sikh men being mistaken for Muslims and becoming the target of verbal and physical abuse. She says, "Since 9/11, [bhangra has] been a medium through which young people express a sense of cultural belonging and unity in the face of a lot of turmoil, a lot of rejection, and conflict."[28] In American college-based bhangra competitions, which have skyrocketed in popularity since 9/11, Punjabi Sikh men have dealt with misidentification and mainstream rejection by performing cultural unity and producing allegedly authentic identities; they do so by seizing onto more traditional versions of bhangra in hypermasculine ways. These findings suggest that perhaps one reason there haven't been such responses in Britain is that, in light of the much longer and publicly visible struggles of British Sikh men for religious freedoms (such as wearing the turban in the workplace), the issue of misidentification has in general distressed them much less than their counterparts in the United States. Singh confirms that "the majority of Sikhs in the U.S. represent a second and third generation while the Sikh population in the U.K. is in the fifth and sixth generation and no longer faces misidentification and discrimination to the extent that U.S. Sikhs are currently facing."[29] Kundnani corroborates the notion that Sikhs haven't been attacked in Britain to the extent they have in the United States. Referring to Britain, he says half-jokingly, "This is because our racists are cleverer—they know the difference now [between turbaned Muslim and Sikh men] ... [that is] one of the weird legacies of cultural awareness."[30] While South Asians in Britain have certainly been attacked for "being brown," there has been relatively less abuse of Sikh men due to misidentification.

British bhangra in the 2000s, then, rather than experiencing a heightened identification along lines of religion, similar to AU music, continues to be a site in which the category of British Asian has a strong life. It is telling, for example, that despite the varying content of the BBC Asian Network, bhangra became its prime symbol: as part of the campaign to protest its closure, organizers coordinated the "first ever bhangra flashmob," in which protestors wore T-shirts printed with that phrase and danced to bhangra music. A newly emergent bhangra band, Tigerstyle, composed of two Punjabi Sikh men from Glasgow, crafted a post-bhangra protest song called "Save the Music" to accompany the campaign. This dub-step track samples classic, or old school, bhangra music from Gurdaas Maan's "Peerh Tere Jaan Di," using faster electronic sounds to make the track more mid-tempo. The lyrics, by the rapper Shizzio, argue that the Asian Network is the only solid platform available to *all* Asian artists. The song calls attention to racism by referring to Britain as being "whitewashed," and it hails the Asian community as a single one, united in its diversity and powerful in its numbers. The chorus powerfully equates saving the music to saving "our people" and, in turn, ending the network as "killing us." The song urges all to protest the threatened closure: "Everybody hold hands, barricade stop them / Time for the protest, gotta get tough / An orange wristband just ain't enough / When we all become one we kick up a fuss / No ifs and buts coz this is a must. . . . If we don't complain it's not gonna faze them."

Cultural Politics

This ethnography rereads the late 1990s, a moment known as Cool Britannia, which many consider the high point of progress against racism and of cultural acceptance. It ruptures a teleological understanding of the situation facing British Asians, that is, as one that moved from good in this era to bad after 9/11 and 7/7. This rereading creates a new genealogy of the present, showing that the project of crafting a British Asian identity has never been either unproblematic or truly successful. It also raises questions about current articulations of Asianness in post-AU and bhangra music, such as how forms of difference shape such articulations. For example, do the responses in the post-AU scene, such as Sawhney's, speak to the racialization of all South Asians? or do they elide diversities in experience owing to such categories as religion? Murthy discusses the political solidarities being expressed in the Asian electronica scene, noting (but not exploring) the fact that this scene is heterosexual, male, and middle class. How, then, do class, gender, and sexuality intersect in such post-9/11 musical articulations of Asianness?

Although gender critiques have been more frequently made of the bhangra scene than of the AU scene (even though, as I have shown, questions of gender pertain to the latter) because bhangra is strongly institutionalized, there have been more forums—such as the BBC Asian Network and panels associated with the *Soho Road* exhibit—through which industry folks have reflected on what DJ Rekha aptly calls, "the gender question."[31] As she said in early 2011, "The gender question is horrible, it sucks, but here I am . . . it's male dominated—but what isn't? You just gotta marshal through and go forward."[32] Recent discussions of gender have highlighted that the bhangra industry continues to be dominated by men. Chana explains that it was difficult to find visuals for the *Soho Road* exhibit that pertained to female artists: "We tried to find photos of female vocalists, but they're very few and far between."[33] He explains that while there have been a few women here and there, "they moved on because of their own family commitments. That's generally what the ladies have done."[34] DJ Vips, who in 2008 released an album featuring a female artist, laments, "It didn't get much attention."[35]

There has been some discussion of a couple of women artists. Miss Pooja, who has recently become prominent, seems to be an ambivalent figure at best. Commentators denounce her dominance and, by implication, her contribution to the current perception that all bhangra tracks sound the same. They also contend that, having been raised in India, she doesn't represent "homegrown" talent. Another woman who has received some attention is the post-bhangra artist Hard Kaur, a hip-hop and rap artist whose music has been influenced by bhangra. She is described as someone who "criticises British racism, relishes the power to play with her culture's sexual rules and roles, and encourages women to make their own choices."[36] But while attention to these artists is important, discussions of gender are still largely limited to the lack (or presence) of women artists.

Little is said about the gendered social relations, including constructions of masculinity and femininity, that shape music production and consumption.

PAYING SUSTAINED ATTENTION to the intersections of race, class, gender, and sexuality, this book has illuminated the contradictory ways in which British Asians negotiate the politics of belonging in Britain. Through this account, the book offers tools for grasping the practices surrounding hybrid cultural forms more broadly. It suggests ways of rethinking the relationship of popular culture to constructions of identity and struggles to belong, particularly for those who are marginalized. Rethinking these relationships will help address more adequately the profound questions of ethnic, racial, and national belonging that shape the world.

Notes

INTRODUCTION

1. The Wag Club, which closed in 2001 after seventeen years in existence, has been deemed an "unassailable temple of cool" (Whitney, "The Wag").
2. Dudrah, "Drum 'n' Dhol."
3. In 1999 the musician Talvin Singh and the band Asian Dub Foundation, who were considered AU artists, were listed as final candidates for the Mercury Prize, Britain's most prestigious album award. Talvin Singh won. The band Cornershop, whose lead singer is British Asian, was also listed. In the competition in 2000 another AU artist, Nitin Sawhney, was a finalist.
4. The phrase had a different valence in the U.S. context, where it was used by artists and activists to condemn the criminalization of South Asian and Arab men post–9/11.
5. Austin and Willard, *Generations of Youth*, 1.
6. The term *postcolonial* has been the subject of great debate. Much discussion has focused on whether or not the term homogenizes histories that vary, assumes an overdetermining role of colonialism, implies a linear narrative of history, or prematurely celebrates the end of colonial relations. For these critiques, see McClintock, "The Angel of Progress"; Prakash, "Postcolonial Criticism and Indian Historiography"; Shohat, "Notes on the 'Post-Colonial.'"

    My use of the word draws from works by Hall, "When Was 'the Post-Colonial'?" and Mani and Frankenberg, "Crosscurrents, Crosstalk" who interpret the prefix *post* to mean not the end of colonialism but its ongoing and nonlinear impact. Also, while *postcolonial* is most often used to describe the lives of people living in former colonies, I join recent work that extends it to people living in the countries of their former colonizers, such as South Asians in Britain. As Sayyid says of this population, "Ex-colonial settlers have to be understood within the context of the postcolonial condition" (Sayyid, "Introduction," 5). For a discussion of how this concept applies to South Asians in the United States, see Mani, *Aspiring to Home: South Asians in America*.
7. Ross, "Introduction," 3.
8. Kundnani, *The End of Tolerance*, 180.
9. McGuire, "This Time I've Come to Bury Cool Britannia," *The Observer*.
10. Bhattacharjya, "The Global Sounds of the Asian Underground" (http://issues.lines-magazine.org/Art_Aug02/Nila.htm; accessed July 10, 2011).
11. Conversation with Arun Kundnani, July 12, 2011.

12 Conversation with Arun Kundnani, July 12, 2011.
13 For critiques of this framework, see Brah, "The 'Asian' in Britain."
14 Majumdar, "Notes from the Asian Underground" (http://media.gn.apc.org/award/felixd99.html).
15 A key study is Hebdige's *Subculture: The Meaning of Style*, which argued that young people resisted such institutions as capitalism through style.
16 Paul Gilroy defines "ethnic absolutism" as an "essentialist understanding of ethnic and national difference which operates through an absolute sense of culture so powerful that it is capable of separating people off from each other and diverting them into social and historical locations that are understood to be mutually impermeable and incommensurable" (Gilroy, *Small Acts*, 65).

Studies highlighting resistance include Ballantyne, "Displacement, Diaspora, and Difference in the Making of Bhangra"; Bennett, *Bhangra in Newcastle*; Bennett, *Popular Music and Youth Culture*; Cooper, "Mix Up the Indian with All the Patwa"; Dudrah, "British Bhangra Music and the Battle of Britpop: South Asian Cultural Identity and Cultural Politics in Urban Britain"; Dudrah, "Drum 'n' Dhol"; Gilroy, *There Ain't No Black in the Union Jack*; Lipsitz, *Dangerous Crossroads*; Sharma, Hutnyk, and Sharma, *Dis-Orienting Rhythms*; and Zuberi, *Sounds English*.

17 Lipsitz, *Dangerous Crossroads*, 119.
18 Though the word *hybrid* began being used regularly in the nineteenth century to describe the offspring of two plants or animals of different species, postcolonial theorists have used it to describe cultural forms that emerged from colonial encounters and resisted them. Homi Bhabha uses hybridity to refer to the ways in which colonial power is disrupted in and through its very attempts to deny other knowledges, the traces of which shape colonial discourse and render it inherently double-voiced. Hybridization thus "reveals the ambivalence at the source of traditional discourses on authority" and "enables a form of subversion, founded on the undecidability that turns the discursive conditions of dominance into the grounds of intervention" (Bhabha, *The Location of Culture*, 112). Bhabha's work celebrates hybridity as subversive and as an "active moment of challenge and resistance against a dominant cultural power" (Young, *Colonial Desire*, 23).

Scholars interested in migration, diaspora, transnationalism, and globalization have used the term to describe the identity of persons of mixed race or cultural origin and influence (i.e., immigrants), the cultural production created by "hybrid" persons (i.e., music, language, style), and the actual processes of cultural mixing. Despite this varying usage, hybridity is often mobilized with a common theoretical intent: that is, hybrid identities, cultural products, and practices are often seen as challenging, in novel and creative ways, essentialist norms of culture, race, and nation.

19 For a detailed account of pre–Second World War emigration, see Visram, *Ayahs, Lascars and Princes*, and Visram, *Asians in Britain*. Compared to the groups that migrated after the Second World War, earlier populations were more heterogeneous, skilled, and smaller in number. The earliest settlers were usually

brought over as ayahs (in 1700) or as lascars (in 1780), or they were nobility who journeyed on their own. Between the First and Second World Wars, many left for England because of their involvement with India's nationalist movements, their pursuit of education, or their professional and business interests.

Overviews of South Asian immigration include Ali, Kalra, and Sayyid, eds., *A Postcolonial People*; Fisher, Lahiri, and Thandi, *A South-Asian History of Britain*; Brown, *Global South Asians*; and Clarke, Peach, and Vertovec, eds., *South Asians Overseas*.

20 Brah cites Sami Zubaida: "These cognitive structures (beliefs, stereotype and 'common-sense' knowledge) in terms of which people in Britain experienced coloured [sic] minorities must be profoundly imbued with accumulations of colonial experience. The beliefs and stereotypes acquired and disseminated by generations of working-class soldiers and middle-class administrators in the colonies are available to our contemporaries. Many of these cognitions are derogatory, some are patronizing, a few are favourable, but there is one theme underlying all of them: the inferiority and servility of 'native' populations. In this respect, immigrant communities from the ex-colonies are not entirely new to the British people" (Zubaida, "Introduction," 4).

21 Thandi, "Migrating to the 'Mother Country,'" 165.

22 Brah, "The 'Asian' in Britain"; Fisher, Lahiri, and Thandi, *A South-Asian History of Britain*.

23 See Parminder Bhachu, *Twice Migrants*.

24 The fact that *Asian* is used to refer to South Asians is most likely because South Asians comprise the largest minority population. However, just as *Asian American* has historically elided South Asians in the United States, in Britain, *Asian* and *British Asian* similarly elide the presence of other Asian populations, such as Chinese, Japanese, Korean, Taiwanese, Turko-Kurdish, and Vietnamese communities.

25 Of the categories of nonwhites enumerated in the census, Indians are the largest group (1,053,411), followed by Pakistanis (747,285), "mixed" persons (677,117), black Caribbeans (565,876), black Africans (485,277), and Bangladeshis (283,063). Smaller populations include other Asian (247,664), Chinese (247,403), other ethnic groups (230,615), and black other (97,585).

26 Http://www.bbc.co.uk/news/uk-20687168 (accessed February 14, 2013).

27 See Hall, *Lives in Translation*, for a detailed account of this legislation.

28 Gilroy, *There Ain't No Black in the Union Jack*.

29 Hobsbawm and Ranger, *The Invention of Tradition*.

30 Quoted by Solomos, *Race and Racism in Britain*, 187.

31 Countering legal and extralegal efforts to exclude nonwhite immigrants, British liberals have variously fought for assimilation or integration, paving the way for a domestic "race relations" industry spawned by the Race Relations Acts of 1965, 1968, and 1976. These acts increasingly defined discrimination and gradually extended its prohibition from "places of public resort" to "indirect or unintentional forms" in areas such as employment and housing. They also created, in 1965, a Race Relations Board (RRB) to respond legally to complaints; in 1968, a Community Relations Commission (CRC) to promote "harmonious community rela-

tions"; and, in 1976, the Commission for Racial Equality, (CRE), assigning to it the combined roles of the RRB and CRC and extending its legal power by granting it the authority to initiate its own investigations. While assessments of these organizations have varied (see Brah, "The 'Asian' in Britain," for a critique), the work they have done is undoubtedly important. Yet white aversion to racial others has continued apace.

32 Hall, *Lives in Translation*, 41.
33 Citing research conducted by Clancy et al., the Website for the U.K. Office of National Statistics highlights the levels of risk experienced by ethnic minority groups versus whites: "In 1999, the risk of being the victim of a racially motivated incident was considerably higher for members of minority ethnic groups than for White people. The highest risk was for Pakistani and Bangladeshi people at 4.2 per cent, followed by 3.6 per cent for Indian people and 2.2 per cent for Black people. This compared with 0.3 per cent for White people. Racially motivated incidents represented 12 per cent of all crime against minority ethnic people compared with 2 per cent for White people" (http://www.statistics.gov.uk/CCI/nugget.asp?ID=267&Pos=1&ColRank=2&Rank=176). For the report, see Clancy et al., *Crime, Policing and Justice: The Experience of Ethnic Minorities*.
34 In April 1979, during a protest in Southall against the National Front, police brutality led to the killing of Blair Peach, a white schoolteacher, and to serious injuries sustained by Clarence Baker, a black Briton and reggae singer; this further galvanized South Asian communities.
35 See, for example, Hiro, *Black British, White British*; Parmar, "Gender, Race and Class"; Brah, "The 'Asian' in Britain"; Fisher, Lahiri, and Thandi, *A South-Asian History of Britain*.
36 More recently, scholars such as Tariq Modood have denounced the use of *black* as a broad political category, arguing that it doesn't address the different ways in which Asian and African communities are victimized (Modood, "Political Blackness and British Asians").
37 Studies I have found particularly useful include Balliger, "Noisy Spaces"; Condry, *Hip-Hop Japan*; Diehl, *Echoes from Dharamsala*; Mahon, *Right to Rock*; Maira, *Desis in the House*; Niranjana, *Mobilizing India*; Sharma, *Hip Hop Desis*; Sterling, *Babylon East*; Thornton, *Club Cultures*; and Walser, *Running with the Devil*.
38 As Stuart Hall writes in the context of discussing black identity and representation, "Identity is not as transparent or unproblematic as we think. Perhaps instead of thinking of identity as an already accomplished fact, which the new cultural practices then represent, we should think, instead, of identity as a 'production,' which is never complete, always in process, and always constituted within, not outside, representation. This view problematises the very authority and authenticity to which the term, 'cultural identity,' lays claim" (Hall, "Cultural Identity and Diaspora," 222).
39 Ibid.
40 Foucault, *Discipline and Punish*; Foucault, *The History of Sexuality*.
41 For a critique of this binary, see Swiss, Sloop, and Herman, eds., *Mapping the Beat*.
42 I draw on the genealogy of feminist scholarship that shows that race and gender

are socially constructed systems that are interlocking in such ways that members of the same racial group may well experience gender and other inequalities in fundamentally different ways. This work was inaugurated by Combahee River Collective, *Combahee River Collective Statement: Black Feminist Organizing in the Seventies and Eighties*, and Crenshaw, "Mapping the Margins: Intersectionality, Identity Politics, and Violence Against Women of Color." Intersectional analyses of South Asian women in Britain include Brah, *Cartographies of Diaspora*; Anthias, Yuval-Davis, and Cain, *Racialized Boundaries*; Puwar and Raghuram, eds., *South Asian Women in the Diaspora*. Wilson, *Dreams, Questions, Struggles*; Intersectionality is undertheorized in work on youth subcultures that sees them as unified groups as opposed to ones that have internal divisions and in which the experiences of differently positioned members vary.

43 Here I join scholars who argue that studies of hybridity often delimit objects of inquiry in ways that elide questions of inequality. That is, hybrid persons, products, and process are sometimes imputed to be resistant simply because of their hybrid properties. For an extensive criticism of these studies, see Hutnyk, "Hybridity." My own research counters theories that assert that cultural mixture is in and of itself resistant.

44 Shukla, "Locations for South Asian Diasporas."

45 See Grewal and Kaplan, *Scattered Hegemonies*.

46 Chatterjee, "Colonialism, Nationalism, and Colonialized Women." Also see Chatterjee, *The Nation and Its Fragments*.

47 Chatterjee, "Colonialism, Nationalism, and Colonialized Women," 623.

48 Ibid., 624.

49 Ibid.

50 Ibid., 629.

51 For further discussion of cultural nationalism, see Maira, *Desis in The House*; Gopinath, *Impossible Desires*; Gopinath, "Bombay, U.K., Yuba City"; Bhattacharjee, "The Public/Private Mirage: Mapping Homes and Undomesticating Violence Work in the South Asian Immigrant Community"; Mani, *Aspiring to Home: South Asians in America*; Puri, "Race, Rape, and Representation"; and Wilson, *Dreams, Questions, Struggles*.

52 Gopinath, *Impossible Desires*.

53 Sunaina Maira's important study *Desis in the House* makes similar claims about how the demand to embody tradition impacts the young women who participate in Indian youth club culture in New York City. But studying production and consumption in two differently class-inflected scenes allowed me to develop a more fully intersectional analysis of how women deal with this demand. I show how working-class and middle-class women face distinctive challenges vis-à-vis cultural nationalism and resolve these challenges in contradictory ways.

54 There are a number of excellent studies of class inequalities in U.S.-based South Asian diasporas. These include Bald, "'Lost' in the City"; Das Gupta, *Unruly Immigrants*; Matthew, *Taxi!*; Prashad, *Karma of Brown Folk*; and Rana, *Terrifying Muslims*. My interest lies in the intersections of class inequalities and cultural nationalism.

55 Atkins, *Blue Nippon*; Condry, *Hip-Hop Japan*; Diehl, *Echoes from Dharamsala*; Mahon, *Right to Rock*; and Sterling, *Babylon East*. I share with these studies an interest in how music is a site through which artists and fans negotiate questions of musical authenticity as these dovetail with those of ethnic, racial, and national authenticity. Diehl's *Echoes of Dharamsala*, for example, examines how Tibetan refugees living in exile in Dharamsala deal with their displacement through music. Exploring how Tibetans engage with various song traditions, she shows that in their in-group criticisms, they exhibit an overwhelming desire for ethnic and cultural preservation that in turn reproduces essentialist notions of Tibetan identity. In *Right to Rock*, Mahon explores how the Black Rock Coalition (BRC), a group of New York–based black musicians and writers formed in 1985, struggled with the hegemonic notion that they and the rock music they performed were not "authentically black." She explores "the cultural productions and cultural politics of the BRC in order to illuminate the ways its members produce, perpetuate, and challenge understandings of black identity and culture" (Mahon, *Right to Rock*, 9).

Atkins, Condry, and Sterling have examined questions of race and authenticity in popular music in Japan. Atkins's *Blue Nippon*, for example, examines how Japanese jazz musicians have historically employed various "strategies of authentication" to "counter powerful psychological, institutional, and sociocultural forces" that point to jazz as being African American and that therefore "cast doubt on the authenticity of the art of Japanese jazzers, as 'jazz' and as 'Japanese'" (Atkins, *Blue Nippon*, 12). Condry's *Hip-Hop Japan* focuses on how young people make and remake hip-hop in sites (or *genba*) such as all-night dance clubs and do so in ways that contest dominant models of globalization. As part of his study, he analyzes debates about "the appropriation of so-called black style," arguing that Japanese rappers are engaged in a "new cultural politics of 'affiliation' that draws inspiration from African American struggles while generating distinctive approaches to race and protest in Japan" (Condry, *Hip-Hop Japan*, 20). Sterling's *Babylon East* places questions of race at the center of his study of Japanese engagements with Jamaican popular culture—a rare account of "the transnational cultural exchanges between Japan and a non-Western country" (Sterling, *Babylon East*, 5) and thus of Afro-Asian exchanges. Ethnographically examining a range of performances of social identity, he identifies how these are "complicit with or challenge structural and other forms of racism" (Ibid. 28).

56 Atkins, *Blue Nippon*; Condry, *Hip-Hop Japan*; Diehl, *Echoes from Dharamsala*; Mahon, *Right to Rock*; and Sterling, *Babylon East*.

57 The report *Play It Right*, by the Greater London Authority, notes "The U.K.'s music industry is centred on London, with 90 per cent of activity located there; five of the six multinational music publishers have a significant presence in London; London is the recording capital of Europe, and has around 70 per cent of the U.K.'s recording studios, including the world famous Abbey Road Studios (LFC, 1997)" (Greater London Authority, *Play It Right*, 22).

58 In 2003 "Indians, Pakistanis, Bangladeshis, Chinese, and people of other Asian

backgrounds made up 11.5% of the city's total population" (Greater London Authority, 5). Indians made up the largest group (5.4%), followed by Bangladeshis (2%), "Other Asian" (1.8%), and Pakistanis (1.6%) (Greater London Authority, *Play It Right*, 8).

59 Bhachu, "New Cultural Forms and Transnational South Asian Women," 229. A report by the Greater London Authority in 2003 shows that "the Asian population has a young age structure" and estimates that, from 1991 to 2011, the population will nearly double, while the white population will decrease (Greater London Authority, *Play It Right*, 8.)

60 Livingston, "Foreword," v.

61 Greater London Authority, *Play It Right*, 22.

62 "In the late 1990s, racial incidents" were on the rise: "In 1997–98, the police recorded 13,878 racial incidents in England and Wales, an increase of 6% over the previous year" (Commission for Racial Equality, Racial Attacks and Harassment).

63 Hesse, "White Governmentality: Urbanism, Nationalism, Racism."

64 Paul Watt investigates how "out-of-town" visits have identifiable ethnic or racialized meanings for youth residing in the southeast of England. However, he conceptualizes race as victimization. He argues that Asian youth avoid travel to predominantly white areas, preferring to travel to Asian-dominated areas such as Slough and Southall: "Despite attachments to their local residential localities expressed by many of the black and especially Asian respondents, coupled with the very real threat of racist attacks against them in certain parts of the town . . . we did not find that Asian or black youths lived a *solely* localist existence . . . Southall and Slough were popular with the Asians" (Watt, "Going Out of Town," 693). He further contends that women travel in part to escape "the communal gaze" of the local neighborhood with its "potential effects on family honor": "The same local Asian neighborhoods which can offer safety from racist attacks and a positive sense of identity could also be seen at the same time as a source of constraints and restrictions on behavior by some of the young women" (ibid., 694). He concludes that "Southall and Slough did act as focal points in a wider regional South Asian geography of the Home Counties west of London in that they represent centers of Asian populations which afford the capacity to partake in youth leisure activities, notably Bhangra gigs, and consume products which are emblematic of 'Asian-ness'" (ibid., 696). In this account, young people's actions are driven by an avoidance of racist areas (race equals racism) and a pull toward Asian areas to participate in what remains an uninterrogated Asian identity.

65 Scott, "The Evidence of Experience."

66 There were two other AU women who were not as prominent but who were nonetheless present "behind the scene": Shazia Nizam, who managed the Outcaste record label for five years, and Sweety Kapoor, who was in charge of running the AU club Anokha.

67 Here my work differs from recent studies of the relationships between South Asian diasporic music producers and blacks. For example, Nitasha Sharma's important book *Hip Hop Desis: South Asian Americans, Blackness and Global Race Conscious-*

ness centers on South Asian American artists and is a largely celebratory account of their racial consciousness and affiliations with blacks. Her book is a critical addition to scholarship that has mostly described antagonistic relationships between South Asians and blacks in the United States. My work, on the other hand, focuses on Britain, where scholars of British Asian music have largely assumed the existence of political solidarities between these groups. By using an intersectional approach to the realms of both production and consumption I provide a more varied account of these relationships, demonstrating that one cannot assume solidarities and that British Asian people's relationships to blacks and black expressive forms can in fact work against the goals of black British politics.

68 For an in-depth analysis of how youth in India are traversing private and public spheres whose gendered meanings are being remade under conditions of globalization, see Lukose, *Liberalization's Children: Gender, Youth, and Consumer Citizenship in Globalizing India*.

69 I have used pseudonyms for the club night and venue.

CHAPTER ONE

1 Wilson, *Dreams, Questions, Struggles*.
2 Unless otherwise specified, quotes are from interviews that I conducted between 1996 and 1998. I examined the 1996–98 editions of *Eastern Eye*, a publication that was launched in 1989 to "cater for Britain's South Asian communities" (http://www.asiansinmedia.org/2009/01/22/eastern-eye-a-history-of-trial-and-tribulations). Since its launch, *Eastern Eye* has had a large circulation: "In 2004 *Eastern Eye's* first officially recorded circulation figures were released, putting sales at 20,661 per week. Of that, the average number of copies sold weekly were 16,518. Subscription accounted for another 375 in sales and an average of 3,768 copies were given out free every week" (ibid).

To clarify, I am not attempting to explain *why* bhangra has not crossed over. There has been some valuable discussion of the external factors, such as racism, and the internal factors, such as the structure of the industry, that have made crossing over difficult. See Banerji and Baumann, "Bhangra 1984–88," and Dudrah, "Cultural Production in the British Bhangra Music Industry," for accounts of how the economic infrastructure of the industry has hindered bhangra from becoming competitive in the mainstream market. Industry folks have also denounced the mainstream media and music industry for being racist. They have argued that bhangra musicians are trying to break into a corporate world that holds racist stereotypes of Asians and that therefore doesn't properly market bhangra music (ibid.; Mark, "Mainstream Dream"). While some of these reasons appear in the interviews and media I examine, I focus on the main categories through which members in the industry in the late 1990s understood this music's failures, successes, and need for change.

3 Baumann, "The Re-invention of Bhangra," 81.
4 These couplets are drawn from poetry and are known as *boliyan* (Banerji and Baumann, "Bhangra 1984–88," 140).

5 Banerji, "Ghazals to Bhangra in Great Britain," 208.
6 Banerji and Baumann, "Bhangra 1984–88," 146. Other popular albums that fused bhangra with disco include Holle Holle's album *Holle Holle* (1986), and Heera's album *Diamonds from Heera* (1986).
7 A song narrating hardship is Kalapreet's "Oos Pradesh" (That foreign land). It expresses the grief that South Asian migrants experienced from being subjected to extensive racism and economic exploitation and from being nostalgic for their homelands. In making these points, the song refers to an incident that occurred during colonial rule at Jallianwala Bagh in Punjab: on April 13, 1919 (the date of *Vaisakhi*), over twenty thousand unarmed Indians gathered in a large park (*bagh*) in the city of Amritsar to peacefully protest British colonial rule. British soldiers marched through the one small entrance to the park, sealed it off, and without warning, opened fire on the crowd:

> In this land, your dignity lies torn to shreds / Even with your pockets full / You wander the streets like beggars / Why straddle on an aimless horse / That gallops on unbridled / And you came to England, my friend / Abandoning your Punjab / Recall that it was these same foreigners / That took their rifles to us / Innocent, fair, flourishing lives / How they stood and destroyed us / And every corner lies in witness / At Jallianwala Bagh / And you, my friend, came to England / Leaving your Punjab

8 Baumann, "The Re-invention of Bhangra," 90. Though Hindi film music and bhangra are seen as distinctly different genres, Banerji and Baumann note that Indian film music has been important to the growth of British bhangra music aesthetically and industrially: "Aesthetically it has fostered an openness to fused musical styles, while industrially it has provided experience and resources for the mass production and marketing of popular music" (Banerji and Baumann, "Bhangra 1984–88," 140).
9 Banerji, "Ghazals to Bhangra in Great Britain," 142.
10 DJ Ritu, "Bhangra/Asian Beat," 84.
11 Ibid., 85.
12 The various schemas used to categorize bhangra indicate the difficulties in characterizing it. It can be mapped in different ways onto time, space, locale, and culture. For example, bhangra can be categorized by generational differences, by local versions versus those from abroad, by the basis of city or region (i.e., London varieties versus those from the Midlands), by notions of pure versus alternative forms of the music, or by differences in the kinds of music that it is fused with.
13 DJ Ritu, "Bhangra/Asian Beat," 84.
14 Kalra, "Vilayeti Rhythms," 93–94.
15 Ibid., 94.
16 DJ Ritu, *The Rough Guide to Bhangra*, 5.
17 Kaur and Kalra, "Xi Amount of Bhangra and Ragga," 5. Cited in Kalra, "Vilayeti Rhythms," 94.
18 Kalra, "Vilayeti Rhythms," 85, 87.
19 Ibid., 87.

20 Ibid.
21 Gopinath, *Impossible Desires*, 34.
22 Ibid.
23 Although I explore similar themes in chapter 3 on the bhangra club scene, my focus here is on the production of the music itself.
24 I have used a pseudonym.
25 I have used a pseudonym.
26 Banerji and Baumann, "Bhangra 1984–88," 145.
27 *Top of the Pops*, a weekly British television program created by the BBC, featured performances from each week's best-selling music artists and gave a rundown of that week's singles chart. It aired from January 1964 to July 2006.
28 Like Thornton, I approach the mainstream in terms of its symbolic meaning for the people who use it but expand it to include how race can inform this use (Thornton, *Club Cultures*).
29 Mark, "Mainstream Dream."
30 Banerji and Baumann, "Bhangra 1984–88," 143.
31 Ibid.
32 While the release of the album *Rough Guide to Bhangra* might seem a sign of mainstream acceptance, its being categorized as world music is arguably further evidence that it is marginalized given that *world music* often serves as a catch-all term for non-Western music. For a critique of world music, see Feld, "From Schizophonia to Schismogenesis"; Feld, "A Sweet Lullaby for World Music"; Hutnyk, *Critique of Exotica*. Moreover, bhangra's characterization as world music is at best an ambivalent one: Banerji and Baumann show that bhangra is often denounced for being "'too westernized' . . . to be acceptable as 'authentic world music'" ("Bhangra 1984–88," 137). Also, in their reach for the mainstream, bhangra artists are not typically aiming for the world music market.
33 "Interview with Sukhinder Shinda," *Eastern Eye*, 15.
34 "Once Upon a Sahota," *Eastern Eye*, 12. These kinds of condemnations abounded in the magazine.
35 "PMC Five Fingers," *Eastern Eye*, 11.
36 "Up the Garden Path of Bhangra," *Eastern Eye*, 7–8.
37 Ibid., 7.
38 Shabbs, "The Boys are Back in Town!," *Eastern Eye*, 8.
39 Ghai, "We're on Our Way to Wembley?," *Eastern Eye*, 12.
40 Ibid.
41 See Banerji, "Ghazals to Bhangra in Great Britain."
42 Dev is a pseudonym.
43 The film *My Beautiful Laundrette* provides an alternative story of South Asian men and their "unethical" economic behavior. Set in 1980s Britain, the film shows how Thatcherism created a culture of hyperindividualism, capitalism, and entrepreneurship at the expense of the social good. The South Asian men protagonists thus learn that to become British means to become unscrupulous businessmen. One of the main characters in the film, Nasser, is a first-generation Pakistani British businessman and part-time slumlord. He employs Johnny, a

young, white working-class lad, to evict one of his poor, black tenants. When Johnny protests, wondering why Nasser is choosing not to act in racial solidarity with his black tenant, Nasser responds, "I'm a professional businessman, not a professional Pakistani."

44 Said, *Orientalism*.
45 Halberstam, *Skin Shows*, 96.
46 Ibid., 92, 98.
47 Ibid., 102.
48 Ibid., 99.
49 Ibid., 105.
50 Ahmed, "Music for the Masses." Scholarship has expressed similar sentiments. In their analyses of bhangra's emergence, Banerji and Baumann state that promoters will have to overcome the "bhangra image" in order for the music to become mainstream: "In the video-intensive [mainstream] music scene of the 1980s, enamoured of lean and sullen young men, it will be a challenge to market the bright, cheerful, jolly-uncle image of even the most musically competent bhangra bands" (Banerji and Baumann, "Bhangra 1984–88," 144).
51 *Sardar* is a title or form of address often used for Sikh men.
52 Wicked Miah, "Wicked Miah: The Man Next Door," *Eastern Eye*, 13.
53 As Wicked Miah writes, "While the Asian Underground has been steaming ahead with professionalism . . . the bhangra front has made a fine art of shoddy work, dodgy promotions and duff attitudes" ("Wicked Miah: The Man in the Fridge," *Eastern Eye*, 13).
54 Sawhney, "It's Time to Move On," *Eastern Eye*, 10.
55 Asian women were bullied too. An anonymous interviewee said, "They were bullied regularly: in schools and college, at bus stops, on busses, sport centers, libraries. You did not have very visible public fights . . . although after school fights involved women too. At school, you always had a group of women who were aggressive and usually expressed their abuse away from the classroom. They were well known. They portrayed themselves as tough by smoking and hung around in the toilet. It was uncomfortable going to the toilet because you got picked on." One could thus argue that because of normative understandings of bullying as an activity involving men, the lack of gendered specificity in Nitin's narratives risks erasing bullying between women.
56 "Letters to the Editor," *Eastern Eye*, 12.
57 DJ Sheikh, "Why Bhangra's Here to Stay," *Eastern Eye*, 10.
58 The monthly magazine *2nd Generation* focused in part on AU music and related youth style.
59 He combines two definitions of lad: "A boy, youth; a young man, young fellow" (OED, 2a); and "Men of any age belonging to a group sharing common working, recreational, or other interests, esp. with the implication of comradeship and equality; *spec.* the rank-and-file members of a trade union" (OED additional series 1993–97).
60 Krishnaswamy, *Effeminism*, 24. Krishnaswamy's work builds on Mrinilani Sinha's discussion of the dynamics of male power in India in her work *Colonial Mas-*

culinity. Sinha writes that in the colonial ordering of masculinity in the late nineteenth century, "the politically self-conscious Indian intellectuals occupied a unique place: they represented an 'unnatural' or 'perverted' form of male identity. Hence this group of Indians, the most typical representatives of which at the time were middle-class Bengali Hindus, became the quintessential referents for the odious category designated as 'effeminate *babus*'" (Sinha, *Colonial Masculinity*, 2).

61 Krishnaswamy, *Effeminism*, 25.
62 Bhabha, "Of Mimicry and Man: The Ambivalence of Colonial Discourse."
63 Mark, "Mainstream Dream."
64 See Back, "Coughing Up Fire"; Cooper, "Mix Up the Indian with All the Patwa"; Ballantyne, "Displacement, Diaspora, and Difference in the Making of Bhangra"; Shukla, *India Abroad*.
65 Lipsitz, *Dangerous Crossroads*, 130.
66 Ibid. 130–31.
67 Shabbs, "Interview [of Apache Indian]," *Eastern Eye*, 8.
68 Bhangra Child, "Editorial," *Eastern Eye*, 9.
69 Shabbs, "Interview [of Apache Indian]," *Eastern Eye*, 8.
70 "When Will I Be Famous?," *Eastern Eye*, 9.
71 Ahmed, "Music for the Masses," *Eastern Eye*, 8.
72 The film *Hip Hop: Beyond Beats and Rhymes*, directed by Byron Hurt, shows how white-owned record companies expected men to perform this kind of male identity.
73 Alexander, *The Asian Gang*.
74 British colonists, for example, distinguished the Bengali babus, whom they saw as effeminate, from the Punjabi men, whom they cast as part of a "martial race"—a strategy used to induct them into the British army. In Britain currently, the mainstream media often portray young Muslim men as violent terrorists (Alexander, *The Asian Gang*).
75 Shabbs, "Interview [of Apache Indian]," *Eastern Eye*, 8.
76 Ibid.
77 Bands such as Stereo Nation and Intermix, for example, have Afro-Caribbean men in them. Yet this didn't cause anxiety in my interviews or in the pages of *Eastern Eye* (Shabbs, "The Nice Boys of Bhangra"). Although some of my interviewees criticized certain artists for being derivative, they only saw Apache Indian as crossing a line—where the problem is his identity and not just his music. One could argue that Apache came under attack because black forms more heavily influence his lyrics, rhythms, and image. However, this argument ignores the fact that his music is still resolutely a remix: he is roundly hailed for creating "bhangramuffin" music, and reggae purists have attacked him for his remixing of reggae. One could further argue that he is more visible because of his mainstream success. But similar rebukes could be made of the other major figure who achieved success remixing bhangra with black music, Bally Sagoo but are not.
78 It debuted at #2 on the German charts, reached #1 on the Italian charts, and debuted at #5 on the top 40 charts in Britain; it was the first bhangra song to reach

the top 10 in Britain. It also went as high as #33 on the Billboard charts in the United States and #10 in Canada's charts.

79. Panjabi MC's website cites 1999 as the year he crossed into the mainstream: "It was in 1999 when PMC began to experience that the western world people other than that of Asian or Indian backgrounds were actually listening to his music. Tim Westwood, a hip hop DJ from Radio 1 UK began to play one of PMC's tracks, Mundian To Bach Ke. From this point onwards more and more mainstream DJ's and radio stations began to pick up on Panjabi MC's style of Music" (http://www.pmcrecords.com/index.php?page=414901).
80. "PMC Five Fingers," *Eastern Eye*, 11–12.
81. Ibid.
82. Ibid.
83. Ibid.
84. Ibid.
85. Ibid.
86. Shabbs, "Jatt Aagiya," *Eastern Eye*, 8.
87. Ibid.
88. Ibid.
89. Their long list of awards include 1998 Pop Awards (Birmingham): *Best Newcomers* B21, *Best Up-coming* B21, *Best Song* Bally Jagpal ("Nakhre Bin Soni Temi"); 1998 Student Poll Awards (Leicester): *Best Newcomers* B21, *Best Album* B21; 1998 Movie Pageant Awards (London): *Best Newcomers* B21, *Best Selling Album Live and Direct* (Bally Jagpal); 1998 Movie Box Records (Birmingham): Exceeding Sales of 25,000.
90. Shabbs, "The Nice Boys of Bhangra," *Eastern Eye*, 10.
91. Industry folks saw other bands as successfully changing the image of bhangra. Ameet Chana described to me a performance at which DCS arrived on stage during an annual bhangra awards ceremony wearing Nehru jackets in the colors of the Indian flag: "They're making statements now rather than just sort of coming on with a little band tied around their head . . . it's like being young, being fresh, being in your face." DCS's clothing style signified not only a pan-Indian identity but also the expectations of youth cultures to make fashion statements. Ameet Chana also said that DCS released "one of the best albums for years" called *Punjabi Dance Nation* and describes the album as "really young, really fresh," referring specifically to their images and lyrics: "The inlay of their card is stunning, like proper photographs, real kind of stylized. . . . It looks professional."
92. OED, March 2001.
93. Wicked Miah, "21st Centyury [sic] Boys," *Eastern Eye*, 8.
94. Ibid.
95. Ibid.

CHAPTER TWO

1. Also see Banerjea, "Sounds of Whose Underground?"
2. Huq, "Asian Kool? Bhangra and Beyond," 206.
3. My use of the term *protest politics* differs from the concept of the protest song, which scholars sometimes define as songs that accompany organized social movements, which the AU was not. I also use *protest politics* to refer to the demands made of artists to contest inequality not only in their lyrics but also in their interviews and performances.
4. For a discussion of similar pressures on black visual artists, see Mercer, *Welcome to the Jungle*.
5. Foucault, *The History of Sexuality*. Citing from this book, Steven Epstein describes Foucault's use of "incitement to discourse":

   > [Foucault] sought to describe not the silencing of sex but the "discursive explosion" surrounding sex in the modern West—the myriad ways in which sexuality has become an object to be administered as well as the stuff of self-knowledge, via the "wide dispersion of devices that were invented for speaking about it, for having it be spoken about, for inducing it to speak of itself" (34)....
   >
   > He was not denying that sex *had* been "prohibited or barred or masked or misapprehended" (12). But to emphasize this negativity—to imagine that power is that which "just says no" to sex—is to miss the wildly productive and heterogeneous character of the "regulated and polymorphous incitement to discourse" (34). Moreover—and crucially, from a political standpoint—if power does not so much negate sex as organize it through the proliferation of discourses about it, then the whole project of sexual liberation must be entirely rethought. If repression is not the problem, then antirepression is not the solution; indeed, if sexual meanings are orchestrated through an injunction that we speak about sex, then the triumphalist, let-it-all-hang-out rhetoric of sexual freedom is embarrassingly and dangerously consistent with dominant cultural forms.
   >
   > (Epstein, "An Incitement to Discourse: Sociology and *The History of Sexuality*," 489–90)

6. This burden was widespread: many non-AU British Asian artists who achieved some measure of success faced it. That my interviews of AU artists positioned me as part of that "incitement to discourse" was a fact I only later fully grasped.
7. Huq, "Asian Kool? Bhangra and Beyond," 203.
8. Pateman and Mills, *Contract and Domination*, 122.
9. Paraphrasing Locke, who provided the theoretical basis for the liberal separation of the public and the private, Pateman explains as follows:

   > A wife's subordination to her husband has "a Foundation in Nature"... the husband's will must prevail in the household as he is naturally the "abler and the stronger." But a natural subordinate cannot at the same time be free and equal. Thus women (wives) are excluded from the status of "individuals" and

> so from participating in the public world of equality, consent and convention....
>
> Locke's theory also shows how the private and public spheres are grounded in opposing principles of association which are exemplified in the conflicting status of women and men; natural subordination stands opposed to free individualism. The family is based on natural ties of sentiment and blood and on the sexually ascribed status of wife and husband (mother and father). Participation in the public sphere is governed by universal, impersonal and conventional criteria of achievement, interest, rights, equality and property—liberal criteria, applicable only to men.
>
> (Pateman, *The Sexual Contract*, 121)

10. Ismail, "'Boys Will Be Boys,'" 1677.
11. Ibid.
12. Fanon, *The Wretched of the Earth*, 74.
13. Post-bhangra is a category some scholars use to refer to *all* forms of British Asian music, including hip-hop and AU forms, that emerged after bhangra's heyday. See Sharma, Hutnyk, and Sharma, eds., *Dis-Orienting Rhythms*; Hyder, *Brimful of Asia*, 41.
14. Hyder, *Brimful of Asia*, 41.
15. Ibid., 43.
16. Ibid., 42.
17. Ibid.
18. Hyder describes the marketing of these categories: "The music industry thrives on the novel; difference can be marketed and sold like any other commodity ... and the emergence of Asian bands during the early 1990s unearthed much potential for marketing in terms of difference.... Two attendant and stereotypical modes of difference emerged ... 'angry young Asians' and 'mystical Indians'" (ibid., 92).
19. Ibid., 95.
20. Hyder notes that the lead singer of Echobelly has done much to avoid being seen primarily as Asian, including refusing interviews with academics and certain presses (ibid., 101).
21. Ibid., 112.
22. Ibid., 111–12.
23. Huq, "Asian Kool? Bhangra and Beyond," 73.
24. Wilson, *Dreams, Questions, Struggles*.
25. Huq, "Asian Kool? Bhangra and Beyond," 74.
26. Hyder, *Brimful of Asia*, 112. Gayle Wald's work suggests that the idea that Asian women rockers cannot be taken seriously as political is widespread (Wald, "Rock Music, Feminism, and the Cultural Construction of Female Youth").
27. Bhabha, "The Other Question: Stereotype, Discrimination and the Discourse of Colonialism."
28. Posted at http://www.nme.com/NME/External/Reviews/ Reviews_Story (accessed May 9, 1998). The full review reads as follows:

It's astonishing to think that a version of this album first appeared in France just over a year ago, at a time when no label in Britain was remotely interested. Most likely labels here feared Asian Dub Foundation were another "global techno" disaster waiting to happen, *the received wisdom was that no one would be interested in an Asian dub group preaching political change.*

Actually, though, the music industry *needn't have been quite so worried.* Because what this newly remixed version of "Rafi's Revenge" reveals is that the explicitly political dub'n'bass punk assault of ADF *owes more to a lineage snaking back through Public Enemy, The Clash and the MCs,* rather than to any farcical and preconceived notion of Asian or world music.

What's more, while the political content of ADF is patently a vital and inseparable part of what they do, *it's certainly not the first thing that hits you about this album. Nor is it the most interesting.* After all, although we might nod sagely when we learn that the opening track, "Naxalite," is about guerilla uprisings in '60s Bengal, it's exactly the sort of information which makes ADF sound like The Levellers. With breakbeats.

No, what strikes you the first time you hear this record is the sheer speed and sound of it.... The only problem is that the mood throughout is frantically relentless. The strength of ADF's convictions combined with the harsh, hammering rhythms and percussion means that by the time you reach the halfway point of "Dub Mentality," you might already find yourself *overwhelmed....*

Still, it seems *churlish* to criticise a group for having the courage of their convictions, and it certainly doesn't mean this LP is any sort of a failure. It's just that, like the first Rage Against The Machine album, *it might be easier to listen to in stages.* Despite this, "Rafi's Revenge" is an admirable record, which—in the wider context of the times—contains exactly the sort of confrontational and defiantly experimental music we've been missing. It's nice to know the British music industry has finally caught up (emphasis added).

29 While scholars don't constitute a part of the music scene in the way other actors I analyze here do, they are a significant part of the discursive field that shapes interpretations of artists.

30 See Sharma, Hutnyk, and Sharma, eds., *Dis-Orienting Rhythms*; Dawson, "This is the Digital Underclass"; Zuberi, *Sounds English;* and Huq, "Asian Kool? Bhangra and Beyond." As Nilanjana Bhattacharjya notes about *Dis-Orienting Rhythms*, an edited collection of articles about British Asian music, "their style of writing and selection of artists have initiated a now regrettably common practice of judging British Asian musicians solely based on their perceived politics, as evident in their lyrics and published interviews.... *Dis-Orienting Rhythms* suggests that if musicians do not profess their political stance in the lyrics, they should not be taken seriously as artists" (Bhattacharjya, "The Global Sounds of the Asian Underground").

Hyder says about *Dis-Orienting Rhythms* that "despite recognizing the pitfalls of essentialist categorization of Asian-ness, the book's authors nevertheless do not resist the temptation to valorize what they interpret as the political agenda of bands such as Fun'Da'Mental and ADF in a way that ignores the complexity of the multiple identities and articulations at play" (Hyder, *Brimful of Asia*, 43). However, while Hyder contends that scholars have sustained a one-dimensional political focus on bands such as Fun'Da'Mental, Black Star Liner, and Cornershop, he nevertheless contributes to this attention by making them the focus of his own study. Further, while he argues that artists are more than political and shows them to be individuals with multiple identities and desires, I see the category of political itself in need of interrogation and artists' responses as structured, not as evidence of the free play of identity.

31 Gopinath, *Impossible Desires*, 30.
32 Dawson, "Dub Mentality," cited in Gopinath, *Impossible Desires*, 44.
33 Gopinath, *Impossible Desires*, 45.
34 Ibid.
35 Hutnyk, *Critique of Exotica*, 68.
36 Gopinath, *Impossible Desires*, 46.
37 By "cultural activism" I'm referring to the self-conscious use of cultural forms that Faye Ginsburg describes as a "means of social action that are powerfully linked to the kinds of activities more traditionally identified as 'political' in the social movement literature" (Ginsburg, "'From Little Things, Big Things Grow': Indigenous Media and Cultural Activism," 123).
38 Some sources cite Shabs Jobanputra and Paul Franklyn as cofounding the label in 1995. Others cite Jobanputra and DJ Ritu as cofounders in 1994.
39 Pateman and Mills, *The Contract and Domination*.
40 This is a wind instrument, classified as a stick zither, used in classical Hindustani music.
41 Hobsbawm and Ranger, *The Invention of Tradition*.
42 Belsey, *The Subject of Tragedy*, 8.
43 BJP stands for Bharatiya Janata Party, which is a right-wing, Hindu fundamentalist and nationalist political party that has gained increasing political control of India since the 1990s.
44 BNP stands for British National Party, which is a right-wing political party that formed as a splinter group of the racist National Front. It is anti-immigrant and has argued that immigrants and their descendants should return to their "home" countries.
45 In this sense, it is reminiscent of Michael Jackson's use of "colorblindness" (i.e., doesn't matter if you're black or white).
46 Barnett's account of Sawhney's philosophy appears in Bilel Qureshi's feature of January 13, 2010, "Nitin Sawhney: In Search of the 'Undersound,'" for National Public Radio's show *All Things Considered*. The NPR feature can be accessed at http://www.npr.org/templates/story/story.
47 Huq, "From the Margins to Mainstream?," 41.
48 Badmarsh graciously agreed to an extensive interview: I discovered I was fortunate to have this opportunity since he typically denied requests from Asian press because of a negative experience he had. Thankfully, mutual contacts with whom I had also conducted interviews cleared me.

49 The East End is one of the poorest areas of London, but in the late 1990s, certain neighborhoods were being gentrified. For a historical account, see Jane Jacobs, "Eastern Trading: Diasporas, Dwelling and Place."
50 Gilroy, *Small Acts*, 35, 38.
51 Ibid., 43–44.
52 This discussion is not intended to imply that all Muslim artists grapple with the same set of issues in the same ways. Rather, Badmarsh's case shows how artists' multiple identities (i.e., of race, ethnicity, and religion) shape how they approach music.
53 Joi released its first album, titled *One and One Is One: Debut Album from the Original Asian Breakbeat Fusionists*, with Real World Records in 1999. Joi went on tour that year to promote the album, but, tragically, Haroon died of a heart attack on July 8 at the age of thirty-four. Partly in honor of Haroon and in recognition of the extensive contributions of Joi over the years, the BBC Asian Music Awards awarded Joi a prize for Album of the Year in 2000. Farook has continued with Joi and has since produced two albums, *We Are Three* (2000) and *Without Zero* (2006). I feel incredibly fortunate to have had the opportunity to meet Haroon, whose integrity, modesty, and warmth struck me as admirable.
54 Farook is sarcastically referring to stereotypes that Asian youth are "smelly."
55 In 1947 the region of Bengal was partitioned: the predominantly Muslim eastern half was designated East Pakistan and made part of the newly independent Pakistan, while the predominantly Hindu western part became the Indian state of West Bengal. A movement for the autonomy of East Pakistan began within a few years of partition because of linguistic and cultural differences as well as economic disparities between West and East Pakistan. The seeds of independence were sown during the Language Movement of 1952 to recognize Bangla as a state language. After a nine-month-long war of liberation beginning in March of 1971, with the help of India, East Pakistan emerged as the sovereign and independent state of Bangladesh.
56 Amir Uddin is a Sylheti composer and singer known for his Baul music.
57 In Gurinder Chadha's film *I'm British But . . .* there are some short clips of Haroon performing. While the film narrates him as performing bangla music, the song "Funky Asian" speaks to all Asians. Realworldrecords.com explains Joi's history: "A couple of early vinyl releases followed, including the neatly named Asian acid vibes of 'Taj Mahouse,' produced by Tony Thorpe (KLF) in 87, whilst the late eighties rap, 'Funky Asian' appeared a year later. However, it was the classic 'Desert Storm,' released on Rhythm King Records [in 1991], which gave the band their first taste of critical success, with NME (National Music Express) declaring it not only Single of the Week, but also 'one of the most inventive records ever made.' The band looked poised for great things—until they were lost in the aftermath of their label's subsequent absorption into BMG" (http://realworldrecords.com/artists/joi).
58 I believe KMD refers to the hip-hop trio Kausing Much Damage.
59 I thank Lutfus Sayeed, Farzana Khaled, and Kasturi Ray for this translation.
60 Openshaw, *Seeking Bāuls of Bengal*.

61 The liner notes explain the album title: "First Equation—Friendship 1 + 1 = 3. Here, one plus one in friendship equals three. The one plus one is in the third, that being the world. Second Equation—Love 1 + 1 = 1. Here, one plus one in love equals one. The one plus one are the total world." Underneath this text is the citation, "Rabindranath Tagore's Metaphysical Mathematics from 'Rabindranath Tagore: A Biography' by Krishna Kripalani (Visva-Bharati, Calcutta, 1980)." Tagore was a Bengali writer who won the Nobel Prize for Literature in 1913.
62 Maira, "Henna and Hip Hop"; Roy, *Alimentary Tracts*.
63 Gilroy, *There Ain't No Black in the Union Jack*; Gilroy, *Small Acts*.
64 Mills, *The Racial Contract*; Pateman, *The Sexual Contract*.
65 Belsey, *The Subject of Tragedy*, 8–9.
66 Duddy, "Impure Aesthetics," http://poems.com/special_features/prose/essay_duddy.php (accessed July 2011).
67 Belsey, *The Subject of Tragedy*, 7.

CHAPTER THREE

1 To "wind up" someone is to deliberately try to annoy or upset her or him.
2 "Open days" are days during which participating universities offer informational sessions and activities for prospective students.
3 Chadha is referring to young people's remixes of Bangladeshi music.
4 See the press page of Third World Newsreel, the distributor of *I'm British But...* (http://www.twn.org/catalog/pages/cpage.aspx?rec=733&card=price).
5 Appadurai, *Modernity at Large*, 22.
6 In "Noisy Asians or 'Asian Noise'?," one of the most extensive discussions of the politics of British bhangra, Sanjay Sharma's questions concerning gender are relegated to a footnote: "The affirmation of a gendered Asian identity for female listeners in the performance of Bhangra would be in constant negotiation and contestation with the patriarchal expressions present in the music" (Sharma, "Noisy Asians or 'Asian Noise'?," 56n2).
7 During the period that I was conducting my research "one off" events were often held at Zenith in West London because of its proximity to the large areas of South Asian settlement and because it was one of the few remaining venues that would host bhangra events.
8 For a review of the bias of subcultural studies toward male subjects, see McRobbie, *Feminism and Youth Culture*. For studies specifically addressing the experiences of white women in rave subculture, see Hutton, *Risky Pleasures?*, and Pini, *Club Cultures and Female Subjectivity*.
9 Laidler and Hunt, "Accomplishing Femininity among the Girls in the Gang"; Miranda, *Homegirls in the Public Sphere*.
10 For example, in her essay "*Homegirls*, *Cholas*, and *Pachucas* in Cinema," Rosa Linda Fregoso illustrates how *pachucas*, "the predecessors of *cholas* and of today's homegirls ... or what are currently referred to as girl gangs" (317), "are trespassers in public spaces, violating the boundaries of femininity" (318). She

shows how they "threatened the foundations of *la familia's* gendered structure by speaking and acting in the public sphere" (318) in ways their families considered provocative and disrespectful of their authority. She charts how they challenged the patriarchal projects of confining women to the home and policing their sexuality (320) and therefore contested patriarchal constructions of public and private spheres. But, given the ways in which communities of color can tie sexual morality to gendered notions of ethnic authenticity, we know less about how these women may have been considered less *ethnic* by their families and communities, and how they dealt with that issue.

11 Wilson, *Dreams, Questions, Struggles*.
12 *Init* is slang for "isn't it so?" Sukh is using it here to refer to the speech of "trashy" (read: unrefined, uneducated) people. *Slag* is a derogatory term for a promiscuous woman.
13 Osterley, located close to Southall, is an area to which many upwardly mobile South Asian families have moved.
14 Foucault, *Discipline and Punish*.
15 Bhattacharjee, "The Public/Private Mirage: Mapping Homes and Undomesticating Violence Work in the South Asian Immigrant Community," 318.
16 Espiritu, "We Don't Sleep around like White Girls Do," 416. Espiritu describes how particular constructions of Asian women have fueled the colonial rule of Asia and the systematic disenfranchisement of Asians in the United States:

> Asian women—both in Asia and in the United States—have been racialized as sexually immoral, and the "Orient"—and its women—has long served as a site of European male-power fantasies, replete with lurid images of sexual license, gynecological aberrations, and general perversion.... In colonial Asia in the nineteenth and early twentieth centuries, for example, female sexuality was a site for colonial rulers to assert their moral superiority and thus their supposed natural and legitimate right to rule. The colonial rhetoric of moral superiority was based on the construction of colonized Asian women as subjects of sexual desire and fulfillment and European colonial women as the paragons of virtue and the bearers of a redefined colonial morality.... The discourse of morality has also been used to mark the "unassimilability" of Asians in the U.S.
> (Espiritu, "We Don't Sleep around like White Girls Do," 425)

17 Ibid., 416, 421, 427.
18 Parmar, "Gender, Race and Class: Asian Women in Resistance."
19 For a discussion of gender and immigration control, see Wilson, *Dreams, Questions, Struggles*.
20 Hall, "The Work of Representation"; Malik, *Representing Black Britain*.
21 Willis, *Learning to Labour*, 29.
22 An extremely popular group, TLC was characterized by the media as "riding a blend of pop, hip-hop, and urban soul to superstardom during the '90s ... with a sassy, sexy attitude" (http://www.mtv.com/music/artist/tlc/artist.jhtml).
23 Byron Hurt's film *Hip-Hop: Beyond Beats and Rhymes* explores how, as hip-hop

became commercialized and controlled by white-owned record labels, it became increasingly misogynist and homophobic.

24 See Fiona Hutton's typology of mainstream versus underground clubs (Hutton, *Risky Pleasures?*).

25 In a story caricaturing the women who frequent bhangra clubs, *Eastern Eye* portrays them as aggressively pursuing men. Describing the "Asian Club Girl," or "AC Girl," it says, "The Asian club girl wants to look 'ard so no one will mess with her or try and fight her for her man.... [Her] dark red lip-liner gives the impression that the AC girl is a man eater who has just sucked her victim's blood. She probably has!... [Her] thin eye brow, like the multi-coloured hair, is a cunning ploy to make the AC girl seem scarier than Grant Mitchell.... When an AC girl is batting her eye lashes at a bloke, she pretends that some of her make up has flaked off in her eye. She then walks over to the bloke, who she has been checking out all night, and asks for some assistance. When the victim has his face close up to the AC girl she attacks him and performs the kind of tonsil tennis that would leave Pete Sampras for dust.... The AC girl looks like she has just mugged Mr T off the A-Team" (Aziz and Maan, "Rude Boys and Party Girls," 40–41). Notwithstanding the fact that these portrayals are sexist, they do show that club-going women are perceived as tough and aggressive.

26 *Securon* is a pseudonym.

27 Sikh youth who keep the symbols of the faith might legitimately be wearing these items.

28 Parmar, "Gender, Race and Class"; Mani, *Contentious Traditions*.

29 Alexander, *The Asian Gang*.

30 Cohen, in writing about mods and rockers in the late 1960s, coined the term "moral panic" to refer to the moment when "a condition, episode, person or group of persons emerges to become defined as a threat to societal values and interests" (Cohen, *Folk Devils and Moral Panics*, 1).

31 By "enough" she means that there's a limit to the abuse men will endure.

32 "Ho" is colloquial for "whores."

33 By "cuttin' a bird" she means insulting a woman.

34 "Loo" is colloquial for "restroom."

35 Many of the less regular women club-goers commonly denied that they ever attended bhangra clubs in the first place, using a variety of reasons to explain why they were there, for example, "I'm just here for my friend's birthday" or "I'm just here for a one-time, girls' night out."

36 As Beverly Skeggs writes, "Respectability is one of the most ubiquitous signifiers of class.... [It] is usually the concern of those who are not seen to have it. Respectability would not be of concern here, if the working classes ... had not consistently been classified as dangerous, polluting, threatening, revolutionary, pathological and without respect" (Skeggs, *Formations of Class and Gender*, 1).

37 Laidler and Hunt find that for young, working-class women in gangs, "respectability involves both appearance and conduct.... [C]lothing, hairstyle, make-up, and stride signify her status as a reputable young woman" (Laidler and Hunt, "Accomplishing Femininity among the Girls in the Gang," 664).

38 Ibid., 665.
39 Miranda, *Homegirls in the Public Sphere*, 79.
40 McRobbie, *Feminism and Youth Culture*.
41 Miranda, *Homegirls in the Public Sphere*, 103.
42 Ibid.

CHAPTER FOUR

The chapter title "Roomful of Asha" is a play on Cornershop's song "Brimful of Asha," which pays tribute to the famous Hindi playback singer Asha Bhosle. I thank Anand Pandian for this playful suggestion.

1 Anokha closed in 2000 after a successful four-year run, its popularity having engendered a variety of similar club nights throughout London. As I explain in the introduction, the term *Asian Underground* has had a problematic trajectory. After the release of Singh's album, mainstream media appropriated the term, using it to characterize any fusion music that British Asian artists created that was not bhangra. It therefore lumped together different styles of music, using the ethnic background of artists to categorize them. Not surprisingly, many artists disliked the term. Nonetheless, *Asian Underground*, in its more careful usage, referred both to electronic dance music that used South Asian instrumentation and to a club scene that featured such music.
2 Ambient and trance are related genres of underground dance music of the late 1990s that feature synthesizers and gradual dynamic builds.
3 Majumdar, "Notes from the Asian Underground."
4 One exception is Banerjea, "Sounds of Whose Underground?" He examines spaces of consumption, like clubs such as Anokha, but sees them as sites in which white, middle-class audiences appropriate South Asian culture: "Marked by the ready appropriation of *bindis, saris,* incense . . . these are spaces which offer a primarily middle-class constituency a sanitized encounter with an imagined Asian 'other'" (65). While this account makes many acute observations, it does not address how British Asians engage with the AU club scene.
5 I have used pseudonyms to protect their identities.
6 Brah, "The 'Asian' in Britain"; Fisher, Lahiri, and Thandi, *A South-Asian History of Britain*.
7 "R&B" is short for "rhythm and blues," which, in Britain, often refers to the equivalent of commercial hip-hop in the United States.
8 Banerjea, "Sounds of Whose Underground?"
9 "Paki" is a common racist epithet first used against the large numbers of Pakistanis who arrived in England in the 1950s and 1960s. The term quickly became used to refer to South Asians of various backgrounds.
10 Bourdieu, *Distinction*.
11 The website for Club Kali describes the club as follows: "Bollywood, Bhangra, Arabic, R&B and Dance classics spiced up by DJ Ritu and Dilz at the world's biggest Asian music based LGBT club!" (http://www.clubkali.com/; accessed July,

2011). In 2001 the club, which has been running at the Dome in London, celebrated its sixteenth year.

12 The presence of British Asian women in production, performance, and promotion was also minimal. The women who *were* present were often marginalized. I once attended a large music concert held by a highly successful AU musician. One of his most popular tracks featured a beautiful, soaring vocal by a young British Asian woman. When he began playing the track on stage, I eagerly looked for the woman singer, but she was nowhere to be found. In lieu of her presence, a male guitarist appeared on stage to simulate her vocals instrumentally. I approached promoters later to ask why the singer was not part of the show, and they replied that her stage presence was "not great," suggesting that it would not satisfy audiences. Stories such as these deepened my sense that dominant representations of British Asians were routinely structured on the erasure of women, even as signs of Asian femininity were central to creating an Asian aesthetic.

CONCLUSION

1 Sandeep Varma, for instance, critiques the ongoing use of the fusion metaphor to describe bhangra and offers a theoretical model based on quantum mechanics. Yet, in urging that scholars need to analyze how bhangra means specfic things to different people, he risks reducing these questions of meaning by mapping them onto categories of people (such as those of nationality, ethnicity, and religion) at the expense of examining questions of power (Varma, "Quantum Bhangra").

   Dhiraj Murthy has written about East London's Asian electronic music scene on the basis of research he conducted in 2004–6. While he explains that "the musicians involved are predominantly young Asian males" and that he conceives of the scene as a "largely heterosexual masculine space," there is little analysis of gender and sexuality. Again, the only mention of women is that they are "rendered 'invisible'" (Murthy, "Representing South Asian Alterity?," 303). While he notes that many participants in the Asian electronic scene are middle class and that this elite aspect is a "failure" of the scene (ibid., 345), class also eludes his analysis.

2 Community Cohesion Review Team, chaired by Ted Cantle, *The Cantle Report*, 20.
3 The full text of Blunkett's speech is available in the *Guardian* for December 11, 2001: (http://www.guardian.co.uk/racism/Story).
4 Conversation with Arun Kundnani, July 12, 2011.
5 Murthy, "Representing South Asian Alterity?" 334.
6 Conversation with Arun Kundnani, July 12, 2011.
7 Britten, "Ethnic Radio Station to Ban 'Asian' Description."
8 Bhattacharjya, "The Global Sounds of the Asian Underground" (http://issues.lines-magazine.org/Art_Aug02/Nila.htm; accessed July 2011).
9 Ibid.

10 See his website, http://www.nitinsawhney.com/nitinsawhney/About.html, for a fuller list of his successes.
11 Bhattacharjya, "The Global Sounds of the Asian Underground" (http://issues.lines-magazine.org/Art_Aug02/Nila.htm; accessed July 2011).
12 Feld, "A Sweet Lullaby for World Music," *Public Culture* 12, no. 1 (January 1, 2000): 145–71.
13 Conversation with Arun Kundnani, July 12, 2011.
14 Murthy, "Representing South Asian Alterity?" 336.
15 Ibid., 337.
16 Steward, "Bhangra Spreads Its Empire."
17 Dudrah, *Bhangra: Birmingham and Beyond*, 18.
18 Hodgkinson, "Bhangra Knights."
19 Panel discussion for the *Soho Road* exhibit, March 18, 2011, 92YTribeca, New York City. I thank DJ Rekha for generously providing me with a videotaped version of this discussion.
20 http://www.bbc.co.uk/asiannetwork/help/whatisasiannetwork/index.shtml.
21 Sharma, "Telling Stories about Bhangra: A Short Review of the Soho Road to the Punjab Exhibition," *Anti-Babel* blog, October 10, 2007 (http://antibabel.wordpress.com/2007/10/04/telling-stories-about-bhangra-a-short-review-of-the-soho-road-to-the-punjab-exhibition; accessed July 10, 2011).
22 Bhattacharjya, "The Global Sounds of the Asian Underground" (http://issues.lines-magazine.org/Art_Aug02/Nila.htm; accessed July 10, 2011).
23 Interview with Ninder Johal, July 2006.
24 Ibid.
25 Panel discussion for the *Soho Road* exhibit, March 18, 2011, 92Y Tribeca, New York City.
26 DJ Vips participated in "The Big Bhangra Debate," an episode of Bobby Friction's program, "Friction," on the BBC Asian Network. This show aired on July 17, 2009. Some information about this show can be found on Friction's blog, http://www.bbc.co.uk/blogs/friction/2009/07/the_big_bhangra_debate.html.
27 Panel discussion for the *Soho Road* exhibit, March 18, 2011, 92Y Tribeca, New York City.
28 Panel discussion for the *Soho Road* exhibit, March 18, 2011, 92Y Tribeca, New York City. I thank Nina for sharing her work with me.
29 Conversation with Nina Chanpreet Singh, July 27, 2011.
30 Conversation with Arun Kundnani, July 12, 2011.
31 Panel discussion for the *Soho Road* exhibit, March 18, 2011, 92Y Tribeca, New York City.
32 Ibid.
33 Ibid.
34 Ibid.
35 DJ Vips, "The Big Bhangra Debate," July 17, 2009.
36 Steward, "Bhangra Spreads Its Empire."

Bibliography

Ahmed, Thufayel. "Music for the Masses." *Eastern Eye*, May 10, 1996.

Alexander, Claire. *The Asian Gang: Ethnicity, Identity, Masculinity*. Oxford: Berg, 2000.

Alexander, M. Jacqui, and Chandra Talpade Mohanty, eds. *Feminist Genealogies, Colonial Legacies, Democratic Futures*. New York: Routledge, 1997.

Ali, N., V. S. Kalra, and S. Sayyid, eds. *A Postcolonial People: South Asians in Britain*. London: Hurst & Company, 2006.

Anthias, Floya, Nira Yuval-Davis, and Harriet Cain. *Racialized Boundaries: Race, Nation, Gender, Colour and Class and the Anti-Racist Struggle*. New York: Routledge, 1993.

Appadurai, Arjun. *Modernity at Large: Cultural Dimensions of Globalization*. Minneapolis: University of Minnesota Press, 1996.

Atkins, E. Taylor. *Blue Nippon: Authenticating Jazz in Japan*. Durham: Duke University Press, 2001.

Austin, Joe, and Michael Nevin Willard. *Generations of Youth: Youth Cultures and History in Twentieth-century America*. New York: New York University Press, 1998.

Aziz, Shaista, and Gursharan Maan. "Rude Boys and Party Girls." *Eastern Eye*, November 27, 1998.

Back, Les. "Coughing Up Fire: Sound Systems in South-East London." *New Formations* 5 (1988): 141–52.

———. *New Ethnicities and Urban Culture: Racisms and Multiculture in Young Lives*. London: UCL Press, 1996.

Bald, Vivek. "'Lost' in the City." *South Asian Popular Culture* 5, no. 1 (2007): 59–76.

Ballantyne, Tony. "Displacement, Diaspora, and Difference in the Making of Bhangra." In *Between Colonialism and Diaspora: Sikh Cultural Formations in an Imperial World*, 121–59. Durham: Duke University Press, 2006.

Balliger, Robin. "Noisy Spaces: Popular Music Consumption, Social Fragmentation, and the Cultural Politics of Globalization in Trinidad." Ph.D. dissertation, Stanford University, 2000.

Bancil, Parv. "Made in England." Manuscript, 3rd draft, 1998.

Banerjea, Koushik. "Sounds of Whose Underground?: The Fine Tuning of Diaspora in an Age of Mechanical Reproduction." *Theory, Culture & Society* 17, no. 3 (June 1, 2000): 64–79.

Banerji, Sabita. "Bhangra, Ghazals and Beyond." *Folk Roots* 9, no. 51 (1987): 30–33.

———. "Ghazals to Bhangra in Great Britain." *Popular Music* 7, no. 2 (May 1988): 207–13.

Banerji, Sabita, and Gerd Baumann. "Bhangra 1984–88: Fusion and Professionalization in a Genre of South Asian Dance Music." *Black Music in Britain: Essay on the Afro-Asian Contribution to Popular Music*, ed. Paul Oliver, 137–52. Philadelphia: Open University Press, 1990.

Baumann, Gerd. "The Re-invention of Bhangra: Social Change and Aesthetic Shifts in Punjabi Music in Britain." *World of Music* 32, no. 2 (1990): 81–97.

Belsey, Catherine. *The Subject of Tragedy: Identity and Difference in Renaissance Drama*. London: Methuen, 1985.

Bennett, Andrew. "Bhangra in Newcastle: Music, Ethnic Identity and the Role of Local Knowledge." *Innovation: The European Journal of Social Science Research* 10, no. 1 (March 1997): 107–16.

———. *Popular Music and Youth Culture: Music, Identity and Place*. Washington, D.C.: Palgrave Macmillan, 2000.

———, Barry Shank, and Jason Toynbee. *The Popular Music Studies Reader*. New York: Routledge, 2006.

Bhabha, Homi, K. *The Location of Culture*. London: Routledge, 1994.

———. "Of Mimicry and Man: The Ambivalence of Colonial Discourse." *October* 28 (1984).

———. "The Other Question: Stereotype, Discrimination and the Discourse of Colonialism." *Screen* 24, no. 6 (November–December 1983): 18–36.

Bhachu, Parminder. *Twice Migrants: East African Sikh Settlers in Britain*. London: Travistock, 1986.

Bhangra Child. "Editorial." *Eastern Eye*, January 19, 1996.

Bhattacharjee, Ananya. "The Public/Private Mirage: Mapping Homes and Undomesticating Violence Work in the South Asian Immigrant Community." In *Feminist Genealogies, Colonial Legacies, Democratic Futures*, ed. M. Jacqui Alexander and Chandra Talpade Mohanty, 308–29. New York: Routledge, 1997.

Bhattacharjya, Nilanjana. "The Global Sounds of the Asian Underground." *lines* (August 2002). http://issues.lines-magazine.org/Art_Aug02/Nila.htm.

Bourdieu, Pierre. *Distinction: A Social Critique of the Judgement of Taste*. Cambridge: Harvard University Press, 1984.

Brah, Avtar. "The 'Asian' in Britain." In *A Postcolonial People: South Asians in Britain*, ed. N. Ali, V. S. Kalra, and S. Sayyid, 35–61. London: Hurst and Company, 2006.

———. *Cartographies of Diaspora: Contesting Identities*. New York: Routledge, 1996.

Brah, Avtar, Mary Hickman J., and Mairtin Mac an Ghaill. *Thinking Identities: Ethnicity, Racism, and Culture*. New York: St. Martin's Press, 1999.

Brett, Philip. "Out with the Old." *Musical Times* 142, no. 1876 (autumn 2001): 3.

Britten, Nick. "Ethnic Radio Station to Ban 'Asian' Description." *Telegraph*, January 23, 2002. http://www.telegraph.co.uk/news/uknews.

Brown, Judith M. *Global South Asians: Introducing the Modern Diaspora*. Cambridge: Cambridge University Press, 2006.

Butler, Judith. *Bodies That Matter: On the Discursive Limits of "Sex."* New York: Routledge, 1993.

CCCS (Centre for Contemporary Cultural Studies). *The Empire Strikes Back: Race and Racism in 70s Britain*. London: Hutchinson, 1982.

Chadha, Gurinder. *I'm British But...* Umbi Films. San Francisco: National Asian American Telecommunications Association, 1989.

Chambers, Iain, and Lidia Curti. *The Post-Colonial Question: Common Skies, Divided Horizons.* New York: Routledge, 1996.

Chatterjee, Partha. "Colonialism, Nationalism, and Colonialized Women: The Contest in India." *American Ethnologist* 16, no. 4 (November 1989): 622–33.

———. *The Nation and Its Fragments: Colonial and Postcolonial Histories.* Princeton: Princeton University Press, 1993.

Clancy, Anna, Mike Hough, Rebecca Aust, and Chris Kershaw. *Crime, Policing and Justice: The Experience of Ethnic Minorities. Findings from the 2000 British Crime Survey.* Research Study 223. Home Office Research Studies. London: Home Office, 2001.

Clarke, Colin G., Ceri Peach, and Steven Vertovec, eds. *South Asians Overseas: Migration and Ethnicity.* Cambridge: Cambridge University Press, 1990.

Clarke, John, Stuart Hall, Tony Jefferson, and Brian Roberts. "Subcultures, Cultures, and Class: A Theoretical Overview." In *Resistance Through Rituals: Youth Subcultures in Post-War Britain,* ed. Stuart Hall and Tony Jefferson, 9–74. New York: Routledge, 1993.

Clifford, James. "Diaspora." *Cultural Anthropology* 9, no. 3 (1994): 302–38.

Cohen, D. M. "The Jew and Shylock." *Shakespeare Quarterly* 31, no. 1 (April 1980): 53–63.

Cohen, Stanley. *Folk Devils and Moral Panics: The Creation of the Mods and Rockers.* London: MacGibbon and Kee, 1972.

Combahee River Collective. *Combahee River Collective Statement: Black Feminist Organizing in the Seventies and Eighties.* New York: Kitchen Table Women of Color Press, 1977.

Commission for Racial Equality. "Racial Attacks and Harrassment: Fact Sheet." London: CRE, 1999.

Community Cohesion Review Team, chaired by Ted Cantle. *The Cantle Report.* England, 2001.

Condry, Ian. *Hip-Hop Japan: Rap and the Paths of Cultural Globalization.* Durham: Duke University Press, 2006.

Cooper, Carolyn. "Mix Up the Indian with All the Patwa: Rajamuffin Sounds in 'Cool' Britannia." *Language and Intercultural Communication* 4, no. 1 (2004): 81–99.

Crenshaw, Kimberlé. "Mapping the Margins: Intersectionality, Identity Politics, and Violence Against Women of Color." *Stanford Law Review,* no. 43 (1991): 1241–99.

Das Gupta, Monisha. *Unruly Immigrants: Rights, Activism, and Transnational South Asian Politics in the United States.* Durham: Duke University Press, 2006.

Dawson, Ashley. "Dub Mentality: South Asian Dance Music in Britain and the Production of Space." *Social Semiotics* 12, no. 1 (April 2002): 27–44.

———. *Mongrel Nation.* Ann Arbor: University of Michigan Press, 2007.

———. "'This Is the Digital Underclass': Asian Dub Foundation and Hip-Hop Cosmopolitanism." *Social Semiotics* 12, no. 1 (April 2002): 27–44.

Dhingra, Dolly. "Bombay Nights: London's Young Asian Community Is Learning to Let Its Hair Down. Dolly Dhingra Samples Two Clubs Capturing the Eastern Imagination," *Independent,* April 4, 1994.

Diehl, Keila. *Echoes from Dharamsala: Music in the Life of a Tibetan Refugee Community.* Berkeley: University of California Press, 2002.

Din, Ikhlaq, and Cedric Cullingford. "Boyzone and Bhangra: The Place of Popular and Minority Cultures." *Race, Ethnicity and Education* 7, no. 3 (2004): 307–20.

Duddy, Thomas. "Impure Aesthetics: Literature, Ideology and Bloom's Canon." *Think Journal* 2, no. 4 (winter, 2010). http://poems.com/special_features/prose/essay_duddy.php.

Dudrah, Rajinder. *Bhangra: Birmingham and Beyond.* Birmingham: Birmingham City Council Library and Archive Service, 2007.

———. "British Bhangra Music and the Battle of Britpop: South Asian Cultural Identity and Cultural Politics in Urban Britain." *Migration: A European Journal of International Migration and Ethnic Relations*, nos. 39/40/41 (2002): 173–93.

———. "Cultural Production in the British Bhangra Music Industry: Music-Making, Locality, and Gender." *International Journal of Punjab Studies* 9 (2002): 219–51.

———. "Drum 'n' Dhol: British Bhangra Music and Diasporic: South Asian Identity Formation." *European Journal of Cultural Studies* 5, no. 3 (2002): 363–83.

Epstein, Steven. "An Incitement to Discourse: Sociology and *The History of Sexuality.*" *Sociological Forum* 18, no. 3 (2003): 485–502.

Espiritu, Yen Le. "'We Don't Sleep around like White Girls Do': Family, Culture, and Gender in Filipina American Lives." *Signs* 26, no. 2 (winter 2001): 415–40.

Fanon, Frantz. *The Wretched of the Earth.* New York: Grove Press, 1965.

Farrell, Gerry. *Indian Music and the West.* New York: Oxford University Press, 2000.

Feld, Steven. "From Schizophonia to Schismogenesis: The Discourses and Practices of World Music and World Beat." In *Traffic in Culture: Refiguring Art and Anthropology,* ed. George E. Marcus and Fred R. Meyers, 96–126. Berkeley: University of California Press, 1995.

———. "A Sweet Lullaby for World Music." *Public Culture* 12, no. 1 (January 1, 2000): 145–71.

Fisher, Michael H., Shompa Lahiri, and Shinder Thandi. *A South-Asian History of Britain: Four Centuries of Peoples from the Indian Sub-Continent.* Oxford: Greenwood, 2007.

Foucault, Michel. *Discipline and Punish: The Birth of the Prison.* New York: Pantheon Books, 1977.

———. *The History of Sexuality.* New York: Pantheon Books, 1978.

Fox, Richard G., and Orin Starn. *Between Resistance and Revolution: Cultural Politics and Social Protest.* New Brunswick, N.J.: Rutgers University Press, 1997.

Fregoso, Rosa Linda. "Homegirls, *Cholas,* and *Pachucas* in Cinema: Taking Over the Public Sphere." *California History* 74, no. 3 (fall 1995): 316–27.

Frith, Simon. "Music and Identity." In *Questions of Cultural Identity,* ed. Stuart Hall and Paul Du Gay, 108–27. Thousand Oaks, Calif.: Sage, 1996.

Ghai, Raj. "We're on Our Way to Wembley?" *Eastern Eye,* June 14, 1997.

Gilman, Sander L. *Difference and Pathology: Stereotypes of Sexuality, Race, and Madness.* Ithaca: Cornell University Press, 1985.

Gilroy, Paul. *The Black Atlantic: Modernity and Double Consciousness.* Cambridge: Harvard University Press, 1993.

———. *Small Acts: Thoughts on the Politics of Black Cultures*. London: Serpent's Tail, 1993.

———. *"There Ain't No Black in the Union Jack": The Cultural Politics of Race and Nation*. London: Hutchinson, 1987.

Ginsburg, Faye. "'From Little Things, Big Things Grow': Indigenous Media and Cultural Activism." In *Between Resistance and Revolution: Cultural Politics and Protest*, ed. Richard Fox and Orin Starn, 118–44. New Brunswick, N.J.: Rutgers University Press, 1997.

Goldberg, David Theo, and John Solomos. *A Companion to Racial and Ethnic Studies*. Malden, Mass.: Blackwell, 2002.

Gopinath, Gayatri. "Bombay, U.K., Yuba City: Bhangra Music and the Engendering of Diaspora." *Diaspora* 4, no. 3 (1995): 303–21.

———. *Impossible Desires: Queer Diasporas and South Asian Public Cultures*. Durham: Duke University Press, 2005.

Greater London Authority. *Play It Right: Asian Creative Industries in London*. London, February 2003.

Grewal, Inderpal. *Transnational America: Feminisms, Diasporas. Neoliberalisms*. Durham: Duke University Press, 2005.

———, and Caren Kaplan, eds. *Scattered Hegemonies: Postmodernity and Transnational Feminist Practices*. Minneapolis: University of Minnesota Press, 1994.

Halberstam, Judith. *Skin Shows: Gothic Horror and the Technology of Monsters*. Durham: Duke University Press, 1995.

Hall, Kathleen. *Lives in Translation: Sikh Youth as British Citizens*. Philadelphia: University of Pennsylvania Press, 2002.

Hall, Stuart. "Cultural Identity and Diaspora." In *Identity: Community, Culture, Difference*, ed. Jonathan Rutherford, 222–37. London: Lawrence & Wishart, 1990.

———. "Fantasy, Identity, Politics." In *Cultural Remix: Theories of Politics and the Popular*, ed. Erica Carter, James Donald, and Judith Squires, 3–9. London: Lawrence & Wishart, 1995.

———. "Minimal Selves." In *Identity: the Real Me*. ICA Documents 6. London: Institute of Contemporary Arts, 1988. 44–46.

———. "Old and New Identities, Old and New Ethnicities." In *Culture, Globalization and the World-System: Contemporary Conditions for the Representation of Identity*, ed. Anthony D. King, 41–68. Minneapolis, Minn.: University of Minnesota Press, 1997.

———. "The Question of Cultural Identity." In *Modernity: An Introduction to Modern Societies*, ed. Stuart Hall, David Held, Don Hubert, and Kenneth Thomson, 595–634. Cambridge, Mass: Blackwell, 1996.

———. "When Was 'the Post-Colonial'? Thinking at the Limit." In *The Post-Colonial Question: Common Skies, Divided Horizons*, ed. Iain Chambers and Lidia Curti, 242–60. New York: Routledge, 1996.

———. "The Work of Representation." In *Representation: Cultural Representations and Signifying Practices*, ed. Stuart Hall, 13–74. London: Sage, in association with the Open University, 1997.

Hebdige, Dick. *Subculture: The Meaning of Style*. London: Routledge, 1979.

Hesse, Barnor. "White Governmentality: Urbanism, Nationalism, Racism." In *Imagin-

ing Cities: Scripts, Signs, Memory, ed. Sallie Westwood and John Williams, 86–103. New York: Taylor and Francis, 1997.

Hiro, Dilip. *Black British, White British*. London: Eyre & Spottiswoode, 1971.

Hobsbawm, Eric, and Terence Ranger. *The Invention of Tradition*. Cambridge: Cambridge University Press, 1992.

Hodgkinson, Will. "Bhangra Knights." *Guardian*. December 17, 2004.

Huq, Rupa. "Asian Kool? Bhangra and Beyond." In *The Popular Music Studies Reader*, ed. Andy Bennett, Berry Shank, and Jason Toynbee, 201–7. New York: Routledge, 2005.

———. "From the Margins to Mainstream?: Representations of British Asian Youth Musical Cultural Expression from Bhangra to Asian Underground Music." *Young* 11, no. 1 (2003): 29–48.

Hurt, Byron. *Hip Hop: Beyond Beats and Rhymes*. Northampton, Mass.: Media Education Foundation, 2006.

Hutnyk, John. "Adorno at Womad: South Asian Crossovers and the Limits of Hybridity." In *Debating Cultural Hybridity: Multi-Cultural Identities and the Politics of Anti-Racism*, ed. Pnina Werbner and Tariq Modood, 106–36. Atlantic Highlands, N.J.: Zed Books, 1998

———. *Critique of Exotica: Music, Politics and the Culture Industry*. London: Pluto Press, 2000.

———. "Hybridity." *Ethnic and Racial Studies* 28, no. 1 (2005): 79–102.

Hutton, Fiona. *Risky Pleasures?: Club Cultures and Feminine Identities*. Hampshire, England: Ashgate, 2006.

Hyder, Rehan. *Brimful of Asia: Negotiating Ethnicity on the UK Music Scene*. Burlington, Vt.: Ashgate, 2004.

"Interview with Sukhinder Shinda." *Eastern Eye*, June 20, 1997.

Ismail, Qadri. "'Boys Will Be Boys': Gender and National Agency in Frantz Fanon and LTTE." *Economic and Political Weekly* 27, no. 31/32 (August 1–8, 1992): 1677–79.

Jacobs, Jane M. "Eastern Trading: Diasporas, Dwelling and Place." *Edge of Empire: Postcolonialism and the City*, 70–102. New York: Routledge, 1996.

Kalra, Virinder S. "Between Emasculation and Hypermasculinity: Theorizing British South Asian Masculinities." *South Asian Popular Culture* 7, no. 2 (2009): 113–25.

———, and John Hutnyk. "Brimful of Agitation, Authenticity and Appropriation: Madonna's 'Asian Kool.'" *Postcolonial Studies* 1, no. 3 (1998): 339–55.

———. "Vilayeti Rhythms: Beyond Bhangra's Emblematic Status to a Translation of Lyrical Texts." *Theory, Culture & Society* 17, no. 3 (2000): 80–102.

Kaur, Raminder, and Virinder Kalra. "Xi Amount of Bhangra and Ragga." Unpublished paper presented at the "Margins within Margins" Workshop. London: School of Oriental and African Studies, 1993.

Krishnaswamy, Revathi. *Effeminism: The Economy of Colonial Desire*. Ann Arbor: University of Michigan Press, 1999.

Kundnani, Arun. *The End of Tolerance: Racism in 21st Century Britain*. London: Pluto Press, 2007.

Laidler, Karen Joe, and Geoffrey Hunt. "Accomplishing Femininity among the Girls in the Gang." *British Journal of Criminology* 41, no. 4 (2001): 656–78.

"Letters to the Editor." *Eastern Eye*, April 11, 1997.

Lipsitz, George. *Dangerous Crossroads: Popular Music, Postmodernism and the Focus of Place*. New York: Verso, 1997.

Livingston, Ken. "Foreword." In *Play It Right: Asian Creative Industries in London*, Greater London Authority. London, February 2003.

Lukose, Ritty A. *Liberalization's Children: Gender, Youth, and Consumer Citizenship in Globalizing India*. Durham: Duke University Press, 2009.

Mahon, Maureen. *Right to Rock: The Black Rock Coalition and the Cultural Politics of Race*. Durham: Duke University Press, 2004.

Maira, Sunaina. *Desis in the House: Indian American Youth Culture in NYC*. Philadelphia: Temple University Press, 2002.

———. "Henna and Hip Hop: The Politics of Cultural Production and the Work of Cultural Studies." *Journal of Asian American Studies* 3, no. 3 (2000): 329–69.

Majumdar, Krishnendu. "Notes from the Asian Underground." National Union of Journalists: London Freelance. Felix Dearden Award Essay, 1999. http://media.gn.apc.org/award/felixd99.html.

Malik, Sarita. *Representing Black Britain: A History of Black and Asian Images on British Television*. Thousand Oaks, Calif.: Sage, 2002.

Mani, Bakirathi. *Aspiring to Home: South Asians in America*. Stanford, Calif.: Stanford University Press, 2011.

Mani, Lata. *Contentious Traditions: The Debate on Sati in Colonial India*. Berkeley: University of California Press, 1998.

———, and Ruth Frankenberg. "Crosscurrents, Crosstalk: Race, 'Postcoloniality.'" *Cultural Studies* 7, no. 2 (1993): 292–310.

Mark, Markie. "Mainstream Dream." Documentaries. BBC Asian Network, 1996.

Mathew, Biju. *Taxi! Cabs and Capitalism in New York City*. New York: New Press, 2005.

McClintock, Anne. "The Angel of Progress: Pitfalls of the Term 'Post-Colonialism.'" *Social Text*, no. 31 (1992): 84–88.

McGuire, Stryker. "This Time I've Come to Bury Cool Britannia." *Observer*, March 29, 2009.

McRobbie, Angela. "Different, Youthful, Subjectivities: Towards a Cultural Sociology of Youth." *Postmodernism and Popular Culture*, 177–97. New York: Routledge, 1994.

———. *Feminism and Youth Culture: From Jackie to Just Seventeen*. Leicester: Unwin Hyman, 1991.

———. "Jackie Magazine: Romantic Individualism and the Teenage Girl." *Feminism and Youth Culture*, 67–117. New York: Routledge, 2000.

———. "Settling Accounts with Subcultures." *Feminism and Youth Culture*, 26–43. New York: Routledge, 2000.

———, and Jenny Garber. *Girls and Subcultures*. New York: Routledge, 2000.

Mercer, Kobena. *Welcome to the Jungle: New Positions in Black Cultural Studies*. New York: Routledge, 1994.

Mills, Charles. *The Racial Contract*. Ithaca: Cornell University Press, 1997.

Miranda, Marie Keta. *Homegirls in the Public Sphere*. Austin: University of Texas Press, 2003.

Modood, Tariq. "Political Blackness and British Asians." *Sociology* 28, no. 4 (November 1994): 859–76.

———, and Pnina Werbner, eds. *The Politics of Multiculturalism in the New Europe: Racism, Identity, and Community*. New York: Palgrave Macmillan, 1997.

Mohanty, Chandra Talpade, Ann Russo, and Lourdes Torres, eds. *Third World Women and the Politics of Feminism*. Bloomington: Indiana University Press, 1991.

Morley, David, and Kevin Robins, eds. *British Cultural Studies: Geography, Nationality, and Identity*. New York: Oxford University Press, 2001.

Murthy, Dhiraj. "Representing South Asian Alterity? East London's Asia Electronic Music Scene and the Articulation of Globally Mediated Identities." *European Journal of Cultural Studies* 12, no. 3 (August 2009): 329–48.

———. "A South Asian American Diasporic Aesthetic Community? Ethnicity and New York City's 'Asian Electronic Music' Scene." *Ethnicities* 7, no. 2 (2007): 225–47.

Niranjana, Tejaswini. *Mobilizing India: Women, Music, and Migration Between India and Trinidad*. Durham: Duke University Press, 2006.

Oliver, Paul. *Black Music in Britain: Essays on the Afro-Asian Contribution to Popular Music*. Philadelphia: Open University Press, 1990.

Openshaw, Jeanne. *Seeking Bāuls of Bengal*. Cambridge: Cambridge University Press, 2002.

Parmar, Pratibha. "Gender, Race and Class: Asian Women in Resistance." In *The Empire Strikes Back: Race and Racism in 70s Britain*, ed. CCCS (Centre for Contemporary Cultural Studies), 235–74. London: Routledge, 1982.

Pateman, Carole. *The Sexual Contract*. Stanford, Calif.: Stanford University Press, 1988.

———, and Charles Mills. *Contract and Domination*. Cambridge: Polity, 2007.

Pini, Maria. *Club Cultures and Female Subjectivity: The Move from Home to House*. New York: Palgrave Macmillan, 2001.

"PMC Five Fingers." *Eastern Eye*, June 20, 1997.

Prakash, Gyan. "Postcolonial Criticism and Indian Historiography." *Social Text* 31 (1992): 8–19.

Prashad, Vijay. *The Karma of Brown Folk*. Minneapolis: University of Minnesota Press, 2000.

Puri, Shalini. "Race, Rape, and Representation: Indo-Caribbean Women and Cultural Nationalism." *Cultural Critique*, no. 36 (spring 1997): 119–63.

Puwar, Nirmal, and Parvati Raghuram, eds. *South Asian Women in the Diaspora*. Oxford, U.K.: Berg, 2003.

Qureshi, Bilel. "Nitin Sawhney: In Search of the 'Undersound.'" *All Things Considered*, January 13, 2010. http://www.npr.org/templates/story/story.php?storyId=122494341.

Rana, Junaid. *Terrifying Muslims: Race and Labor in the South Asian Diaspora*. Durham: Duke University Press, 2011.

Rich, Adrienne. *Blood, Bread, and Poetry: Selected Prose 1979–1985*. New York: Norton, 1986.

Ritu, DJ. "Bhangra/Asian Beat: One-Way Ticket to British Asia." In *World Music, The Rough Guide: Africa, Europe and the Middle East*, ed. Simon Broughton, Mark Ellingham, and Richard Trillo, 83–90. London: Rough Guides, 1999.

DJ Ritu. *The Rough Guide to Bhangra*. London, U.K.: World Music Network, 2001.
Ross, Andrew. "Introduction." In *Microphone Fiends: Youth Music and Youth Culture*, ed. Tricia Rose and Andrew Ross, 1–13. New York: Routledge, 1994.
Roy, Parama. *Alimentary Tracts: Appetites, Aversions, and the Postcolonial*. Durham: Duke University Press, 2010.
Said, Edward. *Orientalism*. New York: Pantheon Books, 1978.
Sawhney, Nitin. "It's Time to Move On." *Eastern Eye*, October 10, 1997.
Sayyid, S. "Introduction: BrAsians: Postcolonial People, Ironic Citizens." In *A Postcolonial People: South Asians in Britain*, ed. N. Ali, V. S. Kalra, and S. Sayyid, 1–10. London: Hurst & Company, 2006.
Scott, Joan. "The Evidence of Experience." *Critical Inquiry* 17, no. 4 (1991): 773–97.
Seop, Elisabeth, and Sunaina Maira. *Youthscapes*. Philadelphia: University of Pennsylvania Press, 2005.
Shabbs. "The Boys Are Back in Town!" *Eastern Eye*, July 25, 1997.
———. "Interview [of Apache Indian]." *Eastern Eye*, September 26, 1997.
———. "Jatt Aagiya." *Eastern Eye*, September 19, 1997.
———. "The Nice Boys of Bhangra [profile of Intermix]." *Eastern Eye*, June 13, 1997.
———. "Once Upon a Sahota." *Eastern Eye*, June 6, 1997.
Sharma, Nitasha Tamar. *Hip Hop Desis: South Asian Americans, Blackness, and a Global Race Consciousness*. Durham: Duke University Press, 2010.
Sharma, Sanjay. "Noisy Asians or 'Asian Noise'?" In *Dis-Orienting Rhythms: The Politics of the New Asian Dance Music*, ed. Sanjay Sharma, John Hutnyk, and Ashwani Sharma, 32–60. Atlantic Highlands, N.J.: Zed Books, 1996.
———. "Asian Sounds." In *A Postcolonial People: South Asians in Britain*, ed. N. Ali, V. S. Karla, and S. Sayyid, 317–26. London: Hurst & Company, 2006.
———. "The Sounds of Alterity." In *The Auditory Culture Reader*, ed. Michael Bull and Les Back, 409–18. Oxford: Berg, 2003.
———, John Hutnyk, and Ashwani Sharma, eds. *Dis-Orienting Rhythms: The Politics of the New Asian Dance Music*. Atlantic Highlands, N.J.: Zed Books, 1996.
DJ Sheikh. "Why Bhangra's Here to Stay." *Eastern Eye*, October 17, 1997.
Shohat, Ella. "Notes on the 'Post-Colonial.'" *Social Text*, no. 31 (1992): 99–113.
Shukla, Sandhya. *India Abroad: Diasporic Cultures of Postwar America and England*. Princeton: Princeton University Press, 2003.
———. "Locations for South Asian Diasporas." *Annual Review of Anthropology* 30, no. 1 (October 2001): 551–72.
Sinha, Mrinalini. *Colonial Masculinity: The "Manly Englishman" and the "Effeminate Bengali" in the Late Nineteenth Century*. Manchester: Manchester University Press, 1995.
Skeggs, Beverley. *Formations of Class and Gender: Becoming Respectable*. Thousand Oaks, Calif.: Sage, 1997.
Smith, Andrea. *Conquest: Sexual Violence and American Indian Genocide*. Cambridge, Mass.: South End Press, 2005.
Solomos, John. *Race and Racism in Britain*. 2nd ed. Basingstoke: Macmillan, 1993.
Sterling, Marvin D. *Babylon East: Performing Dancehall, Roots Reggae, and Rastafari in Japan*. Durham: Duke University Press, 2010.
Steward, Sue. "Bhangra Spreads Its Empire." *Observer Music Monthly*. London, October 14, 2007.

Swiss, Thomas, John Sloop, and Andrew Herman, eds. *Mapping the Beat: Popular Music and Contemporary Theory*. Malden, Mass.: Blackwell Publishers, 1998.

Thandi, Shinder. "Migrating to the 'Mother Country,' 1947–1980." In *A South-Asian History of Britain: Four Centuries of Peoples from the Indian Sub-Continent*, ed. Michael H. Fisher, Shompa Lahiri, and Shinder Thandi, 159–81. Oxford: Greenwood, 2007.

"The Don Raja Returns." *Eastern Eye*, November 20, 1998.

Thornton, Sarah. *Club Cultures: Music, Media and Subcultural Capital*. Cambridge, U.K.: Polity Press, 1995.

"2B or Not to B21." *Eastern Eye*, July 10, 1998.

"Up the Garden Path of Bhangra." *Eastern Eye*, December 5, 1997.

Varma, Sandeep. "Quantum Bhangra: Bhangra Music and Identity in the South Asian Diaspora." *Limina: A Journal of Historical and Cultural Studies* 11 (2005): 17–27.

Visram, Rozina. *Asians in Britain: 400 Years of History*. London: Pluto Press, 2002.

———. *Ayahs, Lascars, and Princes: Indians in Britain, 1700–1947*. London: Pluto Press, 1986.

Wald, Gayle. "Rock Music, Feminism, and the Cultural Construction of Female Youth." *Signs* 23, no. 3 (1998): 585–610.

Walser, Robert. *Running with the Devil: Power, Gender, and Madness in Heavy Metal Music*. Hanover, N.H.: University Press of New England, 1993.

Warwick, Jacqueline. "'Make Way for the Indian': Bhangra Music and South Asian Presence in Toronto." *Popular Music and Society* 24, no. 2 (2000): 25.

Watt, Paul. "Going Out of Town: Youth, Race, and Place in the South East of England." *Environment and Planning D: Society and Space* 16, no. 6 (1998): 687–703.

"When Will I Be Famous?" *Eastern Eye*, May 10, 1996.

Whitney, Anna. "The Wag, Once the Epitome of Eighties Cool, to Become an Irish Theme Pub." *Independent*, April 24, 2001.

Wicked Miah. "A Parting Song." *Eastern Eye*, July 3, 1998.

———. "21st Centyury [*sic*] Boys." *Eastern Eye*, March 20, 1998.

———. "Wicked Miah: The Man in the Fridge." *Eastern Eye*, January 2, 1998.

———. "Wicked Miah: The Man Next Door." *Eastern Eye*, June 20, 1997.

Willis, Paul. *Learning to Labour: How Working Class Kids Get Working Class Jobs*. Farnborough, England: Saxon House, 1978.

Wilson, Amrit. *Dreams, Questions, Struggles: South Asian Women in Britain*. London: Pluto Press, 2006.

Young, Robert. *Colonial Desire: Hybridity in Theory, Culture, and Race*. New York: Routledge, 1995.

———. *White Mythologies: Writing History and the West*. London; New York: Routledge, 1990.

Zubaida, Sami, ed. "Introduction." In *Race and Racialism* 1–16. London: Tavistock Publications, 1970.

Zuberi, Nabeel. *Sounds English: Transnational Popular Music*. Urbana: University of Illinois Press, 2001.

Index

agency, 15, 28, 39, 77–81, 121–22, 129, 157, 183–85
Ahmed, Thufayel, 46
Alaap, 36, 193
Ali, Mohammed Akber. *See* Badmarsh
angry Asian (trope), 28, 75–77, 80, 92, 97, 108–13. *See also* masculinity; politics; race and racialization
Anokha (club), 2–4, 9, 29, 71, 160–61, 163, 169, 173–82, 224n1
Anokha (Singh), 3, 71
Apache Indian, 35, 41, 53–57, 54, 58, 63, 68
Apna Sangeet, 37–38, 47, 66
Apna Sangeet: Greatest Hits, 47
"Arranged Marriage" (Apache Indian), 55
Arts Council of England, 85
Asian Dub Foundation (ADF), 70–73, 76–78, 203n3, 217n18, 218n30. *See also* Singh, Talvin
Asian gang trope, 143–45. *See also* girl gangs
Asians (British): British colonialism and, x, 10–14, 36–37, 52, 67, 74–77, 211n7; class divisions within, 16–24, 51–52, 67–70, 93–96, 126–39, 156, 177–85; definitions of, 205n24; masculinity and, 1, 18–19, 34–48, 53–69, 108–13, 140–51, 173–75, 222n16; racism toward, 2, 5, 7–8, 42–45, 71–72, 74–77, 80–82, 124, 161–62, 167, 187–89; religious differences and, 7–8, 13, 26, 88, 93, 98, 110, 143, 188–92, 199; stereotypes of, 42–45, 49, 52, 74–77, 84–85, 92–97, 105, 108, 110–13, 166–69. *See also* cultural nationalism; diaspora (definitions); gender; hybridity; identity; race and racialization
Asian Underground: authenticity concerns and, 68–69, 86–88, 161–63, 167–69; belonging and, 169–75, 180; bhangra's relation to, 45–53, 80; British press and, 74–77, 81; class associations of, 3, 52, 69, 165, 169–75, 177–85; community representation and, 68–69; cultural nationalism's responses to, 19; definitions of, 160; gender politics in, 72–75, 77–78, 106–7, 160–61, 169–73, 183–85; mainstream acceptance of, 2–4, 21, 27–28, 34–35, 40–42, 48–53, 57–58, 71, 79–82, 107–8, 167–69, 179, 182–85, 189–93, 215n79; political resistance and, 8–10, 71–73, 77–80, 82–92, 99–108, 177–85; race and ethnicity intersections with, 16, 175–85; scholarly attention to, 77–78; women's experiences with, 16, 24, 164, 171, 178
assimilation pressure, 19–20, 186–89, 205n31. *See also* bad Asian girl (trope); belonging; Britain; modernity
Atkins, E. Taylor, 20, 208n55
Atlas, Natacha, 84
Aurora-Madan, Sonya, 76
authenticity (ethnic): Asian Underground and, 68–69, 86–88, 171–73, 175–77; bhangra performances and, 34–39, 53, 67, 171–72, 178–80; black musical forms and, 48–53; club-going and, 129–39, 177–85; gender and, 5–6,

authenticity (ethnic) (*cont.*) 16–21, 29, 167; political resistance and, 73–92, 99–108, 177–85. *See also* cultural nationalism; gender; identity; tradition
Ayres, Ben, 75

B21 (group), 63–69
Babylon East (Sterling), 20, 208n55
bad Asian girl (trope), 29, 130–33, 140–41, 146–59, 164, 221n10
Badmarsh, 28, 73, 80, 82, 92–98, 104–5, 107, 109–11, 219n48
Bancil, Parv, 79
Banerji, Sabita, 36–37, 40, 213n50
Bangla (language), 102, 119
Bangladesh, 11, 13, 99–108
barbarism (trope), 48–53, 86–87, 145
Barnett, Laura, 89
Basement Bhangra (club), 196
Baumann, Gerd, 36–37, 40, 213n50
BBC Asian Network, 33, 195, 200
Beatles, 68
belonging: Asian Underground and, 169–75, 180; assimilation pressures and, 19–20, 188–89, 205n31; bhangra's traditionality and, 48–53, 134–39, 178–79; citizenship and, 11–14, 45, 102, 188–89; gender and, 108–13; hybrid identities and, 6, 9, 16–21, 33–34, 166–69; mainstream appeal and, 27–28; political resistance movements and, 73, 99–108, 177–85. *See also* Asians (British); Britain; ethnicity; race and racialization
Bend It Like Beckham (Chadha), 9
Beyond Skin (Sawhney), 82, 89, 91, 92, 112, 181, 191
bhangra: Asian Underground's relation to, 57–58; belonging and, 134–39, 178–79; black musical influences and, ix–x, 2, 16, 19, 35, 134–35; class identities and, 148–59, 180, 183–85; club scene of, 1–2, 24, 117–24, 129–39, 164, 199; community responsibility and, 6, 19,

34–35, 48–53, 55–56, 68–69; contemporary-, 193–200; ethnic authenticity and, 2–4, 14–15, 24, 34–39, 46–53, 67–69, 80, 84, 86–87, 105, 166–69, 193; mainstream's relation to, ix–x, 21–23, 27, 33–39, 42–45, 53, 80–82, 129, 196, 210n2, 212n32; masculinity and, 5, 34–39, 42–48, 53–69, 110, 140–51; political resistance and, 72–73, 99–108; religious misidentification and, 198–200; violence and, 118–21, 140, 142–51, 187; women's experiences with, 16, 19, 28, 39, 117–24, 151–59, 171–72, 178, 183–85, 201. *See also* cultural nationalism; cultured hard boys; gender; identity; lad-like boy bands; masculinity
Bharatiya Janata Party, 88, 219n43
Bhaskar, Anjula, 75
Bhatia, Anjali, 75–76
Bhatia, Rajni, 75
Bhattacharjee, Ananya, 129
Bhattacharjya, Nilanjana, 190, 196
Bitti, Satwinder, 38
black(ness): as antiracist catchall, 13, 181, 206n36; bhangra's relation to, ix–x, 1–2, 16, 19, 35, 133–39; club experiences and, 121–22, 128–39, 142–45, 180; gendering of, 53–63, 124, 133–39; mainstream appeal of, 53–59, 62–63, 67–69, 175–77; political resistance and, 77–78, 96–98; stereotypes about, 133–34, 139
Black Star Liner, 77, 189
Blue Nippon (Atkins), 20, 208n55
Blue Note (club), 3, 160, 178, 182–83
Blunkett, David, 188
Bobby Friction, 33, 161, 194
Bombay Jungle (club), 1–2, 9, 21, 27, 120
"Bombay Nights" (Mistry), 1
"Boom-Shak-a-lak" (Apache Indian), 41, 55
Bose, Jayanta, 84
Bradford 12, 13
Brah, Avtar, 10

Britain: belonging in, 6, 9, 27–28, 102, 108–13, 205n31; colonial history of, x, 10–14, 36–37, 52, 67, 211n7, 220n55; mainstream press in, 74–78, 81; music industry in, 21–23, 36–45, 57–58, 68–69, 71, 76–77, 80–82, 93–96, 100–108; political resistance in, 71–108, 177–85; racism in, 5–7, 10–15, 21–23, 28, 39, 49, 71, 73–74, 77–86, 93–96, 103–8, 117–24, 128, 130–33, 142–45, 167, 173–75, 187–89, 200–201, 211n7; religious identity and, 7, 93, 97–98, 110, 143, 188–89, 192, 199. *See also* class; colonialism; gender; race and racialization
British Asians (definition), 26. *See also* Asians (British)
British Nationality Act, 12
Britten, Nick, 189
bullying, 49–50, 128, 213n55
Bush, George W., 193

Cantle Report, 188–89
capitalism, 42–45, 53, 80–82, 96–98, 100–108, 182, 197–98
Chadha, Gurinder, 9, 119, 220n57
Chag, Niraj, 85
Chana, Ameet, 14, 39, 46, 63, 66–67, 201
Channa, Gurshuran, 33, 195
Chatterjee, Partha, 16–18
Chiswick, Linton, 84
"Choke There" (Apache Indian), 55
citizenship, 12, 188–89. *See also* belonging; Britain
class: Asian Underground clubs and, 3, 52, 72–73, 165, 169–85; bhangra clubgoers and, ix–x, 1, 4–5, 120, 148–63; class guilt and, 177–78, 180; cultural nationalism and, 6, 17–18, 69; gender's intersections with, 1, 6, 15–17, 19–21, 53, 66–67, 112, 124–28, 144, 165, 169–73, 178, 183–85, 223n36; identity construction and, 14–21, 121–22; liberal humanism and, 112–13; race and ethnicity's intersections with, 21–24, 51–52, 67–70, 93–96, 126–28, 130–33, 156,

177–85; violence and, 145–59. *See also* Asian Underground; gender; race and racialization
Club Kali, 182, 224n11
Club Outcaste, 29
clubs. *See* Asian Underground; bhangra; masculinity; women; *specific clubs*
coconuts (pejorative term), 49, 168. *See also* authenticity (ethnic); ethnicity; race and racialization
colonialism: Asian Underground's relation to, 29; British immigrant populations' relation to, x, 86–87; cool Britannia trope and, 7, 16–17; gender politics and, 76, 111, 145, 213n60, 222n16; Orientalist discourses and, 42–45, 48, 52, 67, 87, 111, 132–33, 145–48, 182–83; political resistance movements and, 73; postcolonial youth and, 4–6, 14–21, 33–39, 73–82, 161, 203n6. *See also* Britain; gender; race and racialization
Colonial Masculinity (Sinha), 213n60
Condry, Ian, 20, 208n55
"cool Britannia" (trope), 7, 21–22, 187, 200–201
Cornershop (group), 74, 76–77
CrazySexyCool (TLC), 137–38
cultural nationalism: bhangra's relation to, 5–6, 140–51; ethnic authenticity and, 16–17, 86–92, 117–24; gender and, 5–6, 16–18, 28–29, 124–28, 130–39, 142–45, 154, 157, 164, 173–75; liberal philosophy and, 73–74; marriage and, 121, 124–30, 139, 142, 175–76
cultured hard boys, 35, 58–59, 77–78, 80. *See also* bhangra; race and racialization

Das, Aniruddha, 70
Dawson, Ashley, 77
daytimers, 118–20, 123, 141
DCS (group), 37–38, 67, 198, 215n91
Dervesh, Aref, 84
Desis in the House (Maira), 207n53

Index **239**

Dhol Jageero Da (Panjabi MC), 61
Diamonds from Heera (Apna Sangeet), 47
diaspora (definitions), 25–26, 77–78, 122. *See also* Asians (British); belonging; ethnicity; race and racialization
Diehl, Keila, 20
DIP (group), 63
Displacing the Priest (Sawhney), 82, 89, 90
DJ Rekha, 196, 201
DJ Ritu, 1, 27, 37–38, 41–42, 51, 80–81, 182
DJ Sheikh, 49–52, 62
DJ Vips, 198, 201
Dragulis, Ella, 75
Dudrah, Rajinder Kumar, 194–95

East End (neighborhood), 22, 93–96
Eastern Eye (newspaper), 24–25, 34–35, 42–43, 46, 54–55, 86–87, 223n25
Echobelly (group), 75–76
Echoes from Dharamsala (Diehl), 20
Elliot, Missy, 196–97
emasculation, 34–39, 45, 50, 52, 62, 76, 110. *See also* bhangra; masculinity; old-timers (in bhangra); race and racialization
Epstein, Steven, 216n5
essentialism. *See* authenticity (ethnic); ethnicity; identity
ethnicity: authenticity concerns and, 5–6, 16–21, 33–34, 48–57, 67, 73–82, 86–87, 129–39, 167, 171–73, 175–85, 197; class concerns and, 177–85; cultural appropriation and, 53–57, 67–69, 107–8, 168, 183; ethnic traitor trope and, 34–35, 49, 52, 55, 62, 80, 133, 167–68; gender and, 34–39, 105–13, 130–39, 164–65; language and, 38, 41, 54–56, 63, 67, 133; religion and, 6–8, 26, 110, 143, 188–92, 199
ethnography, 14–21

Fanon, Frantz, 74
femininity: bhangra performers and, 53–69, 122; good girl femininity and, 122–28, 164; liberalism and, 73–74, 87–92; violence and, 148–59; wayward girl trope and, 117–24, 145–48, 155, 157–59, 164, 221n10. *See also* cultural nationalism; gender; women
fighting, 145–59, 221n10. *See also* violence
"Flight IC 408" (State of Bengal), 4, 161–62
Foucault, Michel, 141, 216n5
Fregoso, Rosa Linda, 221n10
From Soho Road to the Punjab (exhibit), 195–96, 201
Fun'Da'Mental (group), 74–75, 77, 81, 218n30
"Funky Asian" (Joi), 101–2

gender: Asian Underground politics and, 72–73, 75, 160–61, 164, 169–73, 183–85; bhangra club nights and, x–xi, 5, 140–51, 201; capitalism and, 42–45, 182–83; class's intersections with, 1, 15–17, 20–21, 53, 66–67, 112, 124–28, 165, 169–73, 176, 178, 183–85, 223n36; colonialism and, 76, 145, 222n16; cultural nationalism and, 6, 16–18, 28–29, 52, 154, 157, 173–75; gender-bending and, 3, 164, 182; liberal theory and, 73–74, 81, 87–92, 107, 112, 181, 216n9; marriage and, 121, 124–28, 139, 142, 175–76; masculine performance and, 34–39, 42–48, 57–69, 144; modernity and, 57–69; politics and, 74–77, 157–59; race and ethnicity's intersections with, 15, 28–29, 34–39, 49–50, 56, 62–63, 76, 105–13, 130–39, 164–65; violence and, 28, 56–57, 117–21, 124–28, 133–39, 142–45, 157–59, 213n55. *See also* femininity; masculinity; women
Ges-E (artist), 85, 191
"Get Your Freak On" (Elliot), 197
Gilroy, Paul, 96, 204n16
Ginsburg, Faye, 219n37
girl gangs, 122, 156, 221n10, 223n36

good Asian girl (trope), 28, 132–33, 142, 146–59, 164
Goodness Gracious Me (show), 7
Gopinath, Gayatri, 38, 77–78
Grass Roots (Panjabi MC), 60

Hall, Kathleen, 12
Hall, Stuart, 206n38
Hard Kaur, 201
harrassment (of women), 140–52, 165, 171. *See also* gender; masculinity; security (at clubs)
having a laugh, 134–35, 144
Heera (band), 193
Hesse, Barnor, 23
heteronormativity, 28, 38, 46–48, 56–58, 78, 121–29, 157–65, 177
Hindus, 26, 189, 192
Hip-Hop Japan (Condry), 20, 208n55
hip-hop music, 140
Human (Sawhney), 89, 91, 112
Hunt, Geoffrey, 156
Huq, Rupa, 73
Hustler's HC, 77
Hutnyk, John, 78
hybridity: belonging and, 16–21, 33–34; British Asians and, 6–8, 166–69; cultural appropriation and, 20–21, 23, 39, 53–57; definitions of, 5, 204n18; political resistance and, 8–10, 14–21, 54, 93–108, 177–85, 207n43
Hyder, Rehan, 74–75, 217n18, 218n30

identity: Asian Underground club-going and, 173–85; class and, 1, 14, 22–23, 121–22; cultural nationalism and, 117–24; ethnic authenticity concerns and, 16–21, 86–88, 165, 204n16; gender and, 1, 108–13; hybridity and, 7–10, 16–21, 23, 33–34, 166–69; language and, 38, 41, 54–56, 63, 67; liberal theory and, 73–74, 87–92; masculine performance and, 34–39, 55–57, 108–13; music's role with respect to, 24; political resistance and, 74–83, 93–108, 177–85;

postcolonial youth and, 4–6, 14–21, 33–39, 73–82, 161, 203n6; race and racialization and, ix–x, 6–7, 22–23, 82–86, 206n38; religion and, 7, 13, 93, 97–98, 110, 143, 188–89, 192, 199; rude-girl style and, 136–39; sexuality and, 130–33. *See also* class; ethnicity; gender; race and racialization
I'm British But . . . (Chadha), 9, 119, 220n57
Immigration Act of 1971, 11
imperialism. *See* colonialism
Internet piracy, 197–98
Ismail, Qadri, 74

"Jaan" (Singh), 4, 161–62
Jackson, Michael, 101
Jagpal, Bally and Bhota, 63
Jatt, Bindha, 62
Jay-Z, 58, 193
Jobanputra, Shabs, 80
Johal, Ninder, 197
Joi, 28, 50, 70–73, 82, 99–112, 190–91, 220n53
Juggy D, 197

Kaliphz (group), 77–78
Kalra, Virinder, 38
Kapoor, Sweety, 163, 209n66
Kaur, Raminder, 38
Khan, Imran, 166, 173
Krishnaswamy, Revathi, 52
Kundnani, Arun, 6–8, 189, 192, 200

lad-like boy bands, 35, 57, 63–69, 80, 110. *See also* bhangra
Laidler, Karen Joe, 156
language, 38, 41, 54–56, 63, 67, 133
Lawrence, Stephen, 6, 182
League of Joi Bangla Youth, 99
Legalised (Panjabi MC), 58, 61, 196
liberal humanism, 73–74, 79–81, 87–92, 107, 109, 112–13, 181, 216n9
Limelight (club), 178–79
Lipsitz, George, 9, 54, 57

Lit, Avtar, 189
Livingstone, Ken, 22
London, 21–23, 187, 199. *See also* Britain; class; gender; modernity; *specific artists, clubs, and neighborhoods*
London Arts Board, 85
Long Overdue (B21), 64

Maan, Gurdaas, 200
Macpherson, William, 6
Made in England (B21), 65
Made in England (Bancil), 79
Mahajan, Rashmi, 39
mainstream, the: Asian Underground's acceptance in, 2–3, 34–39, 48–53, 71, 79–82, 107–8, 167–69, 179, 182–85, 189–93, 215n79; belonging and, 27; bhangra's relation to, ix–x, 1, 5, 21–23, 28, 33–34, 40–42, 48–53, 67–69, 196, 210n2, 212n32; political resistance and, 8–10, 71–72, 177–85; profit motive and, 42–45
Mainstream Dream (documentary), 40, 53
Maira, Sunaina, 207n53
Majumdar, Krishnendu, 9, 163
marriage, 121, 124–30, 139, 142, 145, 175–76
Masala (club), 28, 120, 122–23, 129, 133, 136–37, 141–42, 164
masculinity: Asian Underground norms and, 173–75; bhangra clubs and, 1, 5, 110, 117–24, 140–51; bhangra's performance and, 34–39; black(ness) and, 6, 53–57, 77–78, 80; bullying and, 49–50; ethnic authenticity and, 18, 67–69; lad-like boy bands and, 57–69, 80; liberal theory and, 73–74, 87–92; modernity and, 5–6, 19–20; old-timers and, 45–48; political resistance and, 82–86, 177–85; race and ethnicity and, 82–86; violence and, 142–45, 164, 187
McGuire, Stryker, 7

Mercury Prize, 82, 189–90, 203n3
Miah, Wicked, 48, 66–67
Migration (Sawhney), 82, 84, 88, 90
Miranda, Marie Keta, 158
Miss Pooja, 201
Mistry, Rajan, 1, 9, 28–29
modernity: Asian Underground's receptions and, 34–35, 167–69, 171; bhangra's relation to, 5–6, 33–34, 197; capitalism and, 42–45, 53, 96–98; cultural nationalism's responses to, 16–17, 19; ethnic authenticity and, 48–53; gender's relation to, 57–69
Modood, Tariq, 206n36
Mo Magic, 85
"Mundian To Bach Ke" (Panjabi MC), 58, 69, 193–94, 196
Murthy, Dhiraj, 189, 193, 201, 225n1
music. *See* Asian Underground; bhangra; black(ness); *specific artists, clubs, and labels*
Muslims, 7, 13, 26, 93, 97–98, 188–92, 199, 220n53, 220n55
"My Beautiful Laundrette" (film), 212n43

National Health Service (of Britain), 7
National Lottery, 85
National Music Express (magazine), 76
Nation Records, 81
Nawaz, Aki, 81
Newham Asian Women's Project, 13
9/11, 8, 13, 21, 187, 189, 192, 199–201
No Reservations (Apache Indian), 53, 57

old-timers (in bhangra), 46–48, 57–58, 62–63
100% Proof (Panjabi MC), 60
One and One Is One (Joi), 71, 104, 220n53
Orientalism, 42–45, 48, 52, 58, 67, 87, 111, 132–33, 182–83. *See also* Asians (British); colonialism; ethnicity; race and racialization

Outcaste (record label), 4, 27, 80–93, 108, 111, 161, 163, 190–92, 209n66

Pandit, John, 70–72, 77
Panjabi MC, 43, 58–63, 60, 67–69, 193–94, 196, 215n79
Pardesi, 33, 37
"Peerh Tere Jaan Di" (Maan), 200
Planet Bollywood (store), 198
"Play It Right" (report), 22
politics: Asian Underground's relation to, 82–98, 177–85; community representation and, 68–82, 87–92, 99–108, 217n18; gender and, 74–77, 157–59; hybridity as resistance and, 8–10, 54–57, 93–108, 177–85; masculine violence and, 144–45; protest music and, 78–82, 217n18
post-bhangra music, 74–78, 193–200, 217n13
postcolonial youth, 4–6, 14–21, 33–39, 73–82, 161, 203n6. *See also* Asian Underground; bhangra
private sphere, 73–74, 94, 98, 110, 121–22, 129, 140, 158–59, 216n9
The Project (Rich), 197
public sphere, 73–74, 120–22, 157–59, 216n9. *See also* liberal humanism; politics
"Pump Up the Bhangra" (Pardesi), 33
Punch Ammo, 195
Punjabi (language), 38, 41, 53, 56, 63, 67
Punjabi Dance Nation (DCS), 67

queer(ing), 46, 52, 58, 164

race and racialization: Asian Underground's mainstream success and, 3, 16, 71–73, 104, 175–85; belonging and, 16–21, 33–34, 51–52, 166–69; bhangra's resistance to, 39, 48–53, 67–69, 199–200; black musical forms and, ix–x, 53–63; British nationalism and, 5–6, 10–15, 45, 54, 80–82, 161–62, 173–75;

187–89, 200, 211n7; class's intersections with, 20–21, 23–24, 51–52, 67–70, 93–96, 126–39, 156, 177–85; gender's intersections with, 20–21, 28–29, 34–39, 53–63, 76, 105–13, 130–33; political resistance and, 77–86, 93–96, 100–113, 177–85; religion and, 6–8, 26, 110, 143, 188–92, 199; segregation and, 21–23, 136–39; sexuality and, 130–33, 137; violence and, 6–7, 85–86, 142–45. *See also* authenticity (ethnic); ethnicity; gender; identity; masculinity
Rafi's Revenge (ADF), 76, 109
Ram, Satpal, 13, 70
Raman, Susheela, 112
Real World Records, 101, 107–8
recognition, 40–42
religion, 7, 13, 26, 88, 93, 98, 110, 143, 188–92, 199
resistance (political), 8–10, 77–86, 93–108, 110–13, 177–85
Rhythm King Records, 104
Rich, Rishi, 40–41, 194, 197
Ross, Andrew, 5, 162
Rough Guide to Bhangra (DJ Ritu), 41, 212n32
Rubayat (writer), 46, 48
Rushdie, Salman, 13, 188

safe woman trope, 151–59
Safri, Balwinder, 43
Sagoo, Bally, ix, ix–x, 38
Sahni, Mits, 44
Sahotas (band), 43
Satanic Verses (Rushdie), 13
Savale, Steve Chandra, 70
Sawhney, Nitin, 28, 35, 49–51, 73, 80–93, 104–10, 189–96, 201
Sean, Jay, 194, 197
2nd Generation (publication), 51, 166
security (at clubs), 142–48
segregation, 21–23
Seize the Time (Fun'Da'Mental), 75
7/7, 8, 13, 21, 187, 189, 192, 199–201

Index **243**

sexuality, 15, 28–29, 58, 124–39, 151–59, 202
Shaanti (club), 195
Shabbs (editor), 55, 57, 62–63
Shamser, Farouk and Haroun, 71, 99–108
Shankar, Ravi, 68
Shepherds Bush Empire (club), 70
Shin (artist), 198–99
Shinda, Sukhshinder, 42
Shiva Soundsystem, 193
Sholay (film), 175–76
Shri, 80, 85, 191
Shylock (metaphor), 45, 48, 58, 67
Sidhu, Jassi, 63
Sikhs, 13, 26, 189, 199
Singh, Malkit, 43
Singh, Nina Chanpreet, 199
Singh, Talvin, 3–4, 71, 82, 86, 160–62, 180, 189–91
Sinha, Mrinilani, 213n60
Skeggs, Beverly, 223n36
"Smack My Bitch Up" (song), 77
The Sound of B21 (B21), 64
Southall (neighborhood), 22, 123, 126, 131, 209n64
Southall Black Sisters, 13
South Asians. *See* Asians
"Star Megamix" (Sagoo), ix, ix–x
State of Bengal (group), 4, 161–62
stereotypes, 42–52, 74–76, 84–85, 92–97, 105–8, 133–39, 189
Sterling, Marvin, 20, 208n55
Sunrise Radio, 189
Suri, Sunny, 33, 37, 40
Swaraj (club), 4, 29, 161

taal (musical form), 49, 51
Tailor, Sanjay Gulabhai, 70
Take That! (group), 63
Tebbit, Norman, 12
Teri Chunni de Sitare (Alaap), 36
terrorism, 187–89
Thandi, Shinder, 10
Thatcher, Margaret, 12, 22
Tihai Trio (group), 82

TLC (group), 137–38
Top of the Pops, 40–41
tradition: Asian stereotypes and, 42–52; bhangra's association with, 5, 33–34, 46–53, 166–69; cultural norms of, 16–17, 86–92, 117–24; gendering of, 28, 34–39, 52, 105–13, 130–39, 164–65. *See also* authenticity (ethnic); ethnicity; femininity; gender

Uddin, Amir, 101
United States, ix–x, 5, 129, 200

Varma, Sandeep, 225n1
violence: bhangra clubs and, 118–21, 140–59, 164; gender and, 28, 56–57, 124–28, 133–39; racism and, 6, 130–33
Voodoo Queens (group), 75–76

Wag Club, 2
Watermans (venue), 79
Watt, Paul, 209n64
wayward girl trope, 117–24, 145–48, 156, 164, 221n10. *See also* bad Asian girl (trope); femininity; gender
Wham Bam: Bhangra Remixes (album), ix–x
whiteness: Asian Underground's relation to, 63–69, 80–82, 104, 168–73, 175–77, 183–85; bhangra and, 49, 130–33, 199–200; British law and, 11–12, 187–89; class and, 126–28; ethnic betrayal and, 34–39, 57–58, 71–72; gender and, 122, 137; modernity's associations with, 19–20, 34, 48–53, 68–69; political protest and, 101–8. *See also* Asian Underground; class; race and racialization
"Why Bhangra's Here to Stay" (DJ Sheikh), 50
Wild Apache, 57
Willis, Paul, 134–35
With Intent to Pervert the Cause of Justice (Fun'Da'Mental), 74–75
women: agency of, 28, 39, 77–81, 121–22, 129, 157, 183–85; Asian Underground

clubs and, 16, 160–61, 166–69; bhangra clubs and, 16, 19, 117–24, 140–51, 171–72, 201; class differences among, 15, 19, 169–73; club security and, 145–48; interethnic relationships and, 130–39; marriage concerns and, 121, 124–28, 142, 175–76; modernity's pressures upon, 17–18, 20–21, 68–69, 111–13; sexuality and, 130–39. *See also* class; ethnicity; gender; hybridity; race and racialization; tradition

Women Against Fundamentalism, 13

Zaman, Deedar, 70